seattle
cheap
eats

300 Terrific Bargain Eateries

The Best Places® Editors

SASQUATCH BOOKS
SEATTLE

Printed in the United States
Distributed in the United States by Sasquatch Books

Sixth edition.
        01 00 99   5 4 3 2 1
ISSN: 1095-9793
ISBN: 1-57061-148-3

Cover Photograph: Rick Dahms
Cover design: Karen Schober
Interior design: Kate Basart
Interior composition: Patrick David Barber

Special Sales Best Places® guidebooks are available at special discounts on bulk purchases for corporate, club, or organization sales promotions, premiums, and gifts. Special editions, including personalized covers, excerpts of existing guides, and corporate imprints, can be created in large quantities for specific needs. For more information, contact your local bookseller or Special Sales, Best Places Guidebooks, 615 Second Avenue, Suite 260, Seattle, Washington 98104, (800)775-0817.

Best Places®. Reach for it first.

SASQUATCH BOOKS
615 Second Avenue
Seattle, WA 98104
(206)467-4300
books@SasquatchBooks.com
www.SasquatchBooks.com

contents

acknowledgments

Many thanks to our contributors who ate their way through the Emerald City with nary a need for Pepto-Bismol: Carl Hanson, Elisa Murray, Jim Goldsmith, and Sumi Hahn earn our highest regards for (literally) biting off all that they could chew. Additional kudos to cheap eaters Rebekah Anderson, Emily Baillargeon, James Bush, Kim Foster, Joan Gregory, Paul Hughes, Gary Luke, Alan Miller, Jim Pollack, Kate Rogers, and John Zilly.

Our after-dinner mint goes to copyeditor Sherri Schultz for her sweet and thorough treatment of the manuscript. Thanks also to Sharon Vonasch for proofreading the whole meal.

Special thanks to Nancy Leson, a long-time contributor, editor, and friend to Best Places®, whose thumb thrums with the cheap eats pulse of this city. Her help and advice was, as always, instrumental. And, finally, we reserve a special nod to Meghan Heffernan, who not only wrote several spiffy reviews, but also guided the total 300 to the finish line.

Let the eating begin!

—The Best Places® Editors

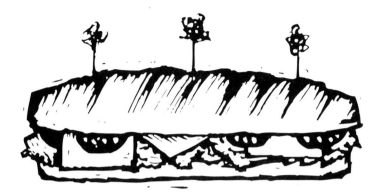

about
seattle cheap eats
and best places®
guidebooks

Seattle Cheap Eats is part of the Best Places® guidebook series, which means it's written by and for locals who enjoy getting out and tasting the food of the region. It's written for smart, hungry people of all ages—people who know it's not necessary to pay top dollar to revel in a four-star experience. When we're eating on the cheap, we look for a lot of different things: restaurants of good value serving tasty food, preferably independently owned and run by lively individuals, perhaps touched with local history, and sparked by fun and interesting decor. In sum, the restaurant has to be worth visiting again. Would we go back? Would we recommend it to a friend? These are the operative questions. Every place listed is not only inexpensive but recommended.

Best Places® guidebooks, which have been published continuously since 1975, represent one of the most respected regional travel series in the country. Each guide is written completely independently: no advertisers, no sponsors, no favors. Our reviewers know their territory, work incognito, and seek out the very best a city or region has to offer. We provide tough, candid reports and describe the true strengths, foibles, and unique characteristics of each establishment listed.

Note: Readers are advised that the reviews in this edition are based on information available at press time and are subject to change. The editors welcome information conveyed by users of this book, as long as they have no financial connection with the establishment concerned. A report form is provided at the end of the book, and feedback is also welcome via email: books@SasquatchBooks.com.

what's cheap?

Seattle Cheap Eats provides 300 honest recommendations on great, inexpensive restaurants in Seattle and its neighborhoods—stretching north to Edmonds, south to Renton, west to Bainbridge Island and including all of the Eastside.

Our price range for choosing these places was based on dinner for two for $30 or less (including tax, tip, and dessert—and sometimes even alcohol). Most cheap eats dinners fall in the $10–$20-for-two range; some spots are even less. Breakfast and lunch at the majority of these eateries in this book fall under $15 for two.

eats tips

Some budget eating tips to remember: Diners and cafes often feature daily or "blue plate" specials that usually include bread, salad, and dessert—all for one great, low price. At more upscale cafes and restaurants, pairing appetizers to make up a meal may be a better deal than an entree. Happy hours in Seattle (mostly at places too cushy for this book) can be a great source of filling, free (or inexpensive) munchies. At establishments that offer wine, consider bringing your own bottle and paying a corkage fee, often a better deal than even the cheapest vintage on their list.

meals/hours

While a lot of cheap eats serve all three squares, some focus on only one or two meals, like breakfast or breakfast and lunch. Some places have a specialty food or particular meal that's not to be missed. As such, we've made a point of telling you which days and meals you'll find a restaurant open. But call ahead for specific hours, as these often change or vary from day to day.

cashing out

Every cheap eat listed here accepts cash. Some take checks; some take only local checks. We've indicated what does which, but note that the usual ID may be required in either case. For those sporting plastic, we've listed which credit cards a place accepts: American Express (AE), Diner's Club (DC), Discover (DIS), Japanese credit card (JCB), MasterCard (MC), and Visa (V).

alcohol

For those who want to know, we tell you, using one of the following: full bar, beer and wine, beer only, wine only, no alcohol.

kids, pets, and other appendages

As a general rule, where the food is cheap, kids are welcome. Many of the cheap eats contained herein, however, are pubs and taverns and, thus, may require a patron to be 21 years old to enter. If you're considering one of these spots and want to take along Junior, call ahead. Fido is, of course, generally not welcome; but also note that some of the aforementioned pubs and taverns, or those places with sidewalk seating, are in fact dog-friendly. Call ahead, though, to be sure. Cats and pot-bellied pigs are frowned upon; a well-mannered parrot on your shoulder is a case-by-case situation.

reservations

Ha!

smoking

Nonsmoking establishments are, of course, very politically correct and Seattle is a very politically correct city. But it's not California and, so, many of the diners, pubs, taverns, etc. listed here do allow smoking. If this is a problem for you, just be sure and call ahead to ask what the policy is. Likewise, if you smoke and don't want to be left puffing in the rain, call ahead.

disabilities

Many of the listings here are smaller cafes, older pubs, and hole-in-the-wall food stands. Not all of them are easily accessible to those with disabilities. At the end of the facts following each review, there is a wheelchair icon indicating spots that are wheelchair-accessible. If you have special needs, however, you may still want to call ahead.

indexes and eatery info

Reviews here are in alphabetical order. When an eatery has three or fewer locations, we list each one. For establishments with more than three branches, we list the original or most recommended branch only; but the location designation indicates where you can find other branches. Each restaurant is indexed in the back of this book by location and type of food served. With some clever cross-referencing, you can find that Mexican spot in Green Lake in a jiffy.

reader's report

Please feel free to use the report form provided in the back of this book (or a copy of it) to let us know what you think. The usefulness of *Seattle Cheap Eats* is dependent upon the hundreds who write to pat us on the back, share a new discovery, or tell us we screwed up.

300
terrific
bargain
eateries

A LA FRANCAISE

2609 NE University Village, Seattle (and branch)
☎ *(206) 524-9300*
University District/Pioneer Square 🍴 **Bakery**

In the style of French boulangeries, A La Francaise stacks its fresh-baked breads (baguettes, country rolls, *pain de paysan*, and more) in deep wooden shelves behind glass cases filled with all manner of pastries and sinful desserts: fruit-filled scones and croissants, danishes, pull-aparts, muffins, cinnamon rolls, cheesecake, and chocolate ganache gâteau among them. Though the bakery items take the cake here, A La Francaise does a fair trade in lunch fare as well.

The lunch menu is chalked on blackboards on the wall—
along with several axiomatic messages trumpeting the glory of bread ("staff of life" stuff). The soup du jour can be had with a slab of fresh bread ($3.50) or a half sandwich. There are several pizzas (the four cheeses with tomato and fresh basil is particularly tempting) and a number of reasonably priced sandwiches on baguette or brioche buns, such as the tuna Niçoise or turkey provolone. Don't expect to dine in at the U-Village locale—the handful of tiny, faux-marble-topped tables (with surface areas barely large enough to hold both a cup of coffee and a croissant) are quickly snapped up. There's a bit more room in the original A La Francaise in Pioneer Square (417 First Ave S, (206) 624-0322). *Light breakfast, lunch every day (Mon–Fri at Pioneer Square); MC, V; local checks only; no alcohol.* ♿

ACAPULCO FRESH

16650 Redmond Way, Redmond (and branches)
☎ *(425) 883-3510*
Redmond/Bellevue/Issaquah/Kenmore 🍴 **Mexican**

Since the Redmond original opened in 1995, three other Acapulco Fresh outlets have sprouted, all emphasizing the use of fresh ingredients, with no microwaves, no lard, no can openers, no freezers. Taquitos arrive so clean, crisp, and dry, you'll swear they've been fried in hot air. Quesadillas, tostados, enchiladas, chimichangas—all healthy as hell. Anything that needs a little zip gets it from Acapulco's best feature, its fresh salsa bar. Piña Pico de Gallo gets its odd spelling from the dose of roasted pineapple. Salsa Negro's robust vegetable flavor lurks in a dark, mysterious brew. Salsa verde and salsa Chihuahua push the bounds of "medium spicy," while Acapulco Heat delivers the heat. They cut chips on site and fry them in canola oil, leaving fingertips dry. It's nice to be free of fat-intake worries here, as the chunky/smooth guacamole improves most anything. But if skimp you must, you can get nonfat yogurt to substitute for sour cream, and extra salsa to compensate for the guacamole. Vegetarians and vegans do well here. *Lunch, dinner every day; no credit cards; checks OK; beer only (branches vary).* &

ADMIRAL WAY CAFE

4323 Admiral Way SW, Seattle
☎ *(206) 937-9530*
West Seattle   ✕ *Diner*

West Seattle's best-kept secret has been continuously serving true-blue diner food since 1979 (it used to be known as Mr. Ed's; the name changed in 1982). The setting is pure (but clean) greasy-spoon, right down to the family booths and stools at the bar. The efficient, friendly, uniformed staff know exactly who the regulars are, what they want, where they want to sit, and how long the turnaround is. Long a stronghold for weekend brunches, the Admiral Way Cafe is popular with older folks in the neighborhood—all the better for the younger, artistic loners who have discovered that the food here pushes all the right nostalgia buttons. Pancakes are fluffy; the Baby Dutchman rises miraculously to a perfect pouf; coffee refills are endless; the freezer jam comes in a three-pack of yummy flavors; sausage patties are generous and hand-shaped; and the authentically chunky corned beef hash house special will convert any doubters. At dinner, expect cafeteria specials like Prime Rib for Two or Roast Beef Special. Sandwiches and burgers here also hit the mark. *Breakfast, lunch, dinner every day; DIS, MC, V; local checks only; no alcohol.* &

AFRIKANDO

2904 First Ave, Seattle
☎ *(206) 374-9714*
Belltown   ✕ *West African*

Men in Senegal don't cook, which is why chef/co-owner Jacques Sarr opened his first restaurant far, far away from home—in Washington state's hippest neighborhood. Seattle's port of entry into West African cooking, Afrikando is decked out in Senegalese prints, imported masks, and salsa music (Sarr has been known to sing and dance in the kitchen). Fervent regulars come for a taste of Senegal's national dish, *thiebu djen*, a stewed white fish, and everyone loves the *mafe*, a stunningly simple combination of jasmine rice, sweet potato, carrots, and yam doused with an oniony, garlicky, peppery peanut sauce. Order the airy fritters as an appetizer, and, if you like fire with the heat, ask for Jacques's "special sauce from hell." No alcohol is served, but there's a selection of homemade juice—ginger, tamarind, and hibiscus—that shouldn't be missed. For dessert, try a bowl of *thiakry*, a thick pudding of couscous, fruit, sour cream, yogurt, and vanilla sauce. It's a rich, creamy mouthful that's gloriously delicious. This is a vegetarian-friendly establishment. Also, note that some menu items push the cheap envelope; order with care. *Lunch, dinner every day; MC, V; local checks only; no alcohol.* &

AI JAPANESE RESTAURANT

1608 N 45th St, Seattle
☎ *(206) 632-7044*
Wallingford   ✕ *Japanese*

Frustrated by the long and growing line at Musashi's, Wallingford's official favorite sushi restaurant? Head two blocks east to Ai, another modest Japanese spot where the sushi is almost as good, the wait is usually nonexistent, and at least one appetizer (often pickled cabbage) is served on the house. The best bet for bargain hunters is the longstanding $8.95 dinner special (which costs $6.90 at lunch). This includes a sesame-dressed salad, miso soup, half a California roll, and a rather huge bowl of sticky rice, plus a choice of two entrees from a list that includes broiled salmon, sushi, tempura, and soba. All other bases are covered on the thorough (but not exhaustive) menu, including sushi, sashimi, teriyaki, yakisoba, donburi, and bento. The decor is whimsical: fake flowers, sumi-brushed postcards, bright yellow touches here and there, and a little patio for when the weather is nice. Service could be quicker at times, but it's friendly, and they've got a generous hand with the ginger. A good choice for take-out. Note: Ai closes for an hour between lunch and dinner. *Lunch, dinner every day; MC, V; local checks only; beer and wine.* &

ALEXA'S ON MAIN

10115 Main St, Bothell
☎ *(425) 483-6275*
Bothell   ✕ *Breakfast*

Alexa's on Main, high above the rivers of commuters on Bothell's new, de facto main drag, is the kind of down-home cafe, by nature and by location, that can anchor and center a small downtown. This is good, because "downtown" here certainly needed one. Alexa's is strictly a large-portion, country-style breakfast-and-lunch spot, with breakfasts served from morning to midafternoon. Experience tells us that if you were to eat both breakfast and lunch here, dinner would not be necessary. Owner Leigh Henderson (whose daughter provides the cafe's name) gutted an old Hallmark card shop, exposing handsome brick walls, and built a kitchen that could handle drop-in trade as well as the catering business she has run since 1991. Henderson's belief in largesse is exemplified by the Calico Grub plate, with its many fat chunks of fried, red-jacket potatoes mixed with little slices of smoked ham and a mess of veggies, its lace top of melted cheddar messy with sour cream, and its lava flow of homemade salsa running down the sides. Even better are her apple pancakes. At lunch, pastas, salads, soups, and sandwiches add to the variety. An extensive, reasonably priced children's menu makes bringing Junior a pleasure. Order tea and you'll be offered a big basket of at least 20 varieties. *Breakfast, lunch every day; MC, V; checks OK; no alcohol.* &

ALIBI ROOM

85 Pike St (on Post Alley), Seattle
☎ *(206) 623-3180*
Pike Place Market

✕ *Bistro*

There's no mistaking that this spot, created by two film-industry types expressly as a venue where would-be screenwriters could congregate, is a place for artistes. Smoke hangs in the air like fog; people in black lean over small tables and converse while drinking wine, looking disdainfully at attractive (and reasonably priced) plates of Brie, fruit, and bread, and ignoring the partial view of the Sound. The menu, featuring Mediterranean-influenced bistro fare, is quite good, with appetizers and light meals such as crostini with tapenade, vegetarian lasagne, a wonderful stuffed ravioli, jerk chicken, and several sandwiches, including a highly satisfying turkey and Brie with cranberry relish (even artistes need comfort food now and then). Most everything is under $10—just remember that smoke is an extra ingredient here. In accordance with its mission, the Alibi hosts an every-other-Monday script-reading series, and at any time of the week, writers can peruse the stacks of scripts that are on hand. Other eclectic happenings—film screenings, live late-night music downstairs, and so on—take place here from time to time; look for flyers. *Lunch, dinner every day (and occasional brunch); MC, V; local checks only; full bar.*

ALKI BAKERY

2738 Alki Ave SW, Seattle
☎ *(206) 935-1352*
West Seattle   ✕ *Bakery*

There's no way a sane soul can simply walk by and ignore this bakery adjunct of the Alki Cafe, nestled alongside one of the busiest beaches in the city. If you're not lured inside by the scent of the famous cinnamon rolls, then you'll eventually saunter in just to figure out why so many people cheerfully line up inside, numbers in hand. You'll learn that they're there for the zippy coffee and colorful salads and sandwiches, not to mention the artfully lighted display case near-to-bursting with cookies, scones, muffins, and slices of cakes and pies. You can take it all to go or hang around hoping for a table or a counter seat with a view of Bainbridge Island and the Olympics. If you just want a nibble without the view, check out the retail outlet in Georgetown, (206) 762-5700. *Breakfast, lunch every day; AE, DC, MC, V; no checks; no alcohol.* ♿

ANGELINA'S TRATTORIA

2311 California Ave SW, Seattle
☎ *(206) 932-7311*
West Seattle   ✕ *Italian*

A busy neighborhood restaurant that serves Italian classics with no thrills or frills, Angelina's (part of the Mitchelli clan) could be considered West Seattle's Italian kitchen. Here you'll find surprisingly decent and affordable renditions of such staples as lasagne, spaghetti and meatballs, linguine with clams, and chicken piccata. So what if they have a heavy hand with the sauces? The pasta itself comes perfectly al dente. Take the whole family or a group of friends—there's plenty of room for everyone in either of the two cavernous rooms or at the sidewalk tables outside. (See separate review for Trattoria Mitchelli.) *Brunch Sat–Sun, lunch, dinner every day; AE, MC, V; checks OK; beer and wine.* ♿

ANGEL'S THAI CUISINE

235 Broadway E, Seattle
☎ *(206) 328-0515*
Capitol Hill   ✕ *Thai*

To sit inside Angel's near the two street-facing banks of windows is to experience Broadway's hustle and bustle from a prime vantage point, with the added bonus of freshly prepared Thai food. From the outside, the window tables set the scene, which is centered on the bar; from inside, the ceiling above the bar is revealed—a cerulean blue with white wisps of clouds (heaven, home of angels, perhaps?)—and the seating area, tucked around the corner from the entrance, is big enough to handle a family reunion. If you like to scrutinize passersby and don't mind an occasional smoker, opt for the windows. As one of the three prominent Thai spots on Broadway, Angel's takes itself seriously, with lots of favorites (phad Thai, swimming angel, and a delicious *tom kah gai* soup) and a host of seafood varieties (squid, scallops, prawns, trout in over 16 dishes). The best deals are the appropriately matched combination dinners—four entrees plus rice for tables of two or more—which squeak in at just under $30 for two (minus tax). *Lunch, dinner every day; AE, MC, V; no checks; full bar.* ♿

ANTHONY'S BEACH CAFE

456 Admiral Way, Edmonds
☎ *(425) 771-4400*
Edmonds   ✕ *Seafood*

The first cheap thrill at Anthony's Beach Cafe, an informal member of the Anthony's chain, is the sunset. It can last up to an hour on clear nights, and the view across the Sound to the Olympics, glimmering blue-purple in the twilight, is truly spectacular. The second cheap thrill is for the kids: two sandboxes set up on the outdoor patio, which can entertain the little ones for even longer than the sunset lasts. And the food is pretty darned good, too. Favorites include fish tacos (there are four kinds, including blackened rockfish, mahi-mahi, and salmon); a wonderful seafood chop-chop salad, rich with Dungeness crab and shrimp; clam chowder served in a sourdough bowl; clams and mussels prepared with white wine, lemon, and garlic; and memorable cobblers, the ingredients of which change with the season. If you really want to get your money's worth, try the all-you-can-eat fish 'n' chips on Monday ($8.95) or the all-you-can-eat prawns on Tuesday ($13.95). The servers are competent and kindly, used to dealing with both cocktail-drinking adults and sand-throwing tots. *Brunch Sun, lunch, dinner every day; AE, DC, DIS, MC, V; checks OK; full bar.* &

AOKI JAPANESE GRILL AND SUSHI BAR
621 Broadway E, Seattle
☎ *(206) 324-3633*
Capitol Hill   ✗*Japanese*

Broadway, better known for its funky restaurants, takes a step in the upscale direction with this long-standing Japanese favorite. Jazz plays softly on the sound system while efficient and smiling servers tend to diners at the modern, well-lighted sushi and robata bars and in the small, serene dining room at the back. A restaurant twice its size could be proud of Aoki's seemingly endless menu, composed of something for everyone: Combination lunches or dinners (highlighting donburi, robata, sushi, or sashimi), soup noodles, and a few dozen *uramaki* (reversed sushi rolls) are among the scores of options available all day and into the night. Most of the menu is available for take-out. *Lunch Tues–Sat, dinner Tues–Sun; AE, DC, MC, V; no checks; beer and wine.* &

A.P. BARBARA'S
4025 196th St SW, Lynnwood
☎ *(425) 672-3666*
Lynnwood   ✗*Inventive Ethnic*

Perhaps owners Barbara and Lee Agelopoulos want to keep their wonderful Greek/Italian/American restaurant a secret, because they've cleverly disguised it as a Denny's-style diner, complete with blue booths, fake plants, and somewhat sterile decor (it even sits next to a KFC in the heart of strip mall country). But this place is something special, as you'll guess the minute one of the kindly waitresses whisks a basket of warm, homemade bread to your table. The pita bread is also made in-house, and the best way to try it is by sampling the appetizer that tops it with mouth-watering strips of gyro meat, tomatoes, onion, and tangy tzatziki sauce. Things only get better from here, from the awesome souvlaki, cacciatore, and moussaka to BBQ baby back ribs worth breaking a diet for. There are amazing fresh pastas, including a fine smoked salmon pasta and a comforting baked spaghetti with Italian sausage; Mediterranean flavors are honored in Athina's Pasta,

a lemon-basil linguine topped with artichoke hearts, onions, mushrooms, broccoli, and feta. Most dinner entrees are priced under $10. The lunch menu adds burgers and grinders, and the place has started serving breakfast, which means

that Lynnwoodites might soon be tempted to let Barbara's do all the cooking. It's a good place for families (the waitstaff will have crayons out for the kids before they're in their booster chairs). Wondering about the name? A.P. stands for Athina and Pete, children of Barbara and Lee. *Breakfast, lunch, dinner every day; DIS, MC, V; checks OK; beer and wine.* &

ARMADILLO BARBECUE

13109 NE 175th St, Woodinville
☎ *(425) 481-1417*
Woodinville   ✕ *Barbecue*

The Armadillo doesn't get by just on its humor, though it could. Droll, wacko, and self-deprecating (the company motto is "Endeavor to Be Adequate"), this Texas-style smokehouse has no pretensions of being anything other than a straightforward purveyor of barbecue. But this joint is more than adequate. The Gill brothers have fine-tuned their craft, serving thoroughly smoked and tender meat (pork, chicken, and beef) with their famous spicy and tangy sauce. Served with sides of molasses-heavy beans and cakey corn bread, it all adds up to a fine Texas feast. The Armadillo is the home of "The Snake Plate," described as "three bucks worth o' stuff," for $4. And the Killer Hot Sauce "concocted by a group of perverts in Texas bent on destroyin' Armadillos" is not for wimps. Ask for extra napkins and be prepared to get messy. The massive oven/smoker doesn't seem to contain all the smoke it produces, so customers usually go home lightly smoked outside as well as in. *Lunch, dinner every day; AE, MC, V; checks OK; beer and wine.* &

ASIA GRILLE

2820 NE University Village Pl, Seattle
☎ *(206) 517-5985*
University District   ✕ *Pan-Asian*

Nestled into the swanky University Village shopping complex, Asia Grille is the Seattle outpost of LeAnne Chin Inc., part of the Minneapolis-based Chinese food chain. For Seattle, Chin has mixed her culinary metaphors, offering a little Thai, a little Chinese, a little

Korean, and a little Vietnamese—among others—in this well-priced take on pan-Asian dining. The atmosphere and service are crisp, bright, and quietly snazzy, but save your wows for the fancy rack of dipping sauces that invariably accompanies the appetizers. There's patio seating for rare sunny days, and singles can opt to sit at the dining bar, with its gleaming view of polished chrome surfaces and kitchen help composing the various elements of a meal here. Whether it be a more traditionally Chinese version of crab with black bean sauce or a clever Asian twist on tacos, Asia Grille has something to intrigue everyone in your family, from the fussiest vegetarian toddlers to well-traveled college-aged know-it-alls. Purists beware: While the end result can often be finger-lickin' good, it may not be exactly what you've had before under the same name. *Lunch, dinner every day; AE, DC, DIS, MC, V; checks OK; full bar.* &

ASSIMBA

2722 E Cherry St, Seattle
☎ *(206) 322-1019*
Central District   ✕ *Ethiopian*

Two can stuff themselves for less than $10 at Assimba—a bargain even by Ethiopian-restaurant standards. It's a modest place, with white-washed walls and a few pieces of folk art, but it's friendly: Although the smiling servers expect you to know that you use pieces of injera, the spongy, pancakelike bread, to scoop up your spicy beef (with your right hand, please), they'll provide you with a fork if you ask. If you're new to the wonders of Ethiopian cuisine, you should know that each dish feeds two to three people. One of the combination platters is a good place to start. The beef combo consists of a large plate of lamb, beef, ground beef, lentils, and collard greens; the vegetable includes the same lentils and collard greens as well as potatoes, carrots, and cauliflower. All dishes are served on injera, with a big dish of it—folded up like a plump towel—on the side. We won't list all the spices and condiments used in cooking, but suffice it to say that two of them are hot red pepper and spiced jalapeño paste. A few beers round out the spare menu. *Lunch, dinner every day; no credit cards; checks OK; beer and wine.* &

THE ASTEROID CAFE

1605 N 45th St, Seattle
☎ (206) 547-2514
Wallingford
✕ *Italian*

Don't pay too much attention to the kitschy name and the Jetsons-like silver walls. The Asteroid, on busy 45th Street, is really your average home-away-from-home Italian restaurant, with eight tables, a small open kitchen, and a friendly, knowledgeable waitstaff. By day, they serve coffeehouse fare and fine panini sandwiches on rosemary focaccia, ranging from the Misto (a kitchen sink–type sandwich that includes salami, prosciutto, turkey, mozzarella, and tomato) to the artful Sorrentina (fresh mozzarella, tomato, basil, balsamic vinaigrette). By night, the kitchen serves pasta. Chef Eric Hulme, who worked previously at Ristorante Buongusto and Relais, presides, offering over 30 varieties, including rigatoni, penne, risotto, fettuccine, ravioli, farfalle, and not-so-humble spaghetti. Prices average around ten dollars a plate and preparations are simple and elegant, with the freshest of ingredients and the most generous of portions (choose something you'll want to eat for lunch for the next three days). Try the rich lasagne di mare or a garlic-lovers special, rigatoni semplici con verdure, with spinach, asparagus, and eggplant in a white wine and roasted-garlic sauce. Risottos are good and change daily. Other touches we like include bruschetta on the house and sorbet served in a whole iced peach. Weekends bring brunch, with Italian-style three-egg omelets, baked frittata, banana walnut pancakes, and tofu scrambles. The Asteroid's three owners are all musicians, one of them ex-Presidents of the United States of America drummer Jason Finn. *Brunch Sat–Sun, light breakfast, lunch, dinner every day; DC, DIS, MC, V; checks OK; beer and wine.*

AT HOME CAFE

17421 139th Ave NE, Woodinville
☎ (425) 481-0140
Woodinville
✕ *American*

If you've got an aching for comfort food, either to take out or to eat in, check out this small, customer-friendly place. Order a meat loaf sandwich and dig into a slab of rich loaf—mixed beef and pork sausage plus a little breading—served between fat slices of wholesome, light-textured, cracked-wheat bread. Time-travel to Thanksgivings past by ordering the Full House sandwich, with stuffing and cranberry sauce, or go deli with a smoked ham sandwich layered with slices of Jarlsberg. Daily specials range from Salis-

bury steak, orange-basil chicken breasts, and apricot-sage pork chops to Athenian lamb kabob, each served with a different pasta salad. Fine soups are all homemade and range from clam chowder to tomato basil. Desserts are big, solid performers, especially the irresistible peach turnovers in summer or the apple strudel most any season. The at home cafe is the direct descendant of Landau's, a classic Old Bellevue fine-dining room, and in this different venue a little of its venerable class shows through. *Light breakfast, lunch, early dinner Mon–Sat; MC, V; checks OK; no alcohol.* &

ATHENIAN INN

1517 Pike Pl, Seattle
☎ *(206) 624-7166*
Pike Place Market   ✕ *American*

The Athenian Inn is a Seattle institution—the kind of restaurant that visitors to San Francisco's Fisherman's Wharf look for and never find. Funky and neighborly, it offers a great view, friendly service, many wines by the glass, all the microbrews you'd ever hope to see in one lineup, and a seemingly endless menu of inexpensive down-home dishes. Don't be misled by the "Athenian" part of the name; founder Papi (Pappadakis) was Greek, but his cooking was all-American. Look for the daily Philippine lunch specials and the 40-plus super seafood snack plates. The long counter in the bar is the favorite watering trough for both Market old-timers and the young hipsters who pop in for a frosty mug. *Breakfast, lunch, early dinner Mon–Sat; AE, MC, V; no checks; full bar.* &

AYUTTHAYA THAI CUISINE

727 E Pike St, Seattle
☎ *(206) 324-8833*
Capitol Hill   ✕ *Thai*

By now it's a cliché that some of the best ethnic food is found in the least aesthetically pleasing of restaurants. Well, we say long live the stereotype! Ayutthaya, located in undistinguished digs just west of Harvard Market, is the type of place the serious aesthete may wish to enter blindfolded, so as not to be offended by the dated wood paneling, track lighting, or Formica-topped tables (with their plastic flowers in bottles filled with colored sand). But aesthetics aren't the point here—food is. And Ayutthaya, with its vast array of finely crafted standard Thai offerings, consistently hits the mark where it counts. The 20 seafood items, including shrimp, halibut, salmon, squid, and scallops, are stir-fried, steamed, sautéed, deep-fried, or grilled, and—as with the chicken, pork, beef, and vegetarian dishes—most are coupled with one of a number of delightfully piquant sauces. With 89 items on the menu, including appetizers, soups, salads, and noodle and rice selections, the challenge is in winnowing your choices to two or three dishes. Come with a good friend who won't mind the drab decor—or your filching a bite or two off his or her plate. *Lunch Mon–Fri, dinner every day; AE, MC, V; no checks; beer and wine.* &

B&O ESPRESSO

204 Belmont Ave E, Seattle (and branch)
☎ *(206) 322-5028*
Capitol Hill ✗ **Coffeehouse**

In a city where coffeehouses breed like caffeine-driven rabbits, B&O Espresso, presiding over Capitol Hill cafe society since 1976, is an institution. This B&O serves breakfast, lunch, and light dinners but is legendary for its homemade desserts and perfectly pulled espresso. It also offers a sublime spot for a romantic tête-à-tête, a good book, or people-watching—either through the window-lined south side, where pierced pedestrians saunter, or within its cozy confines. It's best to come during the slow, dreamy hours between meals, as service at other times can be moody. B&O also operates a small coffee-and-pastry outlet in Broadway Market on Capitol Hill (401 Broadway E, (206) 328-3290). Note: At press time, the Pioneer Square branch has become independent and is changing its name to Cherry Street Coffeehouse, but continues to carry B&O coffee and espresso, as well as serving sandwiches, quiches, and pastries. *Breakfast, lunch, light dinner every day; MC, V; no checks; no alcohol.* &

BACCHUS

806 E Roy St, Seattle
☎ *(206) 325-2888*
Capitol Hill ✗ **Greek**

Bacchus is one of those cozy dens where the world transpires outside in movie-length increments (it's no coincidence that a movie house is directly across the street). The attractive stone building, which also houses a coffeehouse and a hair salon, suits the mood of an authentic Athenian restaurant—the interior is gently lit and offers intimate tables in a relatively small space. Greek specialties abound, and for a drachma or two over $25, two can share a plenty-large spinach salad, complete with tomatoes, cucumbers, mushrooms, green onions, and Parmesan, and a combination platter of entrees.

Choose from the Bacchus (lamb, stuffed grape leaves, and spinach pie), the Athenian (lamb or chicken skewer, spinach pie, stuffed grape leaves, and meatballs in tomato sauce with basil), or the Dionysus (gyros, moussaka, spinach pie, and stuffed grape leaves). All platters run $12–$13 and tend toward generous  portions, so count on leftovers. If you feel confident of your appetite, start with one of a variety of dips, such as the tzatziki, baba ghanouj, or hummus. All are served with oven-warm pita bread, a must for any bacchanalian outing. The soups are delicious, too, both the chicken-lemon-egg and the savory lentil. Of course, the retsina flows freely. *Late breakfast, lunch, dinner every day; AE, DC, MC, V; local checks only; beer and wine.*

BAGEL OASIS

2112 NE 65th St, Seattle (and branch)
☎ *(206) 526-0525*
Ravenna/Fremont   ✗ *Bagels*

Serving some of the best bagels in the city, Bagel Oasis is a favorite for the sporty and sprouty crowd. No interior design magazine will photograph the joint anytime soon, but it's a comfortable, family-friendly place for a nosh. The traditional rounds, served fresh from the oven, are boiled before they are baked and are chewy but not tough (transplanted East Coasters rave about 'em). Try one with a generous spreading of cream cheese, or opt for a breakfast egg dish accompanied by a bagel. Also available are sandwiches (hot and cold) with a bagel base. The Fremont location (462 N 36th St, (206) 633-2676) actually has a parking lot (an appealing feature itself) and is just as down-home as the original in Ravenna. *Breakfast, lunch every day; MC, V; checks OK; no alcohol.* ♿

BAHN THAI

409 Roy St, Seattle
☎ *(206) 283-0444*
Queen Anne   ✕ *Thai*

The cozy, romantic aura created by soft candlelight and the proximity
to Seattle Center make Bahn Thai a great date spot before a night at
the opera or theater. Don't worry about making it to your show on
time; service is speedy and parking is validated (although, since the
dining room closes between lunch and dinner, a call ahead is advised
and reservations are recommended on show nights). The choice of
one- to four-star spice rating makes Bahn Thai's cuisine accessible to
every palate and has earned the establishment a reputation as a place
to bring novice Thai eaters. A variety of curries and vegetarian options
pepper the extensive menu, and the chef, kindly, is open to substitu-
tions. Raves go to the noteworthy *tom kah gai* soup, yellow curry,
peanut sauce with spinach, and sautéed scallops with *prik pao*. We also
love the coconut ice cream as a sweet last dish. Bahn Thai now has a
sister branch across the Sound, in Silverdale. *Lunch Mon–Fri, dinner
every day; DIS, MC, V; no checks; beer and wine.*

BAI TONG

15859 Pacific Hwy S, Seattle
☎ *(206) 431-0893*
South Seattle   ✕ *Thai*

• What may be the area's most authentic Thai restaurant is incongru-
ously housed in a 1960s-style former steak house in the shadow of
Sea-Tac Airport. The menu caters to both American and Thai patrons,
with full-color photographs of dishes as well as listings in Thai script.
You'll find all the familiar favorites here, with a better blend of flavors
for a more full-bodied effect than in versions found elsewhere. Try the
succulent marinated chicken—wrapped in an herb leaf and deep-
fried—that you unwrap like a gift before dipping it into a sweetened
sauce. The noncarnivorous can request curries made with tofu instead
of meat or poultry; the kitchen makes an effort to keep both flavor and
feel. The green vegetable curry with silken cubes of tofu replacing the
advertised chicken is a splendid example. *Lunch Mon–Fri, dinner every
day; AE, DIS, MC, V; no checks; beer and wine.* &

BAKEMAN'S

122 Cherry St, Seattle
☎ *(206) 622-3375*
Pioneer Square   ✕ **American**

Bakeman's is headquarters for the working-class sandwich, now an institution among Seattle's office workers. No sprouts, just shredded iceberg lettuce; no gherkins or cornichons, just crunchy dills; hand-made meat loaf instead of pâté; and real turkey sandwiches made from honest-to-God real, juicy, baked turkey with big hunks of skin sometimes still attached. As you move down the counter, be ready with your choices: white or wheat bread or focaccia; light or dark meat, or mixed; mayo or no mayo; cranberry, double cranberry, or hold the cranberry. If the waiting line is snaking around the room, don't let it scare you off; things move with amazing speed here. You want stats to prove it? Bakeman's employees make  over 500 sandwiches per day—3,000 per week—and move through 240 pounds of turkey daily (that's 30 eight-pounders). Go ahead and order a cup of chili or a bowl of soup to accompany your sandwich (the turkey noodle will remind you of Grandma's), and be sure to say yes when jivemeister Jason tries to fast-talk you into a piece of carrot cake. *Lunch Mon–Fri; no credit cards; checks OK; no alcohol.*

BAKER'S BEACH

3601 S McClellan St, Seattle
☎ *(206) 725-3654*
Mount Baker   ✕ **Bistro**

Some of the many regulars here are so loyal that they appear brain-washed. "This is the *best* restaurant in Seattle," they exclaim repeatedly. Sounds suspicious, but when you're sitting at one of the cafe's nine tables, piling the last bite of a perfectly cooked three-egg omelet on a slice of homemade hazelnut toast, and enjoying a view of leafy Mount Baker Boulevard, you may join the cult. The decor is funky-homey, with an order-at-the-counter policy for breakfast and lunch, and the kitchen turns out comfort food as an art form: plate-size blue-berry pancakes with bacon, big-topped muffins, pizza slices, shepherd's pie, and pesto lasagne. Warning: It's not the cheapest around. While lunch specials—such as the baked salmon with dill sauce for $6—can be true bargains, breakfast averages around $7, and dinner creeps out of cheap-eats territory with entrees up to $13. You could just stop by, as many of the locals do, for a slice of pie, a peanut butter bar, or a loaf of the fresh-baked bread. It's worth hanging out just to enjoy the diversity of the clientele, a reflection of the changing demographics of the neighborhood. *Breakfast, lunch every day, early dinner Tues–Fri; no credit cards; checks OK; no alcohol.* &

BALLARD BAIT & TACKLE BAITHOUSE COFFEE SHOP

5517 Seaview Ave NW, Seattle
☎ *(206) 784-3016*
Ballard ✕ *Soup/Salad/Sandwich*

Need we say there's nothing fancy about this place? It's a bait and tackle shop, after all, where beer and bait are kept behind glass doors in the same self-serve refrigerators. Nevertheless, it serves up one of Seattle's best crab sandwiches, presented open-faced on toasted white bread with a golden dome of melted mozzarella. This is not the kind of lunch spot you stumble across every day. It's set slightly off the road and across the railroad tracks in a squat 1920s-era brick building, so you're likely to drive right past it if you're not paying attention. To get to the baithouse-cum-coffee shop, take the rickety stairs at the side of the building down to the lower deck just above the calm waters of Shilshole Bay. Word of mouth has done wonders for this place. It's not just grizzly old fishermen lining up at the counter; it's anyone who knows a crackin' good crab sandwich when they taste one. Besides crab sandwiches, you'll find a soup-of-the-day selection, caesar salad ($5.99 or $7.99 with crabmeat), and a lineup of the usual deli sandwiches. On sunny days, take your meal out to the deck and watch as a steady stream of yachts and workboats pass into and out of the Sound. Prices for the crab sandwich fluctuate seasonally. On weekend nights, the bait shop opens for live jazz. *Lunch every day, lunch menu Fri–Sat nights; AE, DIS, MC, V; checks OK; beer only.*

BALLET VIETNAMESE AND CHINESE CUISINE

914 E Pike St, Seattle
☎ *(206) 328-7983*
Capitol Hill ✕ *Vietnamese*

The name might hint at a bank account–draining fine-dining experience enjoyed in the lap of luxury. But this is a far cry from the Bolshoi. Ballet Vietnamese and Chinese Cuisine, located just two doors down from the Comet Tavern and around the corner from Harvard Market, is a no-frills operation. The good news is, you won't pay extra for Ballet's lack of opulence. In fact, Ballet has established itself as a tremendous noodles-and-rice bargain, offering loads of familiar Asian food at rock-bottom prices. Of the more than 60 menu items, only a few (all seafood) stretch above the $5 mark—and none venture beyond $6.25. A generous portion of chicken sautéed with broccoli and carrots in a spicy almond sauce runs a mere $4.50 and includes a mound of steamed rice. Or try the delicate rice noodles topped with pork, shrimp, beef, chicken, or tofu—and throw in a four-pack of spicy pork pot-stickers for just a few bucks extra. Not surprisingly, Ballet's take-out business is booming. *Lunch, dinner every day; MC, V; checks OK; beer only.*

BANJARA

2 Boston St, Seattle
☎ *(206) 282-7752*
Queen Anne   ✕ *Indian*

When Indian food finally came to Queen Anne, it came in a big way—two restaurants opened on top of the hill, across the street from one another, almost simultaneously. (To be fair, there's at least one other Indian oasis hunkered down in the lowlands near Seattle Center.) More than a year later, Banjara, the less expensive of the two hilltop options, has firmly anchored itself. Filled with folks from the neighborhood and festooned with brightly colored Indian tiles and bric-a-brac, Banjara serves exactly the kind of Indian food you'd expect to find here: plain fare tricked out in fancy hammered copper bowls and plates. All the greatest hits—naan, *saag paneer*, lamb vindaloo, tandoori chicken—appear on the menu, and all of them will fill you up: partly because of their grease quotient, partly because you'll just keep stuffing yourself. The service is swift, the waitresses wear wonderfully wrapped saris, and everyone always seems to be having a grand old time. *Lunch, dinner every day; AE, DIS, MC, V; local checks only; beer and wine.* ♿

BANZAI JAPANESE RESTAURANT

480 228th Ave NE, Redmond
☎ *(425) 868-1664*
Redmond   ✕ *Japanese*

Throw a kimono over most Japanese restaurants on the Eastside and try to discern their differences. We bet you can't. But up on the

Plateau—deepest suburbia—Banzai has carved a niche with its claim to have the longest Japanese menu around. At well over 200 items, it shames even most Thai and Chinese restaurants. Teriyaki swordfish, one of the many offerings, is served with a thin and dry Japanese-style teriyaki sauce, as opposed to the usual stuff with the consistency—and sugar content—of maple syrup. Not everything works here: the lobster tempura, for example, constitutes an appalling waste of lobster, with more flavor and fun to be had from the battered sweet potato that accompanies it. The sushi menu stretches forever, fattened with a little redundancy—order *hokkigai* (surf clam) or *akagai* (red clam) and you get the same thing, only with slightly different prices. The gizzard shad sushi, however, is one of a kind. There's a wide variety of rolls here, named for some of this great nation's most vibrant urban centers: the Brooklyn roll, the Boston roll, the New York roll, the Philadelphia roll, and—ta-dum—the Redmond roll. *Lunch every day, dinner Mon–Sat; AE, DC, DIS, MC, V; local checks only; full bar.* ♿

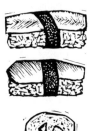

BARBACOA CARIBBEAN GRILL

301 NW 85th St, Seattle
☎ *(206) 784-4699*
Greenwood *Caribbean*

Caribbean cooking in Seattle—the whole idea sounds like a contradiction in terms. But, somehow, that's what this bare-bones storefront dishes up, against a backdrop of riotous color that includes a TV monitor playing travel videos about you-know-where. Yes, this is island food, mon. Families come here, kids in tow, for the mighty portions of greens cooked down to the melting point, the tender ribs, and the grilled shrimp on stewed rice. Working couples unwind with succulent flank steak, smoky potatoes, exotic juices, and all sorts of good-for-you root vegetables. Be forewarned: The popular tortilla chips appetizer comes with a trio of pungent salsas that will bring tears to your eyes—this one definitely ain't for the kids. (Cool yourself off during the experience with a lovely lavender lemonade or a hibiscus cooler.) For a lot less than a plane ticket, Barbacoa will warm you up with Caribbean heat, smoke, and fire. *Lunch, dinner Wed–Sun; AE, DC, DIS, MC, V; checks OK; beer and wine.* ♿

BELLTOWN BILLIARDS

90 Blanchard St, Seattle
☎ *(206) 448-6779*
Belltown ✕ *Italian*

A pool hall–cum–upscale bar with a *nuovo Italiano* menu to match, Belltown Billiards has become hugely popular. In its basement location between First and Western Avenues, it features a dark, trendy, industrial look and a long bar with an excellent view of the 12 pool tables. If you want to cue up and nosh, the best deal is at lunch, when you get free pool with your meal. Try the homemade ravioli, the fettuccine with smoked chicken and asparagus, or the prawns della casa, sautéed with garlic and herbs and finished with a spicy tomato sauce. If you want to spend more and impress your date, there's a fine steak on the  menu and an excellent rack of lamb. Those longing for more ordinary pool hall fare will be content with the gourmet pizzas and the four panini, including a mean blackened chicken. The menu stays the same from lunch until late at night, except for the specials. Bartenders and waitstaff are friendly and cool-headed, even in the throes of a rocking weekend night. *Lunch Mon–Fri, dinner every day; MC, V; checks OK; full bar.* ♿

BELLTOWN PUB

2322 First Ave, Seattle
☎ *(206) 728-4311*
Belltown ✕ *Pub Grub*

This modern, airy pub is housed in the wonderful, old Barnes Building, which was built by Belltown's prominent Austin Bell. With its high-backed, sculpted-wood booths, exposed brick, and a polished rowing scull hanging from the high ceiling, Belltown Pub is an upscale, non-smoking alternative to most bars, offering refined pub fare and 17 different microbrews on draft. Choose from appetizers such as chicken skewers, mussels with fennel sausage, or pita bread with three spreads (Gorgonzola-brie, roasted red pepper, cilantro) to smear. There will be plenty to share, as portions are generous. Burgers come with grilled onions and peppered bacon, but the pork loin with fruit chutney is a nice alternative, as is the straightforward chicken picatta. Pasta entrees are fresh and simple. The long bar is a good spot for solo diners to perch and grab a bite. Service is friendly and efficient. Many patrons seem to have drifted over from the surrounding luxury condos, still sprouting like trees-of-heaven from between the cracks of what was once—long ago—a fairly worn section of town. Desserts are limited but fresh. *Lunch, dinner every day; AE, MC, V; no checks; full bar.* ♿

THE BENTO BOX

15119 NE 24th St, Redmond
✆ *(425) 643-8646*
Redmond   🍴 *Japanese*

One good reason to venture out at noon and brave the frustration of the Overlake Memorial Gridlock Area is this darlin' little place just east of Sears and Fred Meyer. There's nothing pretentious about it, not the fairly limited menu, not the cordial service, and not the decor—tidy and attractive (though we don't recommend sitting at the good-looking but backbreaking wooden, straight-backed banquettes). The stir-fry is another good reason, sharing with the yakisoba the same commitment to fresh vegetables, still crisp and colorfully presented, and a light, pleasing sauce. Salads too. Specialty bentos  are quite a bargain, and there are a few sushi items to choose from, as well as teriyakis and Japanese noodles, both ramen and udon. The Korean influence—which takes the form of *bebim bop* and *bulgogi*, a variation of the famous beef barbecue dish—comes from chef Richard Kim, while wife Kaye, of Japanese ancestry, plays the part of very genial host. Things quiet down considerably after the noon rush. For local software workers, this is a great place to hide out until afternoon rush-hour traffic dissipates, which usually happens by 7 or 8pm. *Lunch, dinner Mon–Sat; AE, DIS, MC, V; checks OK; beer and wine.* ♿

BESO DEL SOL

4468 Stone Way N, Seattle
✆ *(206) 547-8087*
Wallingford   🍴 *Mexican*

Beso del Sol isn't just a neighborhood Mexican restaurant. In addition to burritos, enchiladas, and combination plates, the menu includes a generous selection of Southwestern cuisine favorites, plus an array of grilled items ("Barbacoa"). Reflecting its neighborhood, a good range of vegetarian options is included as well. A full selection of Mexican import beers and a few Northwest tap options are available from the bar—although you might prefer one of the enormous margaritas. The entrees are colorful and well arranged; portions are sizable, prices reasonable. The detailed wooden interior of the restaurant is brightened by plants and colorful decorations. The sunlight streaming through the large streetside windows further contributes to the pleasant atmosphere you'd expect from a restaurant whose name translates to "kiss of the sun." *Lunch, dinner every day; AE, DIS, MC, V; local checks only; full bar.* &

BETH'S CAFE

7311 Aurora Ave N, Seattle (and branch)
☎ *(206) 782-5588*
Green Lake/Bothell ✕ *Breakfast*

The original Beth's is the real deal—a dark, smoky diner on Aurora with cracked-upholstery booths, a long lunch counter, a Coca-Cola clock, and 12-egg omelets. Open 24 hours, it's an old favorite of working-class folks, hungover students, geezers, and everyone else who appreciates mammoth breakfasts in an atmosphere that's about as far away from yuppie Seattle as you can get. The aforementioned 12-egg omelets (around $10) are a true phenomenon, served in a pizza pan and sided by a mess of Beth's wonderful, griddle-crisp hash browns. Other truck-stop-fare favorites include the six-egg omelets, the rib-eye steak and eggs, the chili and onions, the biscuits and gravy (heavenly), and the platter of pancakes with eggs and bacon (all plates around $5–$7). And for the wimps in your group, there's also a list of so-called "mini-breakfasts," a still good-size portion of eggs, bacon, pancakes, and such for only $3. Breakfast here is served all day long, as it should be, but there's also a lunch and dinner menu, which includes burgers,  chili, steaks, sandwiches, onion rings and fries, a few salads, and chocolate cake. Other attractions at Beth's include the ubiquitous wall art—weird drawings and sayings that make for very entertaining late-night reading. A sample: "This is a work-free smoke area. Thank you for not smoking." Beth's is (fortunately?) a bit cleaner since a fire in the summer of '98 forced a brief closure. A second Beth's opened on Bothell Landing in 1998 (10001 Woodinville Way, (425) 482-0537)—but the atmosphere is more Denny's than true greasy-spoon. *Breakfast, lunch, dinner every day (open 24 hours); MC, V; no checks; no alcohol.*

BETTY SUE'S URBAN BAR-B-Q

4508 NE University Village Pl, Seattle
☎ (206) 523-4274
University District   ✗ Barbecue

It may not be a true hole-in-the-wall barbecue joint, but Betty Sue's is still a good antidote to homogeneous University Village. The decor is cowboy-funky—Route 66 souvenirs, Texas flags, and old saddles—and they serve up a mean paper plate of slow-smoked brisket, baked beans, coleslaw, and a crispy-sweet corn muffin. Not surprisingly, take-out is big here. There are a number of concessions to the health-conscious, including low-fat cuts of meat, no MSG, and a selection of smaller-size "lite plates." We like the pulled pork and baby back ribs best, but the spicy sausage, half chicken, and shredded beef are also not to be sneezed at (unless you've poured on too much of Betty Sue's home-made sauce). The sauce, offered in three degrees of fire, is served "Texas-style"—so they say—on the  side, but you can also belly up to the sauce bar at the back. Here you'll find some 45 bottles of interestingly named concoctions from hell, from Crazy Jerry's Brain Damage to Bone Suckin' Sauce. Betty Sue's prices are hole-in-the-wall cheap, topping out at a sampler plate for $11 that easily feeds two, or a complete rib dinner for six for $44.99. Those on the lookout for unusual gifts should note that a corner of the outlet sells all kinds of barbecue paraphernalia, including sauces, cookbooks, and the like. *Lunch, dinner every day; MC, V; checks OK; beer only.* ♿

BICK'S BROADVIEW GRILL

10555 Greenwood Ave N, Seattle
☎ (206) 367-8481
Greenwood   ✗ Bistro

Bick's Broadview Grill celebrated its first anniversary in 1998. And judging from the quality and originality of Bick's grown-up, dressed-up, and spiced-up bar food, and the loyalty of neighborhood patrons, there should be many more anniversaries to come. Warm yellow walls and high ceilings, together with red-brick columns, wooden floors, and stained-wood bar and booths, create a welcoming, relaxing environment in a converted house. Of course, this could be the margaritas talking: They're pint-size and powerful. Unfortunately, prices here can edge out of the cheap zone; your only angle may be the sandwich selection, but don't let that stop you from coming. The Southwest spiced grilled chicken sandwich ($9.50) is absolutely top-notch, a perfect blend of sweetness and spice: A chicken breast grilled with chipotles and cayenne is layered into fry bread with caramelized onions, avocado, Jack cheese, lettuce, and tomato. The tri-level oyster club sandwich (oysters rolled in cornmeal, pan-fried, and then teamed with condiments plus a chipotle aioli) is another delicious winner. The completely loaded Bistro Burger is a bargain at $7.50. There are 18 micro- and macro-brews on tap, a large selection of wines, and a number of specialty drinks. On sunny days, it's pleasant to sit outside on the deck, despite the fact that a large pine tree obstructs most of your view of the Olympic Mountains. *Dinner every day; DIS, MC, V; checks OK; full bar.* &

BIG TIME BREWERY & ALEHOUSE

4133 University Way NE, Seattle
☎ *(206) 545-4509*
University District ✕ **Pub Grub**

This packed, do-it-yourself college watering hole on the Ave has no waitstaff, so step to the saloon-style antique bar to order any of Big Time's dozen or so handmade microbrews. The pale and amber ales, porter, and IPA are always available, and several other specialty brews are rotated weekly. To order grub to go with that brewski, venture over to the kitchen window. Bring along your big, booming voice, as the noise from the TV and jukebox and the rumble of animated conversation necessitates shouting. The sandwiches (which, surprisingly, do not include burgers) and pizzas are decent, but we recommend you stay away from the vegetarian chili (it's like spooning up a bowl full of ketchup). The kitchen, at times, seems to operate on the premise that "hey, you're a college kid, and you're too drunk to care." The best food bet is undoubtedly the nachos—because it's difficult to screw up nachos—but despite all, this longtime U-Dub hangout is an institution, and is a good spot for a brew and more. You'll find a shuffleboard in the smoking room at the back of the saloon. On the Huskies' home game days in fall, this place is a pulsing sea of purple from wall to wall. Check out the Big Time Web site at www.bigtimebrewery.com to receive a virtual coupon good for $1 off any pitcher of beer. *Lunch, dinner every day; MC, V; no checks; beer only.* &

BIG TIME PIZZA
7824 Leary Way, Redmond
☎ (425) 885-6425
Redmond   ✕ *Pizza*

When Big Time—already a neighborhood fixture for years—moved into a solid old brick building in the heart of "downtown," it instantly hit the big time. Even in lesser quarters it had thrived, thanks to its range of traditional and especially its exotic pies, all built on a solid platform of wonderful chewy crusts. Ethnically inspired varieties run from Rajun Cajun to Greek. The Cascade Loop pizza includes smoked chicken, Granny Smith apples,  and dried cranberries, plus mozzarella and Gorgonzola. Wanna get wild on your own? Custom-design something: jerk chicken, mango salsa, and Montrachet cheese, perhaps? With the move to bigger digs came an expansion of the menu, which now offers salads, focaccia sandwiches, and calzones as well as a line of pasta entrees, including a surprisingly harmonic plate of smoked chicken in garlic cream sauce studded with sun-dried tomatoes and mushrooms atop fettuccine. We also never fail to go wild for the wild mushroom pizza, with its forest-load of portobellos, shiitakes, and domestic 'shrooms. *Lunch, dinner every day; AE, DC, MC, V; checks OK; full bar.* ♿

BIMBO'S BITCHIN' BURRITO KITCHEN
506 E Pine St, Seattle
☎ (206) 329-9978
Capitol Hill   ✕ *Mexican*

Don't let the name or decor intimidate you. While not your typical neighborhood taqueria, Bimbo's Bitchin' Burrito Kitchen serves up healthy portions of both tasty food and upbeat attitude. This place makes some of the best (if not the most original) burritos in the city, and serves them in a Mexican-birthday-party-meets-desert-Southwest-meets-Polynesia atmosphere. Black velvet paintings and tacky tourist souvenirs adorn the walls, and Blondie blasts over the speakers. The Basic Burrito is tasty as-is, but  gets even better with extra fixings like the tangy cumin-lime sour cream or—for something really different—sunflower seeds or garlic roasted pota-toes. Don't miss the Down Home Burrito with roasted chicken and potatoes, or the Enchilada Cha-Cha with roasted Ana-heim chiles topped with a homemade sauce. Wash it all down with a delicious margarita made from Bimbo's own homemade sour blend, which you can choose to sip (until 2am, if you choose) in the adjoining Cha-cha lounge next door. *Lunch, dinner every day; MC, V; no checks; full bar.* &

BIZZARRO ITALIAN CAFE
1307 N 46th St, Seattle
☎ *(206) 545-7327*
Wallingford   ✕ *Italian*

There's no better place in town to be a regular than at this funky quasi-Italian cafe off Stone Way, where the decor is garage-sale-explosion and the waitstaff is among the most charming in town. The ambience is shaped in large part by the theatrical, ever-changing decorations that hang from the tall ceiling: You may sit under a re-created vegetable garden (upside-down chairs, giant carrots, twining ivy) or tip a wine glass beneath one of several large dinosaurs. The eating here is quite good too, although to be truthful Bizzaro is more about fun than about food. But the pastas are more than adequate, the risotto specials are flavorful, and the chicken piccata is always tender and moist. (House salad is included with entrees, but we recommend upgrading, for $1, to a tasty small caesar.) For dessert, share a delightfully sticky bananas Foster with someone you love. Bizzarro is open till 11pm on weekends during summer and, at press time, had just begun serving brunch on weekends. *Brunch Sat–Sun, dinner every day; AE, DIS, MC, V; checks OK; beer and wine.*

BLACK PEARL
7347 35th Ave NE, Seattle
☎ *(206) 526-5115*
Wedgwood   ✕ *Chinese*

This neighborhood spot, which used to be Panda's, is still busy, busy, busy, keeping up its reputation as one of the most dependable Chinese restaurants north of the Ship Canal. It's not the atmosphere, which is clean but sterile—it's the food. The serious-looking cooks staffing the woks in the open kitchen definitely know their stuff. Specialties are the thick, satisfying handmade noodles, starring in several chow meins and soups; the tea-smoked chicken or duck; the chicken in black bean sauce; and the shrimp-stuffed tofu. The Lovers Eggplant, a longtime favorite, is also still on the menu. (Is it the crisp, batter-fried outside, the tender inside, or just the name that makes this dish so wonderful? You decide.) Also a winner is the asparagus and mushroom plate in its fermented, rather smoky black bean sauce. Less successful—at least from a non-Chinese point of view—are the Shanghai rice cakes, strangely flavored and easily confused with the cabbage they're stir-fried with; and the oddly bland hot-pot stews of vegetables and meat, tofu, or seafood. Not surprisingly, Black Pearl offers some incredible lunchtime bargains: $4.95–$5.95 for an entree, spring roll, soup, and fried rice. *Lunch Mon–Sat, dinner every day; AE, DC, MC, V; local checks only; beer and wine.*

BLACK SHEEP CAFE

Bothell Landing, 18123 Bothell Way NE, Bothell
☎ *(425) 485-1972*
Bothell   ✕ *Soup/Salad/Sandwich*

Vegetarians and vegans can bring their meat-eating friends along to this breakfast, lunch, and sometimes dinner spot—and everyone will get a darn decent meal. Turkey sandwiches abound, and there's even a Reuben and a BLT. But a glance at the prominent burger section reveals that most of the offerings there are meatless. The Sun Burger, which is made in-house and served on an oversize whole-wheat bun

with lots of veggies, kicks (taste) bud with a hearty and nutty mix of millet, carrot, onion, celery, and "secret spices." The best lunch deal is the Sampler: three samples of soups and/or salads. In the evenings, the menu gets split between meat and  meatless/vegan, with such offerings as chicken stroganoff and pasta primavera. From the deck in pleasant weather, you can see nearby Burke-Gilman Trail snaking along the riverside; doubtless the sight of all those bikers, joggers, and roller bladers will further inspire you to eat healthy. *Breakfast, lunch Tues–Sun, dinner Wed–Fri; DIS, MC, V; checks OK; beer and wine.* &

BLOWFISH

722 Pine St, Seattle
☎ *(206) 467-7777*
Downtown   ✕ *Pan-Asian*

Located in the Paramount Hotel, Blowfish offers a fun and comprehensive, if predictable, take on fusion food: You can get your Korean *bulgogi*, your Chinese pot-stickers, and your Indonesian skewers all right here. (And don't forget your divey cocktail-lounge drinks, complete with mermaid swizzle sticks!) On any given night, the wok station, the robata grill, and the bar are all ablaze with activity. Your fellow diners are an eclectic mix of downtown Seattle—the same crowd you'd see in Westlake Mall—who end up looking anonymous in this setting of red shuttered windows, beige walls, horizontal ceiling fans, hanging "paper" cranes, and pachinko machines. The cleverly priced menu focuses on the greatest hits from a variety of Asian cuisines, though you may have to be clever yourself to keep your meal in the budget realm. All dishes are meant to be shared—the trendiest way to eat right now, but also one that is authentically Asian. Food arrives at the table swiftly, as soon as it's prepared and in no particular order. Both the larger entrees and smaller plates succeed best when they stick close to the traditional, like chicken pot-stickers and Chinese broccoli; many of the smaller plates—satays and sushi—are costlier by comparison. All in all, though, Blowfish is a great place for a large group of people to eat, drink, and be merry. *Breakfast, lunch, dinner every day; AE, DIS, MC, V; local checks only; full bar.* &

BLUE WATER DINER

305 Madison Ave, Bainbridge Island
☎ *(206) 842-1151*
Bainbridge Island   ✕ *Diner*

How can you go wrong eating in an authentic 1940s dining car, nestled in the heart of already charming Bainbridge Island? Owner Al Packard has recovered and painstakingly restored this funky piece of Americana after shipping it back from its former resting place in New Jersey. He's turned it into a fun, full-service restaurant, delivering capably on a promise of food that's "not always fancy, but always great," serving standard diner fare in huge portions. Burgers, sandwiches, soups, and salads fill out the menu, and greasy (but tasty) breakfasts are served all day. Stick with the classics: A one-third-pound cheeseburger with fries and a chocolate malt will leave you sleepy and smiling. If the grease sends you into acute food catatonia, walk it off with a slow stroll through Winslow, or grab a few winks on the dock of a nearby marina. *Breakfast, lunch, dinner every day; MC, V; checks OK; beer and wine.* &

BOAT STREET CAFE

909 NE Boat St, Seattle
☎ *(206) 632-4602*
University District   ✕ *Bistro*

The Boat Street Cafe is a gem in the middle of nowhere, on one of the most difficult-to-find little streets in Seattle. That doesn't mean that no one knows where it is, though: You'll recognize it by the long line outside, especially for weekend brunch. What looks like a fisherman's shack from the outside is utterly airy and light-filled inside. The unfinished ceilings, glowing walls, and open kitchen make this the ideal space for low-toned conversations, newspaper reading, and leisurely cups of tea—in short, the perfect place for a quiet, civilized weekend brunch, a lovers' lunch, or an intimate dinner. On the weekend, break into a coddled egg, using a bit of crusty bread to sop it all up. At lunch, try one of the sandwiches, made with a Le Fournil baguette, or an artfully dressed salad—all favorites with the university folks nearby. Dinner is pricier, but you get more bang for the buck as well: candlelight, a small, perfect wine list, and a rotating selection of dishes that reflects the offerings of the season. *Brunch Sat–Sun, lunch Tues–Sun, dinner Wed–Sat; no credit cards; checks OK; beer and wine.* ♿

BOTTICELLI CAFFE

101 Stewart St, Seattle
☎ *(206) 441-9235*
Downtown   ✕ *Soup/Salad/Sandwich*

Just a block from tourist-trodden Pike Place Market, at the corner of Stewart Street and First Avenue, tiny Botticelli has been doing what it does best for over a decade: providing customers with excellent coffee and tasty toasted panini. And Botticelli's been doing it to a veritable chorus of international adulation. The gray walls are a gallery of gushing reviews from both near and far, from the local dailies and weeklies to *National Geographic's Traveler* magazine, the *New York Times*, and the *London Sunday Times*. Do the sandwiches live up to the hype? You bet, particularly when compared to the fast-food lunch options you might otherwise be faced with downtown. Each panini is made with fresh ingredients by the caring hands of the owner herself, who favors such Italian deli superstars as prosciutto, fontina, provolone, porchetta, bresaola, and mortadella. Focaccia or rustico bread is brushed with olive oil and toasted to golden brown perfection. The Focaccina Farcita is a wonderful gathering of chopped artichoke hearts, diced tomatoes, provolone, and Italian dressing. If you find the lunch hour too advanced for a delicious cappuccino or espresso, try the sparkling San Pellegrino Italian sodas ($1.50) for a refreshing complement to the panini. This is a small place with only a few tiny round tables, so expect to take your sandwich to go during the weekday lunch hour. *Coffee only mornings Mon–Fri, lunch Mon–Fri; MC, V; no checks; no alcohol.*

BOULANGERIE
2200 N 45th St, Seattle
☎ *(206) 634-2211*
Wallingford ✕ *Bakery*

Walk by Boulangerie around 7pm, when the fragrance of fresh brioche is wafting down 45th Street, and you'll know why this French bakery has such a legendary local reputation. Stop by merely to pick up a loaf of crusty walnut bread—or a seeded baguette, or a *pain complet*—and you'll inevitably end up with a white paper bag of goodies such as napoleons, honey-almond tarts, *chausson aux pommes* (apple filling wrapped in puff pastry), and croissants (there are seven kinds to choose from). Boulangerie also has excellent cakes and fruit tarts and a good selection of pâté, Brie, jam, vinegars, mustards, and other French delicacies. Sandwiches—vegetarian, turkey, ham, salami, or roast beef—are the best buys for only $2.50, and day-olds go for $1.50. The small space doesn't invite lingering, but they do have good coffee and the *New York Times* on hand. *Breakfast, lunch, early/light dinner every day; no credit cards; checks OK; no alcohol.* ♿

BRIAZZ
1400 Fifth Ave, Seattle (and branches)
☎ *(206) 343-3099*
Downtown/Bellevue/University District ✕ *Soup/Salad/Sandwich*

Salads, sandwiches, soups, and baked goods feature high-quality ingredients at this chain of sleek urban take-out cafes. The food tastes of attention to detail, from good, locally baked bread to salads fragrant with fresh herbs and dressings with pizzazz. Choose from a wide range of cuisine and a selection of low-fat entrees, from the traditional (ham and cheese sandwiches) to the tantalizing (tandoori-spiced basmati rice, roasted chicken, onion, and dried apricots on a bed of greens). With everything packaged and ready to go, all you need to do is make your selection from the refrigerated cases and form a line to ante up. Fight for one of the few tables if take-out's not your style, or avoid the line altogether by ordering a box lunch for delivery. Suits mob the downtown store on weekdays at lunch hour, but the line moves along efficiently. There are currently nine Briazz cafes, but expect more branches to open soon. *Breakfast, lunch every day; AE, DC, DIS, MC, V; checks OK, no alcohol.* &

BRIGHT STREET PUB & CAFE

4332 Leary Way NW, Seattle
☎ *(206) 706-1443*
Fremont   ✗ *Bistro*

The Bright Street Cafe, located between Fremont and Ballard, is light on the pub, heavy on the cafe. There's a small bar just inside the front door, but the kitchen is obviously the major focus. There's no pub grub here—the Bright Street offers fare ranging from soups and salads to ravioli pie, seafood, and steak; a hamburger and a tuna melt are available for a lighter meal. There are no fries, but a few bucks will get you a large, relatively unadorned salad. Full dinners are fancier and begin to creep out of budget range, but portions are generous. On the beer side, this spot survives its limited tap line by buying local (two varieties from the Maritime Brewery up Leary Way) and going classic (Guinness Stout); there are also more than 40 wines to choose from. *Dinner every day; AE, MC, V; checks OK; beer and wine.* &

BRUSSEAU'S

117 Fifth Ave, Edmonds
☎ *(425) 774-4166*
Edmonds   ✗ *Soup/Salad/Sandwich*

Though original owner Jerilyn Brusseau is long gone, her eponymous cafeteria-style bakery and cafe remains a local favorite. Ferry-bound folks vie for a spot outdoors at umbrellaed picnic tables, while families and elderly patrons relax inside at glass-topped tables over coffee and sweets. The day's menu always includes a couple of soups—perhaps cilantro-and-cumin-spiked black bean—meant to be sopped up with a house-baked roll. Create a sandwich from a short list of options (yes, they make halves), or choose among a sampling of salads lining a glass display case. Save room for a slice of seasonal fruit pie, and don't leave without buying a loaf of fresh bread to savor at home. *Breakfast, lunch every day; MC, V; checks OK; no alcohol.* &

BUCA DI BEPPO

701 Ninth Ave N, Seattle
☎ *(206) 244-2288*
Lake Union ✗ *Italian*

Show up with lots of friends, the patience of Job, the appetite of a sumo wrestler, and an abundant sense of humor, and you will have so much fun you won't know what hit you.

This "concept" Southern Italian restaurant is all party-down and Italian-American kitsch—from the religious icons and walls plastered with photos, to the bar decorated with Chianti bottles, to the Dean Martin version of "That's Amore" that'll have you swaying while waiting for a table and then for your garlicky, oversize portions of family-style chow. The food's as good as it is plentiful, with foot-long pizzas, baseball-size meatballs atop mounds of spaghetti, a slab of lasagne that'd fill a shoebox, and a heap of chicken cacciatore. Beppo is tucked into a space a block or two west of the lake—just look for the neon wine glass endlessly refilling itself. *Dinner every day; AE, MC, V; checks OK; full bar.* &

BULGOGI

Crossroads Shopping Center, 15600 NE Eighth St, Bellevue
☎ *(425) 747-7212*
Bellevue ✗ *Korean*

The menu placard at Bulgogi is right to call Korean food "Asia's best-kept secret," and this establishment is an excellent place to sample a couple of the more popular dishes in this delightfully varied cuisine. What the Crossroads food court lacks in charm, Bulgogi's food more than compensates for with rich flavor. The rice bowl is a full meal by itself. Known as *bebim bop* in Korea, it's a winter favorite: a bowl filled with hot rice, marinated meat, sprouts, and assorted vegetables, topped by an egg that sizzles and fries on the heat of the food below it. Served on the side is the essential element of the dish, a hot red sauce with an earthy taste unique to Korean cuisine. The other major menu option is *bulgogi* itself, a sliced, deeply marinated rib beef. Complemented by a side of fresh kimchi (cabbage pickled in red pepper), it offers a complex, smoky palate of flavors not present in other beef preparations. Shoppers are familiar with one of *bulgogi*'s most appealing attributes, its fantastic aroma, which one encounters when navigating the crowds at the north end of the shopping center's food court. *Lunch, dinner every day; MC, V; no checks, no alcohol.* &

THE BUNGALOW WINE BAR AND CAFE

2412 N 45th St, Seattle
☎ *(206) 632-0254*
Wallingford   ✕ *Bistro*

At most places the wine list is created to complement the cuisine. At this tasteful Wallingford wine bar, however, the menu exists for the sake of the wine—an extensive list of over 60 regular selections plus weekly specials. Keeping dinner low-cost at the Bungalow is no easy chore, as forgoing the vino here seems almost sacrilege, and the least expensive choices are $5 a glass. The menu, which changes slightly from week to week, is arranged by plate size: small-plate items run from $4 for an olive sampler to $8.50 for tiger prawns in a garlic, chipotle, and white wine sauce; medium plates may include a roasted vegetable ensemble with aioli and Romesco sauces, steamed mussels, or a tempting lasagne with butternut squash cream sauce; large plates easily run into double-digit prices. There are also three cheese plates available for around $6. Your best bet is to nab a spot out front on the tiny wooden deck (with views past the neon Dick's Drive-In sign toward the Cascades), nurse a glass of red wine, and nibble on the cheese and olive plates. Or drop in for a homemade chocolate truffle and a cup of coffee or a glass of pricey port. Inside the Bungalow—a converted Craftsman-style home with hardwood floors and cream-colored walls that also houses an excellent poetry-only bookstore—the dining area is divided into three small rooms, with the larger tables in such cozy proximity to one another that you can't help but eavesdrop on every pretentious thing your neighbor is saying about French wine or how this lovely little bungalow reminds her of an absolutely spectacular place in Tuscany. . . . *Dinner Tues–Sun; MC, V; checks OK; beer and wine.*

BURRITO LOCO

9211 Holman Rd NW, Seattle
☎ *(206) 783-0719*
Greenwood   ✕ *Mexican*

Burrito Loco is a big, anonymous storefront in the middle of nowhere with lots of parking, so if you walk in with minimal expectations you'll be jolted out of your seat. All the clichéd plates you find at other family-run Mexican restaurants are served here, too, but with a difference: The ingredients are fresher, the sauces have a clearer, brighter flavor, and the beans are free of lard. A tremendous amount of care is put into the food here. Local chefs are known to make pilgrimages for Burrito Loco's *tortas*, sandwiches served on soft, white Mexican rolls, filled with your choice of fish, fowl, pork, or beef. The refreshing ceviche is sublime, especially in warmer weather, and makes for either a great appetizer or a light meal. *Agua frescas* are also served up here: You can get melon, honeydew, or *horchata*, the sweet drink made from rice and evaporated milk. *Lunch, dinner every day; DIS, MC, V; local checks only; beer and wine.* ♿

CAFE DAVINCI'S

89 Kirkland Ave, Kirkland
☏ *(425) 889-9000*
Kirkland 🍴 *Italian*

It seems as if DaVinci's always has been and always will be the buzz of Kirkland on a weekend night. Even when the weather is dicey and the glass wall that looks out on Lake Street is kept closed, that buzz draws twentysomethings off the street and into the dark, loud bar, where during quieter, more reflective moments, sporting events blare from big TVs. It's the kind of place where love (or at least lust) blooms like summer impatiens; it's also a place that needs a strong arm hanging around, just in case things take a negative turn. But there's another side to DaVinci's as well—the other side of the building, actually— where a dining room looks out on the lake and a large streetside patio area offers some of the best seats in town on a fine day. What a pleasant surprise to find not only decent pizza but some pleasing pasta as well, especially the cannelloni. But face it, nobody comes here for the cannelloni. *Lunch, dinner every day; AE, DC, DIS, MC, V; checks OK; full bar.* ♿

CAFE SEPTIEME

214 Broadway E, Seattle
☏ *(206) 860-8858*
Capitol Hill 🍴 *Bistro*

The owners of Cafe Septieme found the perfect location—right on the Broadway strip—for this hip, clean, and stylish cafe. Contemporary fine art hangs on faux-painted walls, and white tablecloths match the professional, neatly dressed waitstaff. The cafe caters to a clientele that enjoys a cloth napkin but doesn't carry enough of a job to need breakfast before 9am on a weekday. Septieme serves a hearty Seattle-roast coffee, fresh baked treats, and an excellent breakfast—better than you'd expect from a cafe with a full bar. Choices range from simple oatmeals and granolas and eggs to grilled polenta and a nice French toast. Our favorite is the huevos rancheros—black beans, potatoes, and eggs on a tortilla, with a fresh fruit garnish. It can get crowded during the popular weekend brunch. For lunch and dinner, Septieme offers a menu of pastas, salads, sandwiches, and specials until 11pm; dessert is served until closing. During the summer, tables are set up on the sidewalk for the requisite Broadway people-watching. *Breakfast, lunch, dinner every day; AE, DC, DIS, MC, V; no checks; full bar.*

CAFE SOLEIL
1400 34th St, Seattle
☎ *(206) 325-1126*
Madrona   ✗ *Ethiopian*

This aptly named corner cafe is filled with light—even during the dampest part of the year. And if you close your eyes, you can pretend you're sitting in the famous open-air market of Addis Ababa, reveling in the smoky scents of crushed cardamom, cumin, and chile peppers. Tear off a piece of injera, the flatbread that serves as both starch and eating utensil in any Ethiopian dinner, and grab a morsel of vegetable, lamb, or salmon *wat* (stew)—our favorite is the vegetable, made with a hearty assortment of greens, such as Swiss chard or kale. Other fine options include the *tibs,* stir-fried dishes that are kicked up with a hearty red chile paste. Owner Kuri Teshome cooks because she loves to—and it shows. Cafe Soleil is a wonderful place to take the vegetarian in your life for lunch, dinner, or weekend brunch. During the colder months, nothing can beat the invigorating effects of the fresh-shaved ginger tea. *Breakfast, lunch Tues–Sun, dinner Tues–Fri; MC, V; local checks only; beer and wine.* ♿

CAFFE INFINITO
16349 NE 74th St, Redmond
☎ *(425) 883-8855*
Redmond   ✗ *Soup/Salad/Sandwich*

Tucked away in the hypercorporate confines of the Redmond Town Center, Caffe Infinito is a truly welcome surprise. The menu is limited but full of interesting options. Start with the antipasto and assorted cheese platter, large enough to be shared by two or three. Proceed to a tub of hearty chowder or fresh soup; then try a mammoth hot deli sandwich, featuring treats like honey turkey and Black Forest ham, that could satisfy even the most jaded New Yorker. Dining is pleasant inside, where the decor is lush and woody, or out front at the bistro tables. The attractions of Infinito only start with the menu. Owner J. D. Hemmat got the idea for his cafe while working as a roadie on Candlebox's North American tour, and music is a major theme here. The establishment has been wired for acoustics and quickly converts to a live-music venue. The back of your receipt features the ever-changing lineup of performances, which range from swing music to fortune-telling. *Breakfast, lunch, dinner every day; AE, DIS, MC, V; checks OK; beer and wine.* &

CAFFE LADRO

600 Queen Anne Ave N, Seattle
☎ *(206) 282-1549*
Queen Anne ✕ *Coffeehouse*

The term Caffe Ladro is Spanish for "coffee thief." And judging by the throngs of faithful customers who queue up before the barista at this artsy espresso joint on top of Queen Anne Hill, you might guess that it got its name because it's pilfering customers from the banal chain coffeehouses that crowd it on either side. One thing is certain: Caffe Ladro gives you a better coffee in a more hip environment than just about any coffeehouse in the city. Amid rust-colored industrial walls, you'll sit in pretty, painted wood chairs, at tables of amalgamated stone and colored glass; as you review the menu, burnt into a sheet of flexed copper, you can admire the funky stained-glass creation that hangs above the counter. Your drink arrives in a cool coffee cup  with the sleek silhouette of the coffee thief himself. In the mornings, feast on delicate currant and walnut scones, cinnamon rolls, muffins, and granola. A modest selection of sandwiches and homemade soup awaits you for lunch. *Light breakfast, light lunch every day; no credit cards; checks OK; no alcohol.*

CALIFORNIA PIZZA KITCHEN

595 106th Ave NE, Bellevue

☎ *(425) 454-2545*

Bellevue   ✕ *Pizza*

California pizzas—Wolfgang Puck–inspired creations with unusual toppings, sometimes delightfully surprising like hoisin chicken and goat cheese, and sometimes downright malevolent such as potatoes and black beans—had already found their way north before California Pizza Kitchen arrived on the Eastside a few years back. Still, there's something alluring about the glossy place. Maybe it's all the sun-yellow trim, glass, and mirrored surfaces: California transplants can settle into black and blond furniture and dream of windshield shades on cars parked at beaches in December. More to the point, the pizza is quite good, with a thin, crispy crust, though the $9 average is a little hefty for the 10-inch pies. Our favorites include the hoisin duck portobello among the *nuovo* style, and the margherita among the traditional. This spot could well be called California Pasta Kitchen, as much of the pasta is fresh and made in-house. Play it safe with a tomato-basil angel hair, or tempt fate with ginger black-bean angel hair. A kids' menu coddles families (though we don't recommend letting an impressionable youngster witness Mom or Pop ordering kung pao spaghetti). There's nothing mutant about the desserts—Key lime pie or apple crisp as wholesome as all of, uh, Beverly Hills. *Lunch, dinner every day; AE, DC, DIS, MC, V; checks OK; full bar (limited liquor).* ♿

CANTON WONTON HOUSE

608 S Weller St, Seattle

☎ *(206) 682-5080*

International District   ✕ *Chinese*

Located one block east of the Uwajimaya market, the Canton Wonton House is a small, sparse noodle shop—a few simple hangings of calligraphy on cream-colored walls, a dozen or so tables, a counter for a few more folks, and a large window that spies into the workings of the kitchen. Otherwise, it's just you and your noodles. All dishes are prepared in the delicate, understated tradition of Cantonese cuisine—the majority in the Hong Kong style characterized by thin egg noodles in a large bowl of remarkably full-flavored golden broth, garnished with bok choy and topped with wontons stuffed with shrimp and ground pork; thinly sliced beef brisket or barbecued pork; fish or squid balls;

or various mix-and-match pairings. The less soupy alternative is to have your noodles on a plate with the luxurious broth on the side. Large bowls and plates, which run from $3.95 to $5.25, are a surprisingly filling meal. Regular bowls and plates are about a buck less and make a great light lunch. For a bit more, try a bowl of the traditional thin rice porridge called congee—add minced beef, pork, egg, kidney and liver, or chicken for just $1.50 extra. *Lunch, dinner every day; AE, DIS, MC, V; no checks; no alcohol.*

CASCIOPPO'S

2364 NW 80th St, Seattle
☎ *(206) 784-6121, ext. 3*
Ballard   ✕ *Deli*

In 1996, partners Gus Froyd and Peter Glick bought the retail end of Cascioppo Brothers, Ballard's famed sausage maker. With an eye for creating an old-style specialty market, they expanded the menu, started dry-aging steaks in a cedar-lined cooler in the back room, and added more homemade "heat 'n' eat" selections such as meat loaf and garlic-and-basil-stuffed chicken breasts. Most important, they spent many sleepless nights "analyzing"—as Froyd puts it—pastrami. The result is a charmingly unpretentious deli that serves up arguably the best hot pastrami sandwich west of Manhattan, attracting a group of worshipers that includes both blue-collar folk and cell phone–clad businessmen. And it's only $4.95. Other deli treasures abound: fresh mozzarella, smoked turkey, homemade half-sour pickles, Cascioppo's sausage, wonderful bacon, and home-prepared corned beef. Because Froyd worked for 15 years in the wine business, there's also a fine selection of wine and port. In keeping with the partners' philosophy, no bottle is priced more than $2 above cost. Everything is take-out only. *Lunch every day; MC, V; checks OK; wine only.*

CATFISH CORNER

2726 E Cherry St, Seattle
☎ *(206) 323-4330*
Central District   ✕ *Southern*

From the TV perched in the corner playing a documentary-style video of catfish preparation (tons of catfish on factory conveyor belts) to the no-frills dining room (formica tables, bright-orange vinyl booths) and the photo album at the counter with its faded pictures of meal selections—the emphasis here is placed strongly on catfish. And what fish! Whether you go for bits & chips, bits & pups (hushpuppies), or an entire catfish, the lightly breaded fillet is so delicate it melts in your mouth. We love it with a lotta sweet tartar. Catfish Corner sits, appropriately, on the corner of East Cherry and Martin Luther King Boulevard, and also serves buffalo fish, prawns, red snapper, and hamburgers. Whole dinners, ranging from $7.75 to $8.75, include beans and rice, a cornbread muffin (as unimpressive as its side dish price of 25 cents might suggest), and a choice of coleslaw or potato salad (mustardy and filling). The beans and rice are worth getting on the side, or try the collard greens (best with a splash or three of vinegar). But cheap eaters should skip the dinner combos and head straight to the catfish fillet bits & pups. The pups are great—cornmeal dumplings that are deepfried, hot, and sweet. Lots of people take their catfish to go, but, if you eat in, service is warm and welcoming. Don't skip the peach cobbler. *Lunch, dinner Mon–Sat; no credit cards; local checks only; no alcohol.* &

CAT'S EYE CAFE

7301 Bainbridge Pl SW, Seattle
☎ *(206) 935-2229*
West Seattle   ✗ *Soup/Salad/Sandwich*

Conveniently located just down the road from Lincoln Park, this shabby charmer of a cafe is a good place to fortify yourself before or after a long walk. It's got a long lunch counter, a creaky screen door, a menagerie of cat-themed knickknacks, and a young staff who remember exactly how the regulars like their lattes. A simple but effective breakfast menu—try the Potato Works or the focaccia egg sandwich—is served till noon. The afternoon crowd comes in for espresso, frozen-yogurt smoothies, or one of the "catalog" (get it?) of sandwiches listed on the colorful chalkboard. These include the House Cat (bacon, lettuce, tomato, and avocado) and the Cat in Heat (tuna). They also offer a rather typical list of cafe items, including vegetarian chili (quite good!), hummus, quiche, enchiladas, a soup-of-the-day, and several filling focaccia sandwiches. We especially like the Vegetariano and the turkey with havarti and cranberry sauce. Sweet things, such as muffins and Rice Krispie bars, are all baked in-house. *Breakfast, lunch every day; no credit cards; checks OK; no alcohol.*

CHACE'S PANCAKE CORRAL

1606 Bellevue Way SE, Bellevue
☎ *(425) 454-8888*
Bellevue   *Breakfast*

It's easy to speed right past Chace's Pancake Corral without a second glance. For breakfast lovers and golf aficionados, however, that would be a mistake. There's often a wait in the small entryway of this establishment, while businessfolk negotiate deals over Folgers and big plates of hotcakes, but the fine consistency of the pancakes here makes heading to another place far too risky. As the corral in the name indicates, this is your basic breakfast—no ambitious gourmet dishes are offered. The most exotic menu item—coconut syrup— is recommended with certain dishes and is surprisingly good. Potato pancakes are also one of the  specialties. A golf theme decorates the walls, including scoreboards and photos of various small-time tournaments. The service is efficient and friendly: You'll rarely see the bottom of your coffee mug. Parking can be tight. *Breakfast, lunch every day; MC, V; checks OK; no alcohol.* ♿

CHARLIE'S ON BROADWAY

217 Broadway E, Seattle
☎ *(206) 323-2535*
Capitol Hill    *American*

Celebrating more than 20 years as a bastion of late-night eats, Charlie's has retained every bit of the dignified mustiness it had when you spent late Friday nights there in high school, engrossed in "deep" conversations over nachos and fried mozzarella sticks. Smack-dab in the middle of Broadway's hyped-up, caffeinated street scene, it's an oasis of nostalgia. Charlie's harks back to Jimmy Stewart movies and the bygone-era chintz of the American Family House. Once you're ensconced here in a floral-upholstered chair, sitting beneath a formidable chandelier, your thoughts may swing toward MGM-style Sunday suppers, but the best approach to navigating the detailed menu is to keep it simple: You can't go wrong with any of the burgers, appetizers, or desserts (especially the berry pies). The daily specials are more pricey and not usually worth it. Or go for the "breakfast anytime" portion of the menu—the Monte Cristo sandwich (egg-battered bread with cheese, ham, and turkey) never fails to please. Where else can you have waiters sing "Happy Birthday" as you while away the wee hours? *Breakfast, lunch, dinner every day; AE, DC, DIS, MC, V; no checks; full bar.* ♿

CHICKEN VALLEY

1507 Pike Pl, Seattle
☎ *(206) 624-1774*
Pike Place Market
✕ *Chicken*

Chicken Valley, a market stall just a couple of salmon-tosses down from Pike Place Fish, does fried chicken—every poultry part imaginable, from drumsticks (a buck apiece) to thighs and breasts ($1.15 apiece and $4.49 a pound, respectively) to backs, gizzards, livers, and hearts. But though the digs are modest and the fare is limited, this is not Kentucky Fried Chicken we're talking about. The chickens are excellent-quality, free-range birds raised in Washington, baptized in a slightly peppery batter, and fried just until crisp. And they've also got mushrooms, potatoes, and chicken corn dogs—fried, of course. Order a paper bag of treats, douse them with barbecue sauce and/or ketchup, and head to the view-rich public space just south of the Sound View Cafe to munch in bliss. Bring lots of napkins, and expect to eat all the skin, despite your best intentions. Chicken Valley also sells whole uncooked birds, which you can take home and do something different with—if you have the weird idea that something should be done with chickens besides dipping 'em in hot oil. *Lunch every day; no credit cards; no checks; no alcohol.*

CHINOISE CAFE

12 Boston St, Seattle
☎ *(206) 284-6671*
Queen Anne
✕ *Pan-Asian*

As signaled by the name, this cafe is trying to please its world-weary clientele by giving them everything: pan-Asian fare and European flair. A busy sushi bar is backed by a pretty dining room done in warm Mediterranean yellow, with fun, fish-themed art and fresh flowers on the tables. There's also an inviting patio outside. By most accounts, Chinoise is succeeding. It's always crowded with see-and-be-seen folks as well as families, and most dishes are competently turned out, if a bit bland (a three-star dish barely blisters). The cooks are best at sushi:

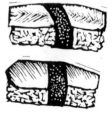

Rolls are plump, seafood is fresh, and the selection is wide-ranging and dotted with unusual specials such as octopus and asparagus rolls. Most of the dishes in the healthy "Good Greens" section are also good bets, such as Vietnamese-style lemongrass chicken, served in a bowl of rice noodles flavored with peanuts, lime, and cilantro. "Wok dinners" are also tasty, including the garlic shrimp (the kitchen has a generous hand with the shrimp), mu-shu chicken, and yakisoba. Specials tend to be eclectic, such as pistachio squid with basil-roasted aioli or sautéed geoduck in lemon-butter sauce. Prices are $7–$10 for most dishes, with sushi dinners ranging up to $20. Lunch is a bargain. Besides blandness, there are only two real problems here, both resulting from the cafe's popularity: Service can be slow, and waits quite long. *Lunch, dinner every day; AE, DC, DIS, MC, V; no checks; beer and wine.* &

CITY THAI

21 Bellevue Way NE, Bellevue
☎ *(425) 452-8554*
Bellevue ✕ *Thai*

In the shadow of Bellevue Square sits City Thai, where diners are greeted at the door by a wall of grinning photos of the owner. Here he is with the Thai prime minister. And look! There's Michael Jackson, for whom City Thai's jovial owner served as personal bodyguard. Inside, the food is excellent without being overly adventuresome. Phad Thai and chicken satay are now as American as pizza to us globalist Northwesterners, but these standbys are worth another look. In fact, all of the old favorites are a little better than usual at City Thai: The sours are a little more sour, the curries have a greater spectrum of flavor, the crushed peanut accents have a fresher taste. The atmosphere is comfortable and warm. The woodsy chalet ceilings of the structure (which seems to have previously contained a pancake house) somehow reach an aesthetic equilibrium with the carved teak musicians (a favorite Thai artistic theme). Justifiably proud of the cuisine, the staff at City Thai practices the philosophy of "hosting" rather than "waiting" tables. The result is a dining experience more elegant than the check would indicate. *Lunch, Mon–Sat, dinner every day; AE, MC, V; checks OK; beer and wine.* &

CJ'S EATERY

2619 First Ave, Seattle
☎ *(206) 728-1648*
Belltown ✕ *American*

Though the atmosphere at CJ's is reminiscent of a food-court dining area in your average suburban mall, the consistently high quality of the food and multitudinous menu keep business hopping at this breakfast and lunch spot. On weekday mornings, expect to see a buttoned-down business crowd chowing on cheese blintzes, potato or Swedish-style pancakes, sausage frittatas, or any one of a dozen omelets. Lunch selections include 11 kinds of salads and over three dozen sandwiches, covering everything from tuna melts to meat loaf, with eight kinds of chicken breast sandwich and ten takes on the common burger. Heartier lunch appetites are appeased by "CJ's Specialties," featuring a roast beef platter with mashed potatoes and gravy or fish 'n' chips with fries and coleslaw (both $6.95). Take-out and catering are also available. Remember, the periwinkle blue walls won't hurt you, and the large windows facing First Avenue give a good glimpse of the Space Needle. *Breakfast, lunch every day; AE, DIS, MC, V; checks OK; beer and wine.* ♿

COASTAL KITCHEN

429 15th Ave E, Seattle
☎ *(206) 322-1145*
Capitol Hill ✕ *American*

The good and bad news about Coastal Kitchen is that it's almost always packed—the food here is sure to please the masses, but to partake of it you may have to stand in a massive line first. (For the fiendishly popular weekend "Blunch," that line can easily spill out the door and onto the street.) But the generous portions of red chard or salmon "rumbles" (scrambled eggs) served with shredded hash-browns and succulent maple-cured bacon are worth the wait. This third addition to the joints owned by neighborhood-restaurant king-pins Peter Levy and Jeremy Hardy may just be their best effort. For lunch and dinner, the menu, along with the restaurant decorations, regularly rotates through regional themes—say Cajun, Southwestern, soul food, or Atlantic seaboard. Some dishes are strongers than

others but any are worth a try because this is where the cooks really get rowdy and imaginative. And, too, there are always classic dishes to fall back on, like ale-battered fish 'n' chips, spicy Louisiana stew, and the All Day Long Breakfast. With a versatile cooking crew and a wait-staff that stumbles only when the restaurant is most crowded, Coastal Kitchen serves up consistently good fare no matter what's on the menu. *Breakfast, lunch, dinner every day; MC, V; local checks only; full bar.* &

CONTINENTAL GREEK RESTAURANT AND PASTRY SHOP

4549 University Way NE, Seattle
☎ *(206) 632-4700*
University District ✕ **Greek**

Clean Plate Club membership is near impossible at the Continental, a U-District favorite since George and Helen Lagos opened it on January 1, 1974. The specialty here is huge portions of Mediterranean dishes at very reasonable prices. Most entrees run $6–$7—prices top out at $12.95—and include salad, a roll, and a pastry. Best bets on the long menu are the spanakopita (spinach and feta wrapped in tender layers of phyllo dough); the kefhtes (Greek meatballs); the dolmathes (grape leaves stuffed with lamb and other goodies); and the chicken with lemon, garlic, and olive oil. In the last couple of years, the Lagoses have also added pasta, including fettucine alfredo and various spaghettis, to the menu. At breakfast, you'll share the dinerlike atmosphere with hungover students who know that a plate of eggs, Greek fries, and a souvlaki skewer is their only hope. At all times of the day, save room for the pastries, especially the baklava, crisp-tender and loaded with nuts. You can also pick up everything from Greek soap to dried chickpeas at the small but fine deli. *Breakfast, lunch, dinner every day; MC, V; no checks; beer and wine.* &

COOL HAND LUKE'S

1131 34th St, Seattle
☎ *(206) 324-2553*
Madrona ✕ **Pan-Asian**

Those who understand the movie reference in this restaurant's name may expect Las Vegas–style food: stuff like gargantuan prime rib specials and all-you-can-eat pancake breakfasts. But Cool Hand Luke's is better described as a soup-and-salad diner that serves pan-Asian fare—quite appropriate when you realize that it's part of the gourmet ghetto of 34th Avenue. Between the cerulean-sponged walls there is plenty to sample at reasonable prices. The Lunch Box, for example, includes a daily meat/vegetable combination and a large bed of sticky rice as well as the soup du jour and a succulent spare rib. It's one of the better deals around, for under $6. Or try the Imperial Mix-Up: grilled Portuguese sausage, scallions, and egg mixed with rice. Breakfast is served all day (8am-4pm) on weekends, which is just one more incentive to stop by. With a friendly, laid-back atmosphere and just enough attention from the waitstaff, this is a neighborhood oasis with a warmer touch than its name suggests. *Breakfast Sat–Sun, lunch, dinner Tues–Fri; no credit cards; checks OK; beer and wine.* &

COSTAS OPA GREEK RESTAURANT

3400 Fremont Ave N, Seattle
☎ *(206) 633-4141*
Fremont   ✕ *Greek*

With its Mediterranean whitewashed walls and classically kitschy decor—including black-figure plates and tiny statues of the gods—Costas Opa feels like a trip to a touristy Athenian cafe. This casual corner spot is one of two eateries owned by Costas Antonopoulos (his other is Nikolas Pizza and Pasta in Wallingford—see the separate review. Costas also shares ownership of Costas Greek Restaurant in the University District with his brother, Chris). As you watch the Fremont Bridge being raised and lowered, enjoy a wide selection of standard Greek food (gyros, spanakopita, lots of garlic-redolent dishes) and listen to "Never on Sunday" for the umpteenth time while sipping retsina and dreaming of sunnier climes. *Lunch, dinner every day; AE, MC, V; checks OK; beer and wine.* &

COYOTE CREEK PIZZA

228 Central Way NE, Kirkland (and branch)
☎ *(425) 822-2226*
Kirkland/Bellevue   ✕ *Pizza*

There was a time not too awfully long ago when a pizza hung with pine nuts, pesto, prawns, and cilantro struck diners as odd. But today nary an eyebrow would raise, never a lip purse, nor a glance look askance at such preposterousness. Funny thing: Some of these admixtures even work, and those at Coyote Creek hit their mark more often than not. Even more mundane combos, involving stuff like tomato sauce and pepperoni, earn rave reviews here. Partly that's due to the delightfully crisp crust that never sogs or sags. Gotta admit it—we love the North by Northwest, a combo of apples, roasted hazelnuts, Gorgonzola, mushrooms, and onion that jams like a jazz quintet. The Southwest theme extends beyond a so-named pizza to the decor, which is spare and suggestive of Native American influences. There's a second location in Crossroads Shopping Center (15600 NE Eighth St, (425) 746-7460). *Lunch, dinner every day; MC, V; checks OK; beer and wine.* &

CUCINA! CUCINA! ITALIAN CAFE

901 Fairview Ave N, Seattle (and branches)
☎ *(206) 447-2782*
Lake Union/Bellevue/Issaquah/Kirkland/Redmond   ✕ **Italian**

People either love or hate exclamation-pointed Cucina! Cucina!—but fans of this local chain of Italian-American restaurants far outnumber detractors. Reasons for the strong feelings include the waitstaff, described as either overeager or attentive, the bar scene—too loud or lively, depending on your point of view—and the dependable and tasty, if not entirely authentic, cuisine. No one can deny that there are many things the restaurants do quite well. It's hard to beat the setting of the flagship restaurant on Lake Union, a colorful warehouse of a space that features a huge open kitchen, a terrific view of the lake, and a constant hubbub of staff, diners, and yuppie barflys. Get a window table in the bar during happy hour (when prices are shaved by a couple of bucks), and order a caesar salad and one of their excellent wood-fired pizzas—one-person pies anchored by a crispy-chewy crust. Pasta dishes come in two sizes, and the portions are generous enough that often the "piccola" will be plenty. Good choices include the linguini with roasted chicken and broccoli in a garlic cream sauce, and the penne with a generous helping of wild mushrooms. Pricier specialties include veal marsala and grilled coho salmon, and there are salads and soups as well (the lentil is excellent). Desserts are mostly overpriced and disappointing. There's almost always a line at this hot spot; food is served until late in the bar. Cucina Presto! is a Cucina! spin-off that offers similar dishes in a speedy, order-at-the-counter atmosphere. Though at times the pasta isn't as presto as it could be, people seem to love the concept, and some 17 locations (in Bellevue, Mercer

Island, Queen Anne, etc.) have opened since 1996. *Lunch, dinner every day; AE, DIS, JCB, MC, V; checks OK; full bar (beer and wine at Cucina Presto!).* &

DALY'S DRIVE-IN

2713 Eastlake Ave E, Seattle
☎ *(206) 322-1918*
Eastlake   ✗ *Burgers*

At Daly's, the register tapes read "Fine Fast Food" and the product drives the point home. Maybe the flame-broiled burger wasn't invented here, but ground beef aficionados will find a Daly burger as close to perfection as three-minute-or-so service allows. No soggy burgers under heat lamps here—everything is cooked to order. The pin-ball machines are to your right; a dining room with a Lake Union view is to the left. The Daly Double, the Big Mac's brawnier, juicier cousin, is always an excellent choice, but Daly's also serves up great fish (or clams) and chips, shakes of many flavors, and the world's biggest onion rings. Veggie burgers, salads, and chicken teriyaki are available for those who keep their distance from red meat. *Lunch, dinner Mon–Fri; no credit cards; checks OK; no alcohol.* &

DELCAMBRE'S RAGIN' CAJUN

1523 First Ave, Seattle
☎ *(206) 624-2598*
Pike Place Market   ✗ *Cajun/Creole*

One bite of Danny Delcambre's spicy blackened prawns will transport you to a backwoods Louisiana cafe complete with a fan swirling lazily overhead, zydeco music thumping, and the smell of jambalaya on its way to the table. Delcambre's bustling little cafe offers a nice rendition of the expected red beans and andouille, creamy catfish étouffée, and gumbo brimming with sausage. It also includes the unexpected—a flutter of hand-signing across the room between the owner/chef and his mostly deaf staff (Del-cambre, who studied under Paul Prud-homme, is both deaf and sight-impaired). Service is pleasant and efficient. At lunch,  the muffuletta sandwich gets raves, and sizable dinners (two could split the massive Ragin' Cajun Combo) come with warm, cheesy slabs of jalapeño bread and a light salad. *Lunch Mon–Sat, dinner Thurs–Sun; AE, MC, V; local checks only; beer and wine.* &

DELUXE BAR & GRILL

625 Broadway E, Seattle
☎ (206) 324-9697
Capitol Hill   ✗ *American*

The Deluxe's storefront home at the north end of the Broadway strip isn't huge, but there's enough space within for a neighborhood hangout bar and a thriving restaurant operation. In this beer connoisseur's paradise, the tap list is generous and changes often, and there are drink specials on any given night. The restaurant fare focuses on sandwiches and burgers (love those condiment trays), but it has plenty of meatless dishes too, including the popular baked potato in various incarnations ($5.95 with a tasty side salad). The Deluxe is that rare neighborhood bar that has plenty of regular customers but isn't stand-offish toward first-time visitors. On a hot summer night, with the front doors open and tables set up on the sidewalk, the Deluxe is a noisily cheerful place to be. *Breakfast Sat–Sun, lunch, dinner every day; AE, DIS, MC, V; no checks; full bar.*

DESERT FIRE

7211 166th Ave NE, Redmond
☎ (425) 895-1500
Redmond   ✗ *Southwestern*

After a long contest to determine what the new name should be, the Canyon Cafe chain opened Desert Fire, the first Northwest outpost of this popular Southwestern chain, in the sprawling Redmond Town Center. Walk past the flaming sconces at the entrance into a room outfitted in peeling, split logs. The place feels like an amusement park with its long lines and loads of kids. But tables turn over quickly, and to ease the waiting you're given a beeper that blinks red when your table's ready. The Pit of Fire in the main dining room is the prefab version of a campfire grill, complete with log fences and waiters with bolo ties. The food is, predictably, South by Southwest, from the grilled meats to the tacos, pastas, and salads. Creative sauces abound, from mild, creamy versions of jalapeño and poblano chiles to tangy relishes on the side. We give a thumbs-up to the quesadillas, the chicken piccata, and the Mohave margarita. *Lunch, dinner every day; AE, DC, DIS, MC, V; checks OK; full bar.* &

DICK'S DRIVE-IN

111 NE 45th St, Seattle (and branches)
☎ *(206) 632-5125*
Wallingford/Capitol Hill/Greenwood/
Lake City/Queen Anne   ✕ **Burgers**

A cheeseburger from Dick's is as genuine and enduring a symbol of Seattle as the mighty Space Needle—and it fits better in the palm of your hand. This local institution is the Jet City's homegrown answer to the burger-and-fries culture, complete with horrid orange decor and cheerful paper-hatted servers. It's a good, cheap place to take a) the kids, b) the fellas/the gals, or c) your barhopping late-night friends (until 2am). It's *not* a good date place past about age 16, even if you do call it "Reee-chard's" (imagine silly French accent here). The cheapest burger in town tastes better if you arrive in a car (especially one that's equipped with fins) and hits the spot when topped with American cheese and a squirt of pickle-specked mayo. Hand-dipped chocolate, vanilla, and strawberry milk shakes are a treat for the ice cream lover. The only difference between the five Dick's restaurants is ambience: Broadway has the amazing streetlife; Wallingford has smooth-faced teens in street rods; Queen Anne is the only Dick's with indoor seating. The Greenwood and Lake City stores are classic roadside burger joints alongside major arterials. *Lunch, dinner every day; no credit cards; no checks; no alcohol.* &

THE DISH

4358 Leary Way NW
☎ *(206) 782-9985*
Fremont   ✕ **American**

Located midway between Fremont and Ballard, this tiny, triangle-shaped breakfast and lunch spot is laid-back enough to appeal to both the gritty Ballard crowd and the artsy Fremont folks (and anybody else who happens along). With a scant dozen or so tables, plus an L-shaped lunch counter that seats a handful, the Dish claims a capacity crowd in a hurry, particularly on weekends. You may have to park yourself out front on one of two stained pinewood benches beneath an old electric Coca-Cola sign, but the wait is worth it. The Dish does diner-style breakfasts as well as anyone, serving the usual lineup of omelets and scrambles plus a few surprise combinations like the Chili (cheddar cheese, onion, and chili), the Hula (Canadian bacon, pineapple

chunks, and Jack cheese), and the Florentine (pesto, cream cheese, and ripe tomatoes). The sausage gravy is slathered high and wide over fluffy biscuits, the breakfast burritos are structural wonders stuffed to the bursting point, and there's no shortage of corned beef in the corned beef hash. Lunch is handled deftly as well. There's a long list of sandwiches, including a burger with au jus dip and a veggie sandwich, plus a soup of the day and a selection of salads. For a buck more, sandwiches come with homemade potato salad, chips, a cup of soup, or salad. *Breakfast, lunch Tues–Sun; no credit cards; checks OK; no alcohol.* &

DIXIE'S BBQ

11522 Northup Way, Bellevue
☎ *(425) 828-2460*
Bellevue   ✗ *Barbecue*

The bad news is you can no longer get your brakes repaired here, as in the early days when Gene Porter of Porter's Automotive Repair first wheeled in a smoker like a steam locomotive and started selling the ribs and such that had long made his family so popular at church picnics. The good news is that while you can get good brake work most anywhere, there's only one Dixie's. It's tucked alongside the northbound ramp from SR 520 to I-405, and it focuses solely on barbecue. Folks seem to appreciate this, especially the ones lining up out the door and across the parking lot as early as 11:30am on weekdays. Dixie's has achieved its popularity not on its good looks, but on its good food. About its only advertising to speak of are the bumper stickers and T-shirts that brag, "I Met 'The Man' at Dixie's BBQ." The Man, by the way, is not Porter but his secret, hot barbecue sauce. So toxic is this brew that rumor has it the state Department of Transportation, fearful of a spill and concerned about the structural integrity of its precious interstate highway, considered banning the stuff from the premises. The beef brisket sandwich really doesn't need it, and neither do the well-smoked ribs and chicken. Sides hold up their end of the plate, and the family's lemon cake recipe is legendary. *Lunch, early dinner every day; no credit cards; checks OK; no alcohol.* &

EGGS CETERA'S BLUE STAR CAFE AND PUB

4512 Stone Way N, Seattle
☎ *(206) 548-0345*
Wallingford   ✗ *American*

One of the first nonsmoking watering holes in town, the cafe that was once just "the Blue Star" now has a dizzying assortment of beer on tap (some served in 20-ounce glasses—yum!) and sophisticated pub grub on its oft-changing menu. The detailed wooden bar fixtures and large, high-ceilinged main room combine to create a space that is cheerful yet not overly noisy. The decor is nostalgic-Seattle, with dozens of photos from the collection of local historian Paul Dorpat decorating the walls. (Even the name is an historic reference—nearby Aurora Avenue was designated a "Blue Star Highway" in honor of members of the armed forces.) The kitchen performs equally well on the fancier fare and the simple stuff, though the latter—burgers, sandwiches, salads, pastas, etc.—rule the day. Big portions too; especially generous on the fries. *Breakfast, lunch, dinner every day; AE, MC, V; no checks; beer and wine.* &

EL PARGO MEXICAN SEAFOOD RESTAURANT
10825 Myers Way S, Seattle
☎ *(206) 241-6182*
White Center   ✕ **Mexican**

Dining at El Pargo is like standing at the Four Corners with your sneaker in four states at once—except here you have an elbow in Burien, a toe in White Center, and a backside firmly planted within Greater Seattle. If pinpointing the location (where First Avenue South turns into Myers Way) is confusing, just look for the glass-block entry, the stucco facade, and a festive glow. El Pargo is Mexico away from Mexico: The marlin is the official mascot (there's a large mural along one wall), piñatas hang from the ceiling, and serapes are draped gracefully over the windows. There's something inexplicably authentic about the place, perhaps because the family-run atmosphere makes eating here feel like a visit with the relatives, complete with requisite indifferent teens and noisy children playing out front. The food is exceptional: traditional and beautifully presented. Seafood is  featured in just about every way imaginable: appetizers include oysters, shrimp cocktails, fish taquitos, and prawns (though some of the fancier seafood sold by quantity may not qualify as cheap, depending on your appetite). Otherwise, prices are reasonable, and the selection includes nonseafood items too, such as Chicken Azado (grilled chicken with quesadillas, rice, and salad) and chile verde (cubed pork in a most delectable green sauce)—both remarkably good. *Lunch, dinner every day; MC, V; checks OK; no alcohol.*

EL PUERCO LLORON

1501 Western Ave, Seattle
☎ *(206) 624-0541*
Pike Place Market   ✕ *Mexican*

This place transports you back to that cafe in Tijuana, the one with the screaming hot pink and aquamarine walls and the bent "Cerveza Superior" tables. Once you find it (it's tucked into the Hillclimb behind Pike Place Market), belly up to the cafeteria line, place your order, and fight for a table—in warm weather, those outdoors are as hard to find as free parking spots. Try the taquitos plate, three excellent masa corn tortillas rolled around a filling and served with rice, beans, and a scallion. The chiles rellenos are fresh and bright with flavor, and the unadulterated guacamole's worth the additional splurge. Pick up lemonade or Mexican beer at the end of the counter. *Lunch, dinner every day; AE, MC, V; no checks; beer and wine.*

ELYSIAN BREWING COMPANY

1221 E Pike St, Seattle
☎ *(206) 860-1920*
Capitol Hill   ✕ *Pub Grub*

Want to graze in the Elysian fields, but don't want to go to the underworld to do it? The Elysian is an aptly named stomping ground for the young and hungry denizens of Capitol Hill, who hang out in this hangarlike, bare-bones industrial space to play pool or partake of the really fine cheap food and the designer suds, which are whimsically named after various mythological figures. If you don't know what you want to drink, a pint of Loki offers an easy swallow; those who want to decide for themselves should get the daily rotating sampler tray. The typical brewpub fare includes crispy chicken wings, garlicky hummus, hearty stews, fish 'n' chips, pasta, and big honkin' sandwiches—all priced well below a ten-spot, and more often less than a fiver. This is fat fry territory: perfect, wedge-shaped pieces of crunchy heat, all the better to enjoy your cool beer with. *Lunch, dinner every day; MC, V; no checks; beer and wine.* ♿

EMMETT WATSON'S OYSTER BAR

1916 Pike Pl, Seattle
☎ *(206) 448-7721*
Pike Place Market ✕ *Seafood*

Occupying a cheery back-alley cranny in the Soames-Dunn Building, the namesake restaurant of Seattle's most curmudgeonly journalist embodies some of the casual irreverence of this town. The tiny flowered courtyard is nice when warm noontime sunlight drifts down to the tables; when the weather is wet, take refuge inside at one of the booths. Part of the draw is the oysters. Regulars drop in just to slip down a few, on the half shell or fried up hot and sandwiched on a French roll. Others love the salmon soup, a clean, clam-based broth with big chunks of the pink fish. Still others come for the chowder and a Guinness (one of many bottled brews and drafts available) or the fish 'n' chips—true cod dipped in a spicy breading, fried in light cottonseed oil, and drizzled, if you wish, with Cajun garlic sauce. *Lunch every day, dinner Mon–Sat; no credit cards; checks OK; beer and wine.* ♿

EUROPEAN GOURMET CAFE & DELI

1882 136th Pl NE, Bellevue
☎ *(425) 641-0818*
Bellevue ✕ *Deli*

These days, *deli* is an oft-misused term: a rack of hot dogs, a Cheez Whiz dispenser, and a few gas pumps—Eureka, you're a deli! Well, here's a *real* deli. Located next to a BMW dealer, Ukrainian immigrant Bronya Lefelman deals in meats, cheeses, candies, olives—you name it. How do you like your herring, pickled or creamed? Gotta craving for an anchovy? Easily satisfied. You want that rye slathered with butter from Germany or butter from Austria? Fetas hail from France, Bulgaria, Russia, Greece, and everywhere else. Lefelman has Czech cheese and German cheese, Danish and Dutch,  just for starters. Like your mackerel cold smoked or hot smoked? Have a halvah; have three. Cat got your calf's tongue? Here's some more. Creating a sandwich here can border on international intrigue. In addition, a case of home-cooked foods tempts with rich stroganoff, *golubsti* (cabbage leaves stuffed with herbs, rice, and chicken), borscht, and blintzes. Past the dessert case, a doorway opens into a large dining room with a high ceiling, formal cut-glass chandeliers, a dance floor, a small bandstand, and gorgeous tile flooring. Here is where eat-in diners take their meals and pick a table; it's also a spot for banquets. *Lunch every day, dinner Fri–Sat; MC, V; checks OK; full bar.* &

EZELL'S FAMOUS FRIED CHICKEN

501 23rd Ave, Seattle
☎ *(206) 324-4141*
Central District/Lynnwood   ✕ *Chicken*

Legend has it that a while back, when Oprah Winfrey taped a few of her shows in Seattle, she fell in love with Ezell's fried chicken. Apparently, she's had their chicken FedEx-ed to her on more than one occasion since. Whether or not this legend is true, it certainly could be (and perhaps should be). More than a few people have fallen for the legendary chicken served up at this renowned Central District eatery. Like all fried chicken, it definitely isn't healthy—not by a long shot. But it is *good* . . . greasy, crunchy, juicy, melt-in-your-mouth good. While the chicken is clearly the main attraction, available in both "crispy" and "original recipe" (with apologies to KFC), don't miss out on the sides. The potato salad isn't particularly exciting, but both the beans and the mashed potatoes with gravy ably fill out your meal. The fish dinners are also good, but second-string (the place isn't called Ezell's Fish, after all). Seating here is nonexistent, so the parking lot often doubles as a dining room. Don't be afraid to pull up a curb and enjoy some of Seattle's best fried chicken with the neighbors. Ezell's has a second location in Lynnwood (7531 196th St SW, (425) 673-4193) which is also take-out only. *Lunch, dinner every day; no credit cards; checks OK (no checks in Lynnwood); no alcohol.* &

FARESTART

1902 Second Ave, Seattle
☎ *(206) 443-1233*
Downtown   ✕ *Soup/Salad/Sandwich*

There are few times in life when you can eat your cake and have it too, but lunch or dinner at FareStart (formerly known as Common Meals) is one of those times. Here you'll eat good food *and* contribute to a social good. Why? Because every dollar you spend benefits the FareStart program, which trains homeless folks for jobs in the hospitality industry. Lunchtime is an all-you-can-eat affair for around $6—and that means limitless runs to the salad bar, soup bar, entrees and dessert bar. But the real steal comes on Thursday nights, when guest chefs from Seattle's finest kitchens whip up three- and four-course prix-fixe meals at a prix that's astounding: $11.50 a head. Everyone in Seattle's culinary glitterati has spent a Thursday evening or two in the cafe; the results are always memorable. There are, however, a couple of things you should know: Make reservations, or be prepared to eat somewhere else. Also, alcoholic beverages are only served on Thursday nights. A redecoration back in 1996 gussied up what had originally been a nondescript space in the Josephinum Hotel; it's not swanky, but it's definitely a restaurant now. This fine program is expected to start up in other cities; don't forget that Seattle launched it first. *Lunch Mon–Fri, guest-chef dinner Thurs; DIS, MC, V; checks OK; beer and wine (only on guest-chef night).* &

FIDDLER'S INN

9219 NE 35th Ave NE, Seattle
☎ *(206) 525-0752*
Wedgwood   ✕ **Pub Grub**

Wedgwood's favorite tavern has a convivial atmosphere and a long history—it was started in the 1930s by a tuba player named Walt Haines—plus a surprisingly solid menu. You can start by ordering a pint or two to wash down a screaming plate of Fire-House Nachos, a serving of pesto bread, or a Bavarian soft pretzel with mustard. The main events are the pizzas—big crisp-chewy pies that will satisfy a crowd—and a selection of sandwiches that are a sharp cut above normal pub fare. The sandwich bread is from A La Francaise bakery, and fillings include smoked turkey and cranberry sauce, hot pastrami, and Italian chicken sausage; the wonderful "harvest sandwich" is a happy union of baguette, pesto, and roasted vegetables that have left most of their oil at home. There are a couple of other nods to Seattle's health-conscious crowd, including several soups and salads (get the Greek) and a whole-wheat quesadilla. The tavern—shingled on the
outside, wood-paneled on the
inside—has a surprisingly airy feel,
and the patio to the side is hopping
with regulars in the summer. Live music
is featured several nights a week. *Lunch,
dinner every day; MC, V; checks OK;
beer and wine.*

THE 5 SPOT
1502 Queen Anne Ave N, Seattle
☎ *(206) 285-SPOT*
Queen Anne ✕ *American*

Most mornings there's a line under the big neon coffee cup outside this neighborhood landmark. It's a Big Fun kind of place at the top of the Counterbalance and, in fact, it counterbalances an architecturally pretty cafe with a kitschy menu and solid service. Expect such standard regional American fare as Southwestern tostadas, Southern-style country ham with sautéed greens, Northwest halibut 'n' chips, and a New England roast chicken supper. A Food Festival Series mixes in a regionally oriented menu (say Florida or Texas) on a rotational basis, and decor tends to change with the menu. A great pair of dinner pork chops comes with rib-sticking mashed potatoes and gravy, though we know folks who can make a meal out of an order of french fries and a Pabst Blue Ribbon in the bar. The updated red flannel hash served at breakfast may be the best you'll ever eat. If you're dining alone, grab a seat at the counter and people-watch. *Breakfast, lunch, dinner every day; MC, V; checks OK; full bar.* ♿

FORECASTER'S PUBLIC HOUSE
14300 NE 145th St, Woodinville
☎ *(425) 483-3232*
Woodinville ✕ *Pub Grub*

Forecaster's, the pub attached to the Redhook Brewery, is the best reward for riding your bike from Seattle to Woodinville along the Burke-Gilman Trail. Once you stumble off your wheeled steed, we suggest first taking the brewery tour, where you can sample four beers for a dollar. Then, when you're sufficiently lightheaded, hunker down inside at a booth or outside at a picnic table, and get down to some serious refueling. Not surprisingly, beer figures in the food as well as the drinks: The bratwurst is boiled in Redhook ESB before it's grilled; the salmon and bread board (a bargain at $4.95) includes ESB-basted smoked salmon; and the scrumptious Triple Black Cake is made with Redhook stout beer—which, in turn, is made with Starbucks coffee. The short but creative menu changes seasonally, but there's always at least one burger option plus sandwiches, a full-fledged entree or two, and salads (though the lack of a deep fryer equals no fries). Nothing is over $10. They also have beer, of course: six or so drafts at a time, plus one or two British-style, dry-hopped, barrel-aged brews. It's worth a trip sans bike, too, and the atmosphere is particularly festive on Friday and Saturday nights, when they have live music and are open late. *Lunch, dinner every day; AE, MC, V; checks OK; beer and wine.* &

14 CARROT CAFE

2305 Eastlake Ave E, Seattle
☎ *(206) 324-1442*
Eastlake   ✕ *Breakfast*

Would-be and will-be diners crowd the sidewalk on Saturday and Sunday mornings because the 14 Carrot Cafe is synonymous with "breakfast" for many locals. A hopping joint when the tables are full and the waitstaff is scurrying, the 14 Carrot pours more syrup on a Sunday morning than most restaurants pour water. The omelets, huge and stuffed with ingredients of your choice, are a favorite. The menu also includes pancakes, cinnamon rolls, and lunch. There's an espresso cart parked out front to attend to more complex caffeine needs, but a coffee cup doesn't stay empty long here. The weekday crowd is more neighborhood-oriented, but plenty of business deals have coalesced over the cafe's eggs and bacon. *Breakfast, lunch every day; AE, MC, V; no checks; beer and wine.* &

THE FRANKFURTER

1023 Alaskan Way, Seattle (and branches)
☎ *(206) 622-1748*
Downtown/Bellevue/North End/
Queen Anne/SoDo   ✕ *Hot Dogs/Sausage*

What our city makes up for in espresso carts, it seriously lacks in hot dog stands. The Frankfurter is no steaming cart run by a wise guy with an accent, but it does offer spanking-clean joints that cook up the dogs of your choice. Such old favorites as bockwurst, kiel-basa, and kosher franks have made way for such "that's-no-hot-dog" inventions as sun-dried tomato, Southwestern, and Thai chicken dogs on a bun. But nothing can beat the spicy Italian Hot, teamed with a fresh-squeezed lemonade—and we continue to ignore the written plea not to heavy-hand the kraut. *Lunch, dinner every day (hours vary seasonally and by branch); no credit cards; no checks; no alcohol.* &

FREMONT CLASSIC PIZZERIA AND TRATTORIA

4307 Fremont Ave N, Seattle
☎ *(206) 548-9411*
Fremont   ✕ *Pizza*

Nothing is taken too seriously at this tiny, cheery trattoria. Servers are fun and feisty, as befits a neighborhood restaurant, while the decor, neither here nor there, is just plain cozy. If you stick to the pizza, you can enjoy an utterly delicious, unpretentious meal. Owner and chef Paul Kohlenberg's pizza dough is thin, crackly, floury, and slightly chewy, and his sauce is of the refreshing, chopped-up-tomato variety—a perfect combination. Choose between traditional pizzas (your choice among the usual suspects) or one of Kohlenberg's inventive concoctions. We tend to prefer the former: The crust and sauce are so good that it's a shame to disguise them under a bunch of goop. The simplest pizza of all, the Margherita—tomatoes, mozzarella, Asiago, extra-virgin olive oil, and basil—is smashing. Pasta dishes are less successful. You get huge piles of chewy, oversauced pasta that are relentlessly flavorful and so robust they're almost tiring. Desserts are fine if you have room, but you won't miss anything if you don't. *Dinner every day; DC, MC, V; local checks only; beer and wine.* ⓹

FREMONT NOODLE HOUSE

3411 Fremont Ave N, Seattle
☎ *(206) 547-1550*
Fremont   ✕ *Thai*

Finally, here's a Thai restaurant whose atmosphere can compete with its food for your sensory pleasure. You can't help but be drawn in off Fremont's main drag to inspect this wood-filled temple of Thai good taste: rice-paper lampshades hang from the ceiling, a curio cabinet displays Thai photos, and mirrors make the oft-crowded room appear much larger than it is. The short menu offers fragrant noodle-based soups and sautés and simple rice dishes spiked with various meats, seafood, and vegetables. Among the half-dozen appetizers is *mieng hahm,* a sensually appealing starter of toasted coconut, ginger, Thai chiles, peanuts, red onion, and lime— all meant to be folded into the accompanying *bai cha plu* (dark green leaves). Service is swift and polite. *Lunch, dinner Tues–Sun; AE, DIS, MC, V; checks OK; beer and wine.* ⓹

GASPARE'S RISTORANTE ITALIANO

8051 Lake City Way NE, Seattle
☎ *(206) 524-3806*
Maple Leaf ✕ *Italian*

A remodel more than doubled the size of this once-funky little trattoria, which now boasts a big, bright kitchen visible from one end of the large, V-shaped dining room. Some may mourn a loss of atmosphere (though secretly applauding the loss of hour-long waits), but no one will complain about Gaspare Trani's food—as comforting and sure-handed as ever. Pastas have just the right touch of garlic; salads are made with interesting fresh produce; the vitello piccata (tender veal with the right balance of lemon, white wine, and capers) is a fine rendition of the classic. The near-perfect pizza features a soft, chewy crust topped with a rich tomato sauce. Gaspare now  spends much of his time at his more pricey downtown venture, Il Gambero, but here in Maple Leaf, service still takes its lead from his amiable wife, Dianne. *Dinner Tues–Sun; MC, V; local checks only; beer and wine.* ♿

GEORGIA'S GREEK DELI

323 NW 85th St, Seattle
☎ *(206) 783-1228*
Greenwood ✕ *Greek*

Stepping into Georgia's Greek Deli—with its whitewashed walls, light blue trim, faux grapevines running up a trellis in the dining room, and numerous plants potted in olive tins—will put you in mind of the sunny Greek isles. This effect is enhanced when you hear Greek being spoken in the kitchen and by the regulars in the small (but not cramped) dining room. The menu features traditional Greek favorites such as moussaka, souvlaki, dolmathes, and the requisite gyro platter, plus baked fish of the season, roast leg of lamb, and roasted half chicken. Available for lunch or dinner, these meals come with pita bread and a choice of roasted potatoes or Greek pasta. Lighter appetites and vegetarian interests are also accommodated by way of pita sandwiches, spanakopita, soups, salads, and a dish of giant Greek baked beans drenched in tomato sauce. Breakfast selections, served daily, include a wide variety of eggs, scrambles, omelets, pancakes, and French toast. You'll also find several shelves stocked with Greek specialties for sale, including white and red wines, olives, olive oil, tins of sardines, pasta, grape leaves, olive spreads, snacks, and more. *Breakfast, lunch every day, dinner Mon–Sat; no credit cards; checks OK; beer and wine.* &

GILBERT'S ON MAIN

10024 Main St, Bellevue
☎ *(425) 455-5650*
Bellevue   ✕ **Soup/Salad/Sandwich**

A couple-block stretch of Main Street in Old Bellevue proves that urbane character can indeed be found here in Edge City. Gilbert's on Main possesses the kind of charming ambience that tempts one to make hanging out an art form. Set streetside on the first floor of a new condo complex, high-ceilinged with utilitarian guts exposed overhead, the room feels large but not cavernous. That's due partly to the walls, which are colored halfway between lemon and pumpkin and hand-painted with stylized animals. They do breakfasts and lunches here: lots of omelets and scrambles to start a day properly, plus a variety of pancakes and French toast. Pizzas are available at lunchtime, but the sandwiches deserve most of your attention. Anytime at all is a good time to relax with baked goods (including fine bagels and muffins), an espresso, and something from the magazine collection. On pleasant days, grab a seat at one of the sidewalk tables and while away an hour or two. *Breakfast, lunch every day; AE, MC, V; checks OK; beer and wine.* &

GORDITO'S HEALTHY MEXICAN FOOD

213 N 85th St, Seattle
☎ *(206) 706-9352*
Greenwood   ✕ **Mexican**

Some people might think this family-run restaurant has become a neighborhood favorite because of the word "healthy" in its name, but we suspect that it's because it's such a happy place. You order your fajita taco, fish burrito, or enchilada plate from a cheerful counter-person wearing a tie-dyed shirt, who then hands you a small piñata named Jorge or Silvestre so you can be found. Make a stop at the well-stocked salsa bar, find a table in the spacious, whitewashed, tile-decorated eating  area, and wait briefly for your plate, drumming your fingers on the table in time to the recorded mariachi music. The quality ranges: Best are the quesadilla plates and the burritos, which come either wet (topped with enchilada sauce and melted cheese), fajita-style (with sautéed bell peppers and onions), or stuffed (with fish or spinach or prawns). "Healthy" does figure in here, as all meats are grilled and no lard is used in the rice and beans, but the portions are so generous that the danger of becoming a *gordito* ("fat one") still looms. Use the handy take-home containers. Also handy are the prices: You'll have a tough time spending $15 on dinner for two. And Gordito's prides itself on catering to picky eaters, so feel free to make special orders. *Lunch, dinner Wed–Mon; AE, MC, V; checks OK; beer and wine.* &

GOURMONDO

1518 Western Ave, Seattle
☎ *(206) 587-0190*
Pike Place Market   ✕ **Soup/Salad/Sandwich**

Lately, what's under and behind Pike Place Market has gotten as interesting as what's on top: little restaurants, tattoo parlors, bird shops, antique stores, and, voilà, Gourmondo. Located near the Hillclimb, this pretty little 12-seat cafe is the definition of European chic and restraint: If you don't already know where it is, chances are you'll never find it. Which is a shame, because the food served here is delightfully simple and plain: sandwiches, salads, and pastas made using fresh, high-quality ingredients. You'll love the chicken salad with its colorful array of peppers, green beans, and snowy chicken meat, and you'll swoon over the tender house ravioli. Like all good things, Gourmondo is available only in limited quantities—lunch is the only meal that's served here. Fresh flowers and sunny colors turn this into the best of secret places to meet for a noontime tryst. Dinners for larger groups can be privately arranged. *Lunch Mon–Fri; no credit cards; checks OK; no alcohol.* &

GRAND CENTRAL BAKING COMPANY

214 First Ave S, Seattle
☎ *(206) 622-3644*
Pioneer Square   ✕ **Bakery**

Grand Central holds grand status among Seattle's many bakeries, and may be responsible for the rustic-bread craze that has turned this town into a bread-lover's paradise. Classics here include the Como loaf (a moist, rustic Italian baguette), rosemary rolls, and whole-grain and walnut loaves. At lunch, grab a grinder filled with meat and cheese or roasted veggies and explore Pioneer Square, or slide a tray past the cafe counter and choose from salads, panini (on homemade focaccia), soups, and built-to-order sandwiches accompanied by clever side salads. Marble-topped tables accommodate arcade seating beneath the building's handsome exposed brick walls and soaring ceilings. Or, in warmer weather, you can take your meal to one of the few little tables out back in Occidental Square, in sight of the totem poles. *Breakfast, lunch Mon–Sat (deli open Sun); MC, V; checks OK; beer and wine.*

GRAVITY BAR

415 Broadway E, Seattle
☎ *(206) 325-7186*
Capitol Hill ✕ *Vegetarian*

Meet George Jetson. His boy Elroy. Daughter Judy. Jane, his wife. Need we say more about Seattle's slickest vegetarian restaurant and juice bar, with its conical tables of galvanized metal and green frosted glass lit from within for the ultimate Jetsons effect? Entrees are luscious, healthful, and beautifully presented: mounds of brown rice and steamed vegetables with a glistening lemon tahini sauce; chapatis rolled with hummus and fresh vegetables; miso soup with buckwheat noodles. The freshest of fresh juices can get expensive (and the rejuvenating wheat grass might taste pretty vile to virgin palates), but indulge. You'll feel like a million bucks later. *Breakfast, lunch, dinner every day; MC, V; local checks only; no alcohol.* ♿

GREEN CAT

1514 E Olive Way, Seattle
☎ *(206) 726-8756*
Capitol Hill ✕ *Vegetarian*

This bright, airy, funky little cafe near Denny and Olive boasts a unique and healthy menu. The green in Green Cat, you see, refers to the fare—all vegetarian (with many items available in a vegan form) and all fresh. But even if you're a meat eater, you'll find something to love. The menu is vibrant and varied, and just about everything is good: No matter what time of day you find yourself here, the Green Cat satisfies. If you're just passing by in the morning, pop in and grab coffee and a scone (the scones alone merit a visit, with such heavenly combinations as pear-ginger and blueberry-banana). At lunch, sandwiches and wraps are king, with many regulars going for the Green Cat Sandwich, a baked, open-faced combination of pesto, avocado, tomato, provolone, and sunflower seeds on rye. Your best bets at night are the empanada, a sort of Latin American potpie, and the Buddah Bowl, steamed veggies and bean sprouts served with peanut sauce over brown rice. As you might imagine, salads are always good: crisp and fresh, accompanied by bread hot out of the oven. *Breakfast, lunch, dinner every day; MC, V; checks OK; beer and wine.*

GREENWOOD BAKERY

7227 Greenwood Ave N, Seattle
☎ *(206) 783-7181*
Greenwood ✕ *Bakery*

This postage stamp of a bakery does business at a rapid clip all day long: suits stopping in for a marionberry danish and coffee in the morning; kids lingering at one of the handful of tables with a bag of triple chocolate chip cookies in the afternoon; and guilty-looking folks ordering an eclair or a slice of decadent Grand Marnier cheesecake any old time. At lunchtime, try one of the inventive sandwiches, such as the hot chicken club: a three-fisted sandwich with chicken, bacon, and melted Swiss on six-grain bread. The best lunchtime deal might be a huge, buttery ham-and-cheese croissant for $2.75 or a slice of excellent quiche. Sweets are excellent, especially the cookies (try the vanilla Susans, shortbread dolloped with frosting) and anything in the rotating pastry case. They've also got lots of lovely loaves, although some—such as the sour walnut— are a mite heavier than they would be in, say, France. There are a few pleasant tables, some with a view into the industrious kitchen and some located outside, where you can watch the local populace meander by. The bakery is owned by a husband-and-wife team who also own the Ballard Baking Company. They've had the Greenwood Bakery only since 1996, but it has been here, churning out cakes and such, for more than 70 years—a real piece of Seattle history. *Light breakfast, lunch, early/light dinner every day; no credit cards; checks OK; no alcohol.*

GUISEPPE'S ITALIAN RESTAURANT AND LOUNGE

144 105th Ave NE, Bellevue
☎ *(425) 454-6868*
Bellevue ✕ *Italian*

Guiseppe's makes good on its "Big Portions, Great Prices" motto without compromising on authenticity or variety. Hidden in the lower level of a mall complex just a few doors from Pete's Wines, the place has been here forever. The dining room is as funky as can be, with primitive murals of Italian scenes and three vineyards' worth of fake grapes hanging everywhere, along with straw-wrapped Chianti bottles. Meanwhile, the dark bar remains its own little world, smoke included. While the kitchen suffers from occasional blips and yips, you can trust a half-dozen house specialty pastas, such as the excellent Penne al Amatriciana—quill-shaped pasta with a rich chile pepper and pancetta sauce. Meat and fish dishes can be surprisingly well executed and reasonably priced. And the pizzas aren't bad: Try the barbecued chicken studded with mushrooms and almonds, which easily surpasses its counterpart at the nearby California Pizza Kitchen. *Dinner Mon–Sat; AE, DC, MC, V; checks OK; full bar.* &

HALE'S ALES BREWERY & PUB

4301 Leary Way NW, Seattle
☎ *(206) 782-0737*
Ballard ✗ *Pub Grub*

This brewery pub is an oasis of sorts along the Leary Way stretch between Fremont and Ballard. The green doorway offers a dramatic entry into the pub: Beyond a window, huge steel brewing tanks occasionally spew the grist of the beer-making process. A moment after you see the guts of the brewery, the acrid aroma of nascent beer becomes overwhelming. Thankfully, the restaurant itself is sealed off from the beer tanks and the accompanying smell. A step above bar food, Hale's fare includes just one burger: one Hale of a Burger, that is (yuk-yuk). The rest of the menu consists of hot sandwiches, salads, and pizzas; we recommend sticking with the basics, such as the excellent ham and Swiss. For each of its sandwiches, which run the gamut from your standard Reubens and turkey combos to the less conventional grilled bratwurst, Hale's recommends one of its own microbrews as an accompaniment. Service is efficient and friendly. Taking efficiency a step further, Hale's uses spent grain from the brewing process to make the dough for their pizzas, which are a crowd favorite. And taking efficiency to an extreme, they mix stout beer into their famous Stout Cheesecake, one of the most requested menu items. Sometimes extremes are a good thing. A banquet room upstairs can be reserved for larger groups. *Lunch, dinner every day; MC, V; checks OK; beer and wine.* &

HARBOUR PUBLIC HOUSE

231 Parfitt Way SW, Bainbridge Island
☎ *(206) 842-0969*
Bainbridge Island   ✕ **Pub Grub**

When standard pub grub grows up and gains a measure of respectability, it moves to Bainbridge and takes up residence at the Harbour Public House. This charming waterfront pub, nestled beside the marina on Eagle Harbor, is beloved by island locals and vacationing sailors for its microbrews, water views, and tasty eats. Other features unlikely to turn patrons away are the high ceilings, wood floors, large open windows, and the deck out back with its gorgeous views of both the marina and (on clear days) Seattle's skyline across the Sound. You may have to wait a few minutes for those prime deck seats, though. If so, pull up a stool at the bar—where the talk is likely to turn to sailing—and nurse a microbrew. Order the Pub Nachos as an appetizer and allow this colossus  of chips, cheese, diced tomatoes, olives, and onions, with a hefty measure of sour cream and homemade salsa piled on, to completely albeit pleasantly destroy your appetite for lunch or dinner. Recognizable pub favorites, like the cheeseburger and fish 'n' chips, appear on the menu alongside less traditional offerings like the peppered snapper sandwich or the warm red potato salad, whose kick comes courtesy of the kielbasa sausage and spicy stone-ground mustard vinaigrette. Most sandwiches come with flavorful, thick, hand-cut fries. Daily dinner specials and the day's soup selection are scrawled on the chalkboard. *Lunch, dinner every day; MC, V; checks OK; beer and wine.* ♿

HATTIE'S HAT

5231 Ballard Ave NW, Seattle
☎ *(206) 784-0175*
Ballard   ✕ **Diner**

One thing is immediately apparent upon setting foot in Hattie's Hat: This is no place to order a latte. Nonsmokers shuffle past the hand-carved dark-wood bar, the jukebox favoring old honky-tonk tunes, and the long wooden lunch counter (set beneath an expansive mural of a Scandinavian alpine scene) to the smoke-free back-room dining area, an unappealing ensemble of stucco, peculiar-colored prints of 1950s-era country life, wood paneling, Formica tables, and cushioned aluminum chairs. Yes, this is strictly a drip-coffee dive, serving

straightforward greasy-spoon breakfasts all day, plus diner-style sandwiches, hearty daily specials like pot roast or chicken-fried chicken,
and a daily selection of stews. (It's actually not a bad place for a
casual beer come Saturday night, either.) The occasional Cajun
emphasis, apparent in such favorites as the andouille scramble or the
spicy oyster po'boy, comes courtesy of Rip, a Louisiana native who is
also the mastermind behind Rice and Beans of the Day and the veggie
muffuletta. Going to Hattie's, set as it is amid the two-story red-brick
and stone buildings of Old Ballard, feels a bit like strolling down the
quiet main street of some small rural town and stopping into the local
diner to mingle with the hungry old-timers. *Breakfast, lunch, dinner
every day; MC, V; no checks; full bar.* &

HI-SPOT CAFE

1410 34th Ave, Seattle
☎ *(206) 325-7905*
Madrona   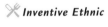 *Inventive Ethnic*

Since Joanne Sugura and Michael Walker took the helm in 1994, the
Hi-Spot Cafe has transcended its granola-and-Birkenstocks image, but
the multilevel Victorian house and its outdoor deck are ever-inviting.
Breakfast is still breakfast: same long lines, same baked eggs, same
great cinnamon buns. Lunch includes the requisite soups, salads, and
groovy '90s sandwiches. But dinner (with its menu that changes
monthly) is the real reason to head here. You'll find
appetizers such as Gorgonzola cheesecake with roasted
red pepper sauce, or *brandade de morue*—a classic ren-
dering of the warm potato and salt-cod spread. Coconut
milk mellows the fiery-hot harissa in the spicy Caribbean
seafood stew, and the mixed grill comes with an innova-
tive version of dolmathes. Entrees won't set you back
much more than $10, and wine list prices hover at the low
end. *Breakfast every day, lunch Mon–Fri, dinner Tues–Sat;
DIS, MC, V; local checks only; beer and wine.* &

HING LOON

628 S Weller St, Seattle
☎ *(206) 682-2828*
International District   *Chinese*

Voices rise above the clatter in this sunny, modest spot in the ID, where
families order steaming bowls of congee and *chow fun* in a cafeteria-like
setting. A swift and friendly staff keeps late hours, serving Chinese

standards and bargain-priced specials (advertised on handwritten signs at the rear of the big room) such as quail in salt or duck feet with mushroom hot pot. Soup purists will appreciate the strong chicken stock; shrimp lovers will like the shrimp-filled wontons; and vegetarians can indulge in bright *gailan* (Chinese broccoli) that has been given the quick-wok treatment. Live crab swim in a small tank for the seafood-inclined, and the adventuresome will find something of interest on the extensive menu. Braised beef organs, perhaps? *Lunch, dinner every day; MC, V; no checks; beer and wine.* &

HOKI'S TERIYAKI HUT

3624 Leary Way NW, Seattle
☎ *(206) 634-1128*
Ballard   ✕ *Teriyaki*

At first glance, Hoki's Teriyaki Hut has two obvious shortcomings: It's orange and it's a hut. But while such bright and unusual markings might mean inedibility in the wild, don't make that mistake here. A fixture on the Fremont-Ballard border for nearly 20 years, Hoki's has built a loyal following with its unusual mix of Hawaiian and Korean cuisine. The menu leads with teriyaki, but unlike the kind you'll find anywhere else in Seattle (and in this teriyaki-happy town, that's saying something). Like much of Hoki's menu, the teriyaki is distinctly different but inarguably good. The chicken and pork katsu are also excellent, but the real find on the menu is the eclectic and affordable bento: teriyaki beef, ginger chicken, mahi-mahi, rice with spicy-hot *furikake*, and kimchi. If you're feeling really adventurous, try the Locomoco, a favorite of many regulars: a hamburger patty, a sunny-side-up fried egg, and brown gravy, all over rice. *Lunch, dinner Mon–Sat; MC, V; no checks; no alcohol.* &

HONEY BEAR BAKERY

2106 N 55th St, Seattle
☎ *(206) 545-7296*
Wallingford   ✕ *Bakery*

Despite more competition in the neighborhood, Seattle's favorite coffeehouse is as lively as ever, with a steady stream of customers lining up to grab a larger-than-life slab of chocolate layer cake before hunkering down for an hour or three at one of the scarred wooden tables. The baked goods—an astonishing array—continue to be the Bear's raison d'être. Some loyalists swear allegiance to the molasses cookies, pumpkin muffins, and marionberry pie, while others have found God in the poppyseed cake, the morning glory muffins, or the mocha-pecan torte. (Watch out for the croissants and some of the breads and cakes, which can be a mite stonelike.) There are plenty of other options (all vegetarian) for those who believe in "real meals," including various casseroles, rollups, soups (black bean chili is a staple), and pasta salads. These tend to be heavy but filling, in a *Moosewood Cookbook* kind of way. No alcohol, but good coffee, juices, and shakes. People-watching is part of the fun: coeds in natural fibers perch in corners scribbling in journals, folksingers croon on weekend nights, and folks catch up on local gossip or hunt down a date for Saturday evening. You probably already know about the regulars who get to hang their mugs up in back. *Breakfast, lunch, dinner every day; no credit cards; checks OK; no alcohol.*

HONG'S GARDEN

64 Rainier Ave S, Renton
☎ *(425) 228-6332*
Renton   ✕ *Chinese*

The former owners of the International District's House of Hong have taken their expertise south to Renton. The strip-mall setting doesn't offer much in the way of atmosphere (Formica and mauve tones), but the daily dim sum lunches, the extensive menu, and the faultless service are more than inviting. While gloppy hot and sour soup proves neither hot nor sour, clams and crab fresh from the tank, generous portions of fragrant steamed cod, garlic-kissed long beans, and the chance to dine on dim sum midweek make this place worth a detour. *Lunch, dinner every day; AE, MC, V; no checks; full bar.* &

HUONG BINH

1207 S Jackson St, Seattle
☎ *(206) 720-4907*
International District   ✕ *Vietnamese*

While other less successful eateries come and go, this tidy Vietnamese restaurant, in one of the many strip malls marking the ever-expanding Vietnamese commercial area near the ID, continues to hold its own. We've had feasts here, huge brimming tables full—for under $20. One such consisted of *banh beo* (a steamed rice cake topped with brilliant orange ground shrimp), *cha hue* (a steamed pork roll), *bahn hoi chao tom* (grilled shrimp on sugar cane—hint to novices: you eat the shrimp and then suck the cane), and a couple of dishes starring pork and shrimp skewers with rice. Pork is particularly nicely done: tender, pounded thin, and marinated in garlic and lemongrass. Best of all, these grilled dishes come in traditional Vietnamese fashion with an accompanying fragrant garden of herbs, allowing you to dress your food to your liking. *Lunch, early dinner every day; no credit cards; local checks only; no alcohol.* &

THE INCREDIBLE LINK

1511 Pike Pl, Seattle
☎ *(206) 622-8002*
Pike Place Market   ✕ *Hot Dogs/Sausage*

Located in the market's main arcade just north of the big bronze pig, the Incredible Link serves up a wide variety of homemade sausages for sale by the pound or grilled up individually as a sandwich. You will simply not find better sausages in Seattle or ones that are made with more care. The owners, the Dorseys, use organically grown herbs and permit no fillers, meat by-products, preservatives, nitrates, or MSGs to sully their sausages. New Orleans natives, the Dorseys specialize in spicy links such as the Old Style Louisiana Hot Sausage (an original recipe gleaned from the French Quarter) and the popular Cajun Beef, a mouth-tingling sensation made with 11 spices and herbs. You will also find international favorites like bratwurst, English bangers, and chorizo, plus locally inspired links like the Sailboat Salmon or the Vegetarian's Delight. There are several low-fat options and a number of wild-game sausages (you might see alligator, venison, duck, or kangaroo). Call for a one-pound freezer pack of your favorites, and be sure to check out the Dorseys' tips for grilling the perfect sausage. Additional information can be found at the Incredible Link's Web site at www.incrediblelink.com. *Lunch every day; AE, MC, V; local checks only; no alcohol.* &

ISSAQUAH CAFE

1580 NW Gilman Blvd, Issaquah (and branches)
☎ *(425) 391-9690*
Issaquah/Monroe/Redmond/Woodinville   ✕ *American*

At this small local chain of '40s-style cafes, a traditionalist can sit down at chrome-trimmed tables, in squeaky-clean surroundings amid

Americana knickknacks, and enjoy generous helpings of griddle cakes, biscuits and gravy, or liver and onions, washed down with freshly mixed milk shakes. A cheerful and cooperative staff serves breakfast all day long and coffee as soon as you sit down. Choose from many varieties of thick French toast, small-checked waffles, and generous stacks of buttermilk pancakes, plus a dozen omelets. Lunches lean toward burgers and sandwiches, while dinners would seem awfully familiar to Harry S. Truman: classics like meat loaf, hot roast beef sandwiches, and chicken-fried steaks. Ladles of dark but unmysterious gravy cover just about everything, and just about everything comes accompanied by a fluffy buttermilk biscuit and a crisp salad. Servers probably wouldn't even mind if you yelled, "Hey Mabel!" Note: Each branch is named for the city in which it resides (Issaquah Cafe in Issaquah, Monroe Cafe in Monroe—you get the picture); the exception is the Redmond branch, which is known as the Village Square Cafe. *Breakfast, lunch every day (Redmond branch only), breakfast, lunch, dinner every day (other branches); MC, V; checks OK; no alcohol.* &

JACK'S FISH AND CHIP SPOT

Pike Place Market, Seattle
☎ *(206) 467-0514*
Pike Place Market ✕ *Fish 'n' Chips*

This fishmonger's stall captures the working soul of Pike Place Market. Two dozen stools line the back, and here you can sidle up to the fish bar for a cup, bowl, or pint of gut-warming clam chowder—a chunky, peppery concoction of vegetables and clams that might benefit from more cream in the broth. Jack's also serves a seafood-rich cioppino, a fabulous deal at $3.99 a bowl, which is accompanied by sliced sourdough bread—perfect for sopping up every last drop. Of course, you're probably here because you've got a hankerin' for fish 'n' chips. Well, you can't get them much fresher than this. The fish (cod or halibut) is hot, moist, and lightly covered in an ale batter. The menu also includes crab or shrimp cocktail, steamed mussels or clams, oysters on the half shell, scallops, and fresh cracked Dungeness crab. The drink selection is limited (the Market Creamery next door has a few additional choices). Three Girls Bakery, across the way, will serve you well for dessert. But for fish this catch-of-the-day fresh, amid the busy hustle and commerce, you can't do better than Jack's. The stall closes at 5pm (4pm on Sundays). *Lunch every day; AE, MC, V; local checks only; no alcohol (BYOB OK).*

JAK'S GRILL

2352 California Ave SW, Seattle (and branch)
☎ (206) 935-8260
West Seattle/Issaquah   ✕ American

Two guys had a dream about owning their own restaurant, signed the lease on a former restaurant graveyard, redecorated, and changed the whole karma of the place. How? With simply grilled burgers, steaks, chops, ribs, and sandwiches, sided with perfect fries or baked potatoes—all sure things if you respect the basics. The folks at Jak's do just that, turning out everybody's favorite comfort foods in large, well-seasoned portions, along with generous complimentary salads with most dinner entrees. Located across the street from the Admiral Theater in West Seattle, Jak's has the kind of casually hip atmosphere—dark wood tables, well-upholstered booths, wall sconces—that just might turn one-time visitors into regulars. And while Jak's is best suited to fans of red meat (which begin to climb out of budget range), the menu also offers seasonal fish options, grilled chicken done in various ways, and a perennial veggie burger. The great little bar in back is just the place to nurse a beer while you wait for friends to show up. There's a Jak's in Issaquah too (38 Front St N, (425) 837-8834). *Dinner Tues–Sun; AE, DIS, MC, V; checks OK; beer and wine (full bar in Issaquah).* ♿

JALISCO

122 First Ave N, Seattle (and branches)
☎ (206) 283-4242
Queen Anne/Bothell/Capitol Hill/Kirkland/
Lake City/White Center   ✕ Mexican

In one of the stranger franchise setups going, lower Queen Anne plays host to two Jalisco Mexican restaurants, one directly across the street from the other. Most folks flock to the flashier, faster-paced, louder, and significantly larger Taqueria Jalisco—home of the cantina—leaving the cozier, border town–like original Jalisco for a quieter, more intimate crowd. The original Jalisco is a familiar arrangement of adobe-colored walls, with tile accents here and there and the odd sequined sombrero hanging from the wall. No matter which Jalisco you choose, you'll find that the predictable but comforting Mexican fare comes in huge portions. Order a combination plate, which comes with rice and beans, and unless you're the starting center for the Seahawks, you'll be taking home a doggie bag. The house margaritas are a tasty bargain at $3.50. Check out the other Jalisco joints in Bothell, Capitol Hill, Kirkland, Lake City, and White Center. *Lunch, dinner every day; AE, DC, MC, V; checks OK; full bar.*

JITTERBUG

2114 N 45th St, Seattle
☎ *(206) 547-6313*
Wallingford   🍴 ***Inventive Ethnic***

This stylish sliver of a place just across the street from the Guild 45th movie theater, has knocked through a side wall and added a full bar and a handful of tables, increasing its size by half. With white linen napkins, terra-cotta-colored walls and a cast-iron chandelier in the bar, and the waitstaff dressed in white shirts and ties, Jitterbug is a diner that's gone higher, if not high, society. Like its siblings the Coastal Kitchen and The 5 Spot, Jitterbug could not resist the urge to take a rotating, thematic approach to its dinner menu (while retaining a selection of permanent entrees). The Barcelona tapas theme, for instance, features various nifty nibbles from Catalonian country, nicely priced between $3.50 and $6.50; a person of modest appetite could easily put away three of these charming plates for dinner. With dinner entrees ranging in price from $7.75 (charbroiled burger) to $16.50 *(carne asada)*, the inventive breakfast and "blunch" offerings remain the best options for keeping the tab respectable—and the most popular as well (the line forms early and remains well into the afternoon). Ginger-bread waffles with maple syrup are a nice treat, as is the Spanish omelet with serrano ham, white beans, pecorino cheese, tomatoes, and asparagus. Film fans with a sweet tooth are encouraged to hop across the street and then return to round out the evening with a decadent dessert and coffee. There may be no better spot to hash over the virtues and vices of a movie than one of Jitterbug's cozy booths, with a hot cup of coffee and the neon Guild sign reflecting pink and blue patterns in the windows. *Breakfast, lunch every day, dinner Mon–Sat; MC, V; checks OK; full bar.* ♿

JOHN'S WOK

1100 Western Ave, Seattle
☎ *(206) 621-0944*
Downtown   🍴 ***Pan-Asian***

What looks like a midscale minimart tucked away in the shadow of the Alaskan Way viaduct actually houses some of the best Asian food for your buck. Part convenience store, part take-out kitchen, the inside of John's Wok is ringed with windows and barstool seating for patrons who have a yen for Asian food and a moment to stop and partake. The menu is divided into the "Hot Submarine" side and the "Oriental Cuisine" side. All menu options are available as whole orders or cheaper (and smaller) half-orders. Beef is the specialty here; the Seoul Beef is incredibly rich and, even as a $4 half-order, it's a heaping helping. Not that there aren't options for those ill-inclined toward red meat: Tokyo Chicken comes with rice and vegetables or piled on a sub; even calamari makes it onto the sub sandwich menu. Meat-free stir-fried vegetables and rice are a lighter way to go, and there's always Teri Mocki for all the flavor without all the guilt. Shelves are stockpiled with soft drinks, beer, wine, and snack foods to accompany your take-out— or appease those junk-food cravings. Deli service is fast, but, come lunchtime, lines start forming. *Lunch Mon–Fri; MC, V; checks OK; beer and wine.* &

JUDKIN'S BBQ & RESTAURANT

2608 S Judkins St, Seattle
☎ *(206) 328-7417*
Central District ✕ *Barbecue*

Seattle's barbecue mecca is not much to look at, just a few tables and some vinyl chairs crowded into a plain little room south of Jackson Street and east of 23rd Avenue. But the Southern-style food is first rate, and the menu—offering various barbecue dinners, sandwiches, and fried chicken—gets right to the point. The restaurant's trademark spicy-sweet sauce covers meaty pork bones with just the right amount of fat for the barbecued ribs. Herbs and flour trap a good amount of grease under the savory chicken's skin. Side dishes, which include traditional red beans, runny greens, and macaroni and cheese, are *sometimes* terrific. Service, though somewhat spacey, is warm and welcoming. Dinner is unfashionably early, so don't be late. *Lunch, dinner every day; no credit cards; no checks; no alcohol.*

JULES MAES SALOON & EATERY

5919 Airport Way S, Seattle
☎ *(206) 763-0570*
Georgetown ✕ *Diner*

The boarded-up storefronts, lonely sidewalks, and abandoned red-brick buildings make this stretch of Airport Way South seem like something out of a Bruce Springsteen song. But despite the desolate, hard luck-hits-small town feel of the area, Jules Maes Saloon & Eatery has somehow managed to chug along, laying down basic, greasy-spoon egg breakfasts, Salisbury steak dinners, and the like at this very location since 1889. The restaurant's interior is a veritable shrine to its longevity. Ceramic beer steins and cast-iron skillets dangle from the ceiling; ornamental plates, assorted implements of the lumber and fishing industry, and dozens of black-and-white photographs of Seattle's inchoate days hang from plywood and cigarette smoke-stained walls, along with various other mementos and bits of junk documenting the past 100 years of operation. The crowd is a colorful assortment of just plain folks who know a good, hot meat-loaf sandwich when they see one, and who recognize that the scales are tipped best when portions are large and prices are small. The corned beef sandwich—thick slices of tender meat with shredded Swiss and a great deal of mayo—comes with a generous bowl of soup or a hefty helping of potato salad for $4. Full dinners include soup or salad, mashed potatoes, and veggies for a paltry $5.25. *Breakfast, lunch Mon–Sat; no credit cards; no checks; full bar.*

JULIA'S IN WALLINGFORD

1714 N 44th St, Seattle
☎ *(206) 633-1175*
Wallingford   ✕ *Breakfast*

When friends agree to lunch only if they can eat something "healthy," take 'em to Julia's. Wallingford's signature restaurant has an impressive array of salads and vegetarian entrees, as well as chicken, pork, and seafood meals. Most are very good, reasonably priced, and not at all fussy in their preparation. (Cleverly hidden among the various kinds of veggie burgers are a delicious real-beef hamburger with fries, and a quite good, generous portion of fish 'n' chips for us unhealthy types.) Julia's makes a specialty of breakfasts, however, with a huge, separate menu for morning visits. A juice machine and espresso machine are also in operation on the premises. The tables are close enough together to give the place a sense of coziness, but the clientele is low-key, so you won't get blasted by your neighbors' conversations. Service is uniformly good, even on crowded days. It's enough to make you want to eat healthy all the time. *Breakfast, lunch, dinner every day; DIS, MC, V; local checks only; beer and wine.* ♿

KABUL

2301 N 45th St, Seattle
☎ (206) 545-9000
Wallingford
✗ *Afghan*

In ancient Afghanistan, the king's cooks marinated and grilled the finest meats, infusing dishes with mint, cilantro, and dill and applying the cooling touch of yogurt and the zing of scallions. Cooks guarded recipes jealously and passed them down through the generations. Today Sultan Malikyar, who emigrated from Afghanistan in the late '70s, prepares his family's recipes here in Wallingford. Menu staples include his father's kabobs (which come sandwiched in pita at lunch and with lovely heaps of basmati rice at dinner) and his mother's *chaka* (garlic-yogurt sauce). With partner Wali Khairzada, Malikyar offers fragrant, elegant food such as crisp *bolani* (scallion-potato turnovers) and *ashak* (delicate scallion dumplings topped with either a beef sauce or a vegetarian tomato sauce). The dining  room's simple decor with its colorful accents feels as soothing as the cardamom-and-rosewater custard served for dessert. Service is friendly, and the restaurant offers live sitar music on Tuesdays and Thursdays. *Dinner Tues–Sun; AE, DIS, MC, V; checks OK; beer and wine.* &

KIDD VALLEY

531 Queen Anne Ave N, Seattle (and branches)
☎ (206) 284-0184
Queen Anne/Bellevue/Bothell/Capitol Hill/Green
Lake/Kirkland/Lynnwood/North End/Ravenna
✗ *Burgers*

The fame of this local burger chain can be summed up in five words: milk shakes and onion rings. The former come in two sizes and 11 varieties, from peanut butter to root beer to boysenberry. They are especially beloved by families and the post-softball crowd. The onion rings come as big as your fist, and much crispier. You'll also find well-prepared burgers ($2.59–$3.59), including a tasty veggie burger, and fries that are a sharp cut above the usual chain spuds. The decor is purple and yellow plastic (though the notorious rotating pinup girl sign has been replaced at most branches), but some outlets have jukeboxes and outdoor seating. A few serve breakfast too. *Breakfast, lunch, dinner every day (meals served vary at different branches—call ahead); no credit cards; checks OK; no alcohol.* &

KIKU TEMPURA HOUSE

5018 University Way NE, Seattle
☎ *(206) 524-1125*
University District   ✕*Japanese*

Getting a cheap meal in the U-District is easy, but getting a good one can be a little more difficult. Take a walk up the Ave around mealtime, though, and restaurants that meet both criteria stand out: They're the ones that are crowded. Despite unassuming storefronts and nondescript interiors, a few restaurants have the good food and the good deals that consistently pack in students and other locals. After 15 years in the same location, Kiku Tempura House definitely falls into this category. With its bar-style seating and sparse decor it may not seem like anything special when you first walk in, but take this as a reassuring sign that the owners' real talents lie not in decorating but in cooking. The best dishes here are the simple ones: Beef over Rice and Chicken over Rice are old-school teriyaki, well prepared and delicious. The tempura is likewise predictable but excellent, nonetheless. Don't pass up the tempura-style gyoza, either. Do make sure you're hungry (the portions are enormous, a must for students on a budget), and if you come around the lunch or dinner rush, you may want to order take-out to avoid the crowd. *Lunch, dinner every day; no credit cards; checks ok; no alcohol.* ⓖ

KING STREET BAR & OVEN

170 S King St, Seattle
☎ *(206) 749-9890*
Pioneer Square   ✕ *Pub Grub*

This is just the place for out-of-luck Kingdome ticket seekers: clean, well lit, and serviced by cable TV. Though known for its various and delicious pizzas and calzones (the individual-size eggplant with garlic, basil, and tomato is particularly good, for $5.50), any selection from the menu will fortify you to cheer your local team to victory—or at least have a good time trying. The full bar complements the menu, which has all sorts of surprises—especially for a sports bar. The grilled King Fish Shish Kabob (at $7.95, the most expensive food item) was, on one visit, slightly overcooked but still delicious, soaked as it was in rice and honey-soy sauce. Salads, sandwiches, Italian-style grinders, and appetizers of all kinds abound. The subterranean bar/dining room is warm, friendly, and

filled with the white noise of the tube and glasses clinking behind the bar. You might feel as if you're in a place where, before long, everybody will know your name. *Lunch, dinner Mon–Fri (open weekends when there's a game); AE, MC, V; local checks only; full bar.*

KINGFISH CAFE

602 19th Ave E, Seattle
☎ *(206) 320-8757*
Capitol Hill   ✗ *Southern*

Lines start forming outside the Kingfish well before it opens. Where else will you find soul food this elegant, made with so much love? Although the cafe feels like it's been around forever, it's actually a fairly recent venture—it opened in 1997. Dreamed into being by the Coaston sisters (they only look like triplets), the cozy storefront in the heart of Capitol Hill is decked out in warm colors and hung with large portraits of family members from way back when. Maybe the reason all the relatives are so good-looking is the food: Classics like pork chops with greens and fried chicken with mashed potatoes are updated and reinvented here—just right for citified tastes. Have a hankering for fried green tomatoes and red beans and rice? They have 'em. Shrimp fritters—any kind of fritters? Right here. The salad dressing should be bottled for posterity—or at least for the rest of us to take home. If the dinner queue deters you, try Sunday brunch. *Brunch Sun, lunch Mon, Wed–Fri, dinner Wed–Mon; no credit cards; checks OK; beer and wine.* ♿

KING'S BARBECUE HOUSE

518 Sixth Ave S, Seattle (and branch)
☎ *(206) 622-2828*
International District/Beacon Hill   ✗ *Barbecue*

Situated just across Sixth Avenue South from Uwajimaya, this tiny storefront, with no room for tables, counters, or seats, serves up big barbecue flavor for the road. In the front window, illuminated by hot lights, hang glazed chickens, ducks, sausages, and pork ribs. Standing at a chopping board behind a glass-partitioned counter, the cleaver-wielding butcher patiently awaits your decision. The Lunch Box Special is a tremendous value for the downtown lunch crowd seeking take-out. For $3.50 you get a choice of two kinds of meat, sliced and diced over a generous portion of rice. The barbecued meats are coated in a glossy, burgundy-colored, sweet barbecue sauce, and the roast chicken is tasty, moist, and tender. Consider taking home a whole roasted duck or chicken (there are also soy sauce–glazed or baked salty chickens) for a quick-fix dinner. The pork ribs and sausages are available by the pound. No drinks are served here, and you won't find a single vegetable in sight. Check out King's other location on Beacon Hill (2710 Beacon Ave S, (206) 720-4715). *Lunch, dinner every day; no credit cards; no checks; no alcohol.*

KITTO JAPANESE NOODLE HOUSE

614 Broadway E, Seattle
☎ *(206) 325-8486*
Capitol Hill   ✕ *Japanese*

Kitto has oodles of noodles, offering Japanese basics such as soba, udon, and ramen in soups and stir-fries. Try zaru soba on a hot day, slurp ramen when it's relentlessly gray, or share a steaming platter of yakisoba with friends before a movie. Combination dinners for two are fabulous bargains. Bustling Kitto attracts a varied clientele; you'll see Japanese grandmothers waiting in line with some of Capitol Hill's most colorful and pierced denizens. But since noodles make for 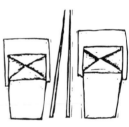 quick eats, the wait's never too long. Udon devotees should steer clear of their favorite dish here; the broth always seems skimpy and the noodles sadly overcooked. *Lunch, dinner every day; MC, V; local checks only; beer and wine.* &

KOLBEH PERSIAN & MEDITERRANEAN CUISINE

1956 First Ave S, Seattle
☎ *(206) 224-9999*
SoDo   ✕ *Middle Eastern*

With the pretty tilework framing its front door and potted plants bordering the entryway, Kolbeh appears like an oasis along this gritty strip of warehouses and industrial shops south of the Mariners' new ballpark. Once inside, step past Persian rugs hung from the ceiling into a dining room redolent with exotic spices and a decor of scarlet carpet, carved wood chairs, and alcoves holding a museum's worth of icons, brass urns, hookahs, ornamental platters, and other Persian bric-a-brac. It doesn't require much imagination to feel as if you've been transported halfway around the world. Of high priority here is the *kashk-o-bademjan* appetizer ($6.50), a creamy, garlicky delight of roasted eggplant sautéed with tomato, mint, and garlic and topped off with a homemade yogurt and sour cream sauce. (Served with pita bread, it makes a delicious and satisfying lunch as well.) Dinner entrees, ranging from pungent vegetable stews to kabobs ($6.99 for ground beef; $11.99 for chicken breast), appear with a generous mound of fragrant basmati rice and are preceded by a comparatively uninspiring green salad (at dinner only). Slow-baked oven selections (Cornish game hens and lamb shanks) take you into a pricier category. The friendly and knowledgeable waitstaff will assist you with recommendations and explanations of the more exotic offerings. Kolbeh's take-out option and proximity to the city make it a particularly good lunch alternative for the downtown work set. Lunch selections are a few dollars less than their corresponding dinners, and gyro, chicken, and ground beef pita sandwiches round out the lunch menu. *Lunch, dinner every day; MC, V; checks OK; beer and wine.*

KORYO RESTAURANT
12020 Aurora N, Seattle
☎ *(206) 362-5009*
North End   ✕ *Korean*

Locals know that for the best Korean food you have to go south to Federal Way or north to Edmonds. But there are fine options closer to the city, one of them being Koryo. The square brown exterior of this place doesn't promise much, but once you walk inside, there's nothing but good cheer and mouth-watering smells. Ask for tabletop grilling if you'd like to cook your own *bulgogi* and *galbi* (marinated rib eye and ribs); otherwise, ask for *galbi jim*, Koryo's exquisite stove-top version of marinated English short ribs. Sit at a regular table or call ahead for the Korean-style dining areas, where you sit on the floor, sans shoes, and eat from a table that is knee high. Like most Korean restaurants, Koryo serves its kimchi and other kinds of *banchan* (side dishes) gratis with many dishes—just remember that these intense, palate-stimulating extras are intended to put some life into your rice. In other words, take them in small doses. *Lunch, dinner every day; AE, MC, V; no checks; no alcohol.*

KOSHER DELIGHT

1509 First Ave, Seattle
☎ *(206) 682-8140*
Pike Place Market   ✗ **Kosher**

This tiny deli has excellent falafel sandwiches, good chicken schnitzel, and jars of homemade kosher dills, but its real appeal is its charming owner, Michel Chriqui. "Eat your knish while it's warm! You can pay me later," he says. "Why don't you sit at one of the tables outside, where you can keep an eye on your bike," he suggests. "Here, try some of this hummus. I just made it," he offers. At $2.35 each, the knishes might be the best bargain, but though the savory turnovers are comfort-food filling, they are sometimes a bit bland. Instead, get a falafel sandwich ($3.95), which is crisp, satisfyingly spicy, and well sauced, or a spiced-eggplant sandwich, or a plate of the breaded and spiced schnitzel. Other specialties on Chriqui's New York–authentic menu include pastrami, corned beef, and turkey sandwiches, bagels and lox, halvah, and poppyseed cake. *Light breakfast, lunch Sun–Fri; MC, V; local checks only; no alcohol.* ♿

KRITTIKA NOODLES & THAI CUISINE

6411 Latona Ave NE, Seattle
☎ *(206) 985-1182*
Green Lake   ✗ **Thai**

Tracking down a Thai place in this town is a little like trying to find a convenience store in the suburbs—there's virtually one on every corner. But if you thought we'd already hit our saturation point, guess again. A scant three months after Krittika opened in early 1998, its take-out business was already at full throttle and the wait for a table on weekends was half an hour—all before they'd even managed to land their liquor license. Who needs beer or wine when the food is this good? The tastes and textures are delightful: crisp, colorful veggies, slippery noodles, and sauces that complement rather than overpower the flavors of the dishes' main ingredients. The menu is vast, with selections deftly covering a range of noodle and rice dishes, meat and poultry, seafood, vegetarian options, curries, soups, and salads— and the daintily displayed dishes are transported to your table on festive Fiestaware. For starters, try the *pla moug tod* appetizer ($4.95), a tasty Thai take on calamari, served with a sensational sweet and

red chile sauce sprinkled with peanuts. The flaxen walls are painted with colorful patterns of ribbons and spheres, and above you, delicate paper lanterns hang over lacquered wood tables in booths of carved wood. *Lunch Mon–Fri, dinner every day; AE, MC, V; checks OK; no alcohol.* &

LA COCINA DEL PUERCO

12046 Main St, Bellevue
☎ *(425) 455-1151*
Bellevue ⚔ **Mexican**

When a restaurant's name translates to "kitchen of the pig," one does not expect an immersion in elegance. And baby, you ain't gonna get one, either! Not unless your idea of sophistication is folding metal chairs and bare bulbs dangling from shades constructed of old license plates, along with dust-gathering piñatas and ratty birdcages. The tiny kitchen turns out just a few items, simple and cheap fare. But they are good, and about as authentic as you can get in white-bread Bellevue.

The cooks hand-make the tamales, filling them with chunks of roasted pork or tomato-sauced chicken. Pollo taquitos and *taquitos de carne asada* both deliver meaty pleasure, accompanied by a heap of soft rice and beans. This is the home of the bargain dessert, too: a cuplet  of burnt cream for a buck and a few nickels. Windows open wide onto Main Street in Old Bellevue rather than Old Mexico, but squeeze another lime into another Dos Equis, hombre, and you might catch yourself whistling, "South of the border . . . down Mexico way. . . ." *Lunch, dinner every day; MC, V; checks OK; beer only.* &

LA GUADALUPANA TAQUERIA MEXICANA

8064 Lake City Way NE, Seattle
☎ *(206) 517-5660*
Lake City ⚔ **Mexican**

La Guadalupana is actually a Mexican grocery store that has added a small taqueria to the back, but it takes only one tostada de ceviche here to realize what's wrong with most of the Mexican food in Seattle: goopiness. You won't find goopy here. The aforementioned tostada is an artful construction of marinated shrimp, onion, cucumber, carrot, tomato, and cilantro on a toasted corn tortilla. The *pozole*, another house specialty, is a chile-spiced soup of pork and hominy accompanied by a plate of cilantro, lime, onion, and two kinds of sauces. Even the burritos are elegant creations, with the ingredients never getting too involved with each other. And food adventurers will be happy with the menudo (tripe soup) and tongue burritos and tacos. The service is a bit erratic (dishes come out one at a time, and you have to nag the counterpeople occasionally), but the one real problem here is space: Since the only place to dine is a six-stool counter, most of La Guadalupana's business is take-out. Don't forget to pick up a Mexican B-movie, a piñata, or a jar of seasoned pig's feet at the grocery on your way out. *Lunch, dinner Fri—Wed; no credit cards; local checks only; no alcohol.* &

LA MEDUSA

4857 Rainier Ave S, Seattle
☎ *(206) 723-2192*
Columbia City   ✗ *Italian*

Offering the beguiling promise of "Sicilian Soul Food," La Medusa is the dream project of co-owners Lisa Becklund and Sherri Serino, both chefs with a long history in Seattle restaurants. They've created a quintessential neighborhood hangout in Columbia City, an off-the-beaten-track, multi-ethnic neighborhood that's finally coming around to better times. The ever-helpful staff aims to please. Want an honest opinion on what's good today? They'll tell you, no holds barred, no tongue in cheek. Start with a cracker-crust pizza or the crisp-fried cod fritters, made from mashed taters and salt cod, and then progress to a well-composed pasta such as the  Arab-style penne with cheese. But if you want a sure hit, choose from the nightly specials, which can range from wild salmon—grilled with a touch of lemon, oil, and garlic—to a catch-of-the-day risotto. *Dinner Tues—Sat; MC, V; no checks; beer and wine.* &

LE FOURNIL

3230 Eastlake Ave E, Seattle
☎ *(206) 328-6523*
Eastlake   ✗ *Bakery*

Le fournil literally means "bakery," so it's an apt name for this bright little Eastlake gem. Brittany native Nicolas Pare hooked up with a baking buddy from New York, Kevin Thompson, so he could open a place of his own. "You have to love what you do," Pare declares, "especially if you want to make bread." Every night the two labor side by side, in syncopated motion, to create the most ethereal pastries this town has ever tasted: divine chocolate cream puffs, brioches, croissants, breads, fruit tarts, eclairs, and other classic French creations. It's all as authentically Gallic as Pare's charming accent. Anything they make with almond paste is bound to be delicious, and those who think they don't like quiche will quickly change their opinion when they sample one here: Made with ham and Swiss or blue cheese and roasted leeks, these quiches are silky smooth and seductively delicious. Lunchtime offers an excellent deal: a sandwich or quiche, a pastry, and a drink for $6. *Light breakfast, lunch Tues–Sun; no credit cards; checks OK; no alcohol.* &

LESCHI LAKECAFE

102 Lakeside Ave S, Seattle
☎ *(206) 328-2233*
Leschi   ✕ **Pub Grub**

With only a smattering of restaurants along Lake Washington's scenic western shore, the Lakecafe's choice waterfront location—amid Leschi's parks, marinas, condos, and tiny commercial center—is its greatest asset. Seafood dominates the menu at this neighborhood restaurant-bar: calamari appetizers, clam chowder starters, seafood caesars, mixed grill entrees. The choices are many and tempting, but the quality and the service can be spotty. For best results, sample several appetizers (such as shellfish simmered in a creamy broth, oysters topped with crab, or cioppino) along with a salad and one of the 18 brews on tap. At lunch, you'll be mingling with the leisure-lunch set from nearby upscale neighborhoods; evenings draw active crowds of local singles and families, many fresh off their boats or bicycles. During the summer, the outdoor patio is extremely popular despite the fact that it fronts the street, not the lake, and is plagued by inadequate service. Indoors, the large, roomy bar has a comfortable pub atmosphere. Best views are from the coveted window tables in the rather dark, low-ceilinged restaurant proper; arrive early to snag one. *Lunch, dinner every day; AE, DC, DIS, MC, V; checks OK; full bar.*

LIBERTY DELI

2722 Alki Ave SW, Seattle
☎ *(206) 935-8420*
West Seattle   ✕ **Deli**

The first white settlers to reach Seattle landed on Alki Beach, an event commemorated today by the beach's miniature Lady Liberty—who was donated by the Boy Scouts and also serves as the logo of this casual beachside stop. During the day, the deli is strictly a sandwich joint: East Coast transplants nostalgic for a sandwich piled high with paper-thin, hand-sliced meat should take a walk down memory lane with the Liberty Grinder or the pressed, grilled Reuben, considered by many to be the best in town. In the evening, tables are moved aside to turn the space into a quasi-cabaret. Performances have included a play, a musical act, and a stand-up comic—served up with a special dinner. When temperatures rise, pop in to stare at the manna in the refrigerated cases, which contain the most intriguing assortment of microbrewed sodas in town. *Breakfast Tues–Sun, lunch, dinner every day; AE, DIS, MC, V; local checks only; beer and wine.* ♿

LOCKSPOT CAFE

3005 NW 54th St, Seattle
☎ *(206) 789-4865*
Ballard   ✕ **Fish 'n' Chips**

You might dispute the Lockspot's slogan—"World-Famous Fish 'n' Chips"—but it's hard to beat its location, right next to the parking lot of the Hiram B. Chittenden Locks. The Lockspot has been here in various incarnations since the Locks were built in 1917; its mermaid sign is the first thing the hordes see when they descend upon the Locks and the last thing they see when they leave. The Lockspot's specialty is a basket of deep-fried cod and fries for $5.95; we advise that you order from the outdoor window and abscond immediately to the lovely park grounds. Other recommended items include the simpler dishes: the burgers (try Ballard's Biggest, a half-pounder), the fried calamari, the nicely spicy shellfish stew, the grilled pesto salmon platter, and the soft-serve ice cream. All entrees are under $10. There's also a full bar, if you're so inclined, that's open till 2am. Happy sailing! *Breakfast Sat–Sun, lunch, dinner every day; AE, DIS, MC, V; no checks; full bar.* ♿

LONGSHOREMAN'S DAUGHTER

3508 Fremont Pl N, Seattle
☎ *(206) 633-5169*
Fremont   ✕ **Bistro**

Longshoreman's Daughter pulls off the rare trick of offering great weekend brunches during the day and elegantly romantic dinners in the evening. Brunches include omelets, specialty waffles, and crowd-favorite Texas Eggs: poached, with black beans, salsa, and corn bread or tortilla. This is all very well and good, but dinner is the real treat here. Start with the mussels or a well-dressed caesar salad. Entrees range from the tame and expected (for example, a roasted half chicken or the ravioli of the day—both nicely done) to the more adventurous (linguine in saffron cream sauce with chicken sausage and lavender sprigs—excellent). Weekend brunches can be crowded: If you're with a group, you may want to get coffee next door to sip while you wait outside; if you're alone, you'll probably be able to grab a stool at the counter right away. Breakfast during the week has a more limited menu, but the space is not as jam-packed. Service here can vary wildly, but the bustling waitstaff is *almost* always full of Fremont cheer. *Brunch Sat–Sun, breakfast, lunch, dinner every day; MC, V; local checks only; beer and wine.* ♿

LUNA PARK CAFE
2918 Avalon Way SW, Seattle
☎ *(206) 935-7250*
West Seattle ✕ **Diner**

Not for those afraid of clutter, Luna Park Cafe is filled with stuff—some of it, like the incredible tin lunchbox collection, actual collectibles; the rest of it, well, just junk. This is a space where time has stood still: The vinyl booths have retained their springiness, and the tableside jukeboxes still work. And one of the waitresses knows the local girl who got a date with Elvis when the World's Fair was in Seattle—if you ask her, she'll tell you all about it. The food is, for the most part, as retro as the atmo. The spicy-but-not-too-interesting meat loaf is terrific, as are the burgers and other hot sandwiches. For non-meat eaters, the veggie burger makes a great vehicle for condiments. Note: If you get the delightfully lumpy mashed potatoes, request extra gravy—you won't need it, but it's so good that you'll welcome the excuse for more. Servings here are enormous (when they say jumbo hot fudge sundae, they mean it), and shakes are served up in a frosty metal shaker, right out from under the mixer. A great place to take your grandparents, your swing-dancing partner, or anyone with a '50s Americana fetish. *Breakfast, lunch, dinner every day; MC, V; checks OK; beer and wine.* ♿

MACRINA BAKERY AND CAFE

2408 First Ave, Seattle
☎ *(206) 448-4032*
Belltown   ✗ *Bakery*

Leslie Mackie has gained national acclaim as a bread baker, first as originator of the rustic bread program at Grand Central Bakery and later with her own ovens at Macrina. Today, she and her small army of bakers can hardly keep up with the demand for her gutsy, exceptional breads, which you'll find on the tables at the city's finest restaurants. Mornings, neighborhood regulars show up for buttery pastries, bowls of fresh fruit and house-made granola, and creamy lattes, enjoyed in the sunny Euro-chic cafe setting; a more substantial brunch is served on weekends. Others make haste with a loaf of potato bread, warm from the oven. Lunch brings simple, artful soups, salads, and panini, and a classy meze trio of daily-changing Mediterranean-inspired noshes. A fair number of vegetarian dishes are offered as well. *Brunch Sat–Sun, light breakfast, lunch Mon–Fri; MC, V; local checks only; beer and wine.* ♿

MAC'S SMOKEHOUSE

1006 First Ave S, Seattle (and branch)
☎ *(206) 628-0880*
Pioneer Square/South Seattle   ✗ *Barbecue*

What Mac's Smokehouse lacks in atmosphere, it makes up for by being slap next to the Kingdome. This means that on game days, the place is packed with kids clutching miniature footballs, guys in baseball hats heatedly discussing batting averages, and couples on a sports date sipping beers. Line up, order a pitcher of Bud Lite and a Boston pork butt sandwich, and join in. Best buys are the smokehouse sandwiches, especially the Razorback shredded pork or the smoked beef brisket ($5.50), slathered with Jack Daniels mustard and the kicky house barbecue sauce. Or make a meal out of the fine side dishes, such as tart coleslaw crisped up with red peppers, or the superb red beans and rice, done Louisiana-style with chunks of pork sausage and hot links. (The corn bread, on the other hand, is a bit dry.) For a few bucks more, you can also get plates of maple-glazed ribs, smoked chicken, brisket, and breast of turkey. They've got a decent kids' menu, too. The food is cafeteria-style, and the line goes fast, so be ready with your order. If you're not off to a game, make a night of it; there are pinball machines, blues music, and a few outdoor tables. There's a second Mac's down in Tukwila, too (10315 E Marginal Way S, (206)

763-4645). *Lunch, dinner Mon–Sat (open Sun for Mariners games only); AE, MC, V; checks OK; beer and wine.*

MAD PIZZA

4021 E Madison St, Seattle (and branches)
☎ *(206) 329-7037*
Madison Park/First Hill/Fremont *Pizza*

Sure, you can get a pepperoni or cheese pie, but why would you want to, when you can order one of Mad Pizza's signature exotic combinations? It's not quite pizza madness, although this pizzeria claims to be "committed." The pies are good, if not great, and are handled by an unfailingly cheerful staff. Join the hip young crowd showing off their piercings and tattoos while waiting for their orders. Or dash in for a slice of pie, and then sit back and have fun watching the other customers. The popular Fremont branch (3601 Fremont Ave N, (206) 632-5453) is tucked into a spare, clean space in a multiuse building underneath Doc Watson's. The original Mad Pizza is in Madison Park, and there's another on First Hill (1314 Madison St, (206) 322-7447). *Lunch, dinner every day; AE, MC, V; checks OK; beer and wine.* &

MADISON PARK CAFE

1807 42nd Ave E, Seattle
☎ *(206) 324-2626*
Madison Park *Breakfast*

Indulging in a morning repast at this charming house-turned-cafe has been a local ritual for more than 20 years. Seated at one of the too-few tables inside—or out in the brick courtyard in warm weather—you might wrap your hands around a latte, smear butter on a warm scone, and await baked eggs bubbling with ham and cheese or a grand, soufflélike strata. Neighbors gossip while children toy with their coloring books, eating homemade granola and wiping sticky hands on checkered tablecloths. At lunch, real estate agents do soup and salad with clients, shopkeepers share inventive sandwiches, and you can still get a proper quiche and a glass of wine to go with it. On weekend evenings, the cafe turns into a country-French bistro. Though the menu is lovely (oysters with Pernod cream sauce, rack of lamb, steak au poivre), prices soar out of cheap range, so enjoy the cafe's atmosphere over breakfast or lunch and save dinner for a splurge. *Breakfast Tues–Sun, lunch Tues–Sat, dinner Fri–Sat; MC, V; checks OK; full bar.*

MADISON'S CAFE

3803 Delridge Way SW, Seattle
☎ *(206) 935-2412*
West Seattle ✕ **Pub Grub**

Madison's Cafe was a single-story brick storefront sinking into a big urban funk when it was rescued and lovingly restored by a young couple who wanted to turn it into a great neighborhood space for music and food. It's still family-run (Madison is the owners' daughter), and the place has since evolved into a fixture on the acoustic rock and folk scene. The food here is honest cafe/pub fare served in sizable portions. Aside from very satisfying burgers, sandwiches, and salads, there are cafe favorites that bring in the locals time and again, like the mouthwatering Korean-style steak and the sinfully rich Madison Bar. It's a great space to hang out and nosh until you're feeling brave enough to try the open mike. Ample parking outside and plenty of tables and seats inside are an added benefit—though if you want a good vantage point for the musical acts, you may want to get there a bit earlier to nab the best spots. *Brunch Sat–Sun, lunch, dinner every day; DIS, MC, V; local checks only; beer and wine.* ♿

MAE PHIM THAI

94 Columbia St, Seattle
☎ *(206) 624-2979*
Pioneer Square ✕ **Thai**

Fast-paced and dirt cheap, this friendly, family-run restaurant, tucked right next to the Highway 99 on-ramp, offers about a dozen simple Thai dishes to eat in or take out. Lower-downtown office types can sit down to an enormous plate of phad Thai, swimming Rama, or curry (and, more often than not, a complimentary bowl of soup as well) and still have time to window-shop before the clock strikes "You're late!" This is straightforward Thai food at its best. *Lunch, dinner Mon–Sat; no credit cards; local checks only; no alcohol.*

MAE'S ON PHINNEY RIDGE

6412 Phinney Ave N, Seattle
☎ *(206) 782-1222*
Phinney Ridge   ✕ *Breakfast*

Would you prefer to eat your omelet and hashbrowns in the booth shaped like a gaping mouth, or the one clothed in animal skin? Perhaps you'd like a seat in the Moo Room, one of four separate dining rooms? It's all part of the experience at Mae's, a place that prides itself on its awe-inspiring breakfast, its portions, and its personality (all three are combined in the dish called Green Eggs and Ham). Best bets are the humongous, yeasty cinnamon rolls, the old-fashioned shakes and malteds, the biscuits and gravy, and the vast plates of "spuds." You can also get decent renditions of all the usual diner fare, including pancakes, scones, omelets, and enough granola-and-fruit combos to make the vegan crowd happy. At the other end of the spectrum is the Cinnamon Roll French Toast, which, rumor has it, once sent someone into insulin shock. Although breakfast is the thing at Mae's, there is a good lunch menu too, with large salads, chicken and biscuits, and burgers. *Breakfast, lunch every day; AE, MC, V; checks OK; beer and wine.*

MAHARAJA CUISINE OF INDIA

500 Elliott Ave W, Seattle (and branches)
☎ *(206) 286-1772*
Queen Anne/Greenwood/West Seattle   ✕ *Indian*

The success of the original Maharaja in West Seattle spawned this sibling branch located near the grain elevators between Queen Anne and Magnolia, just a stone's throw from Elliott Bay. The location has certainly improved the dining prospects of those living in the numerous apartment complexes along this largely industrial strip of Elliott Avenue. Housed in a pink corrugated-metal shell of a building, with an interior of soft pinks and purples, Maharaja hardly dazzles the eye with its decor. No matter: Impressing the palate is what counts, and the dishes, inspired by the traditional cooking of the Punjab region of northern India, stand up on their own. The Special Dinners for two are both popular and a good value: At $20.95 for the vegetarian and $22.95 for the nonvegetarian, these meals could probably feed three adults adequately. They come with the works: a choice of appetizer, three hearty main dishes, naan, basmati rice, and either *gulab jamun* or rice pudding for dessert. The menu abounds with a wealth of aromatic sauces ranging from the exotic to the sublime, making every dish the waitstaff carries past you seem a lost chance at bliss. The clay tandoori charcoal oven renders the variously marinated meats tender and tasty—the Mixed Grill is a fine sampler of the tandoor's magic. Curry fanatics can choose from a "Festival of Curries," with your choice of lamb, poultry, seafood, or vegetables in the supporting role. The fully loaded lunch buffet ($4.95) operates seven days a week, and free delivery is available. Check out Maharaja's other locations in Greenwood (8518 Greenwood Ave N, (206) 782-7890) and West Seattle (4542 California Ave SW, (206) 935-9443). *Lunch, dinner every day; AE, DIS, MC, V; local checks only; beer and wine.* ♿

MALENA'S TACO SHOP

620 W McGraw St, Seattle
☎ *(206) 284-0304*
Queen Anne   ✗ *Mexican*

This tiny hole-in-the-wall in an old two-story red-brick building might seem more in character tucked into the lonesome barrio of a Mexican border town than perched atop swank Queen Anne Hill. Malena's follows the unwritten rule that the best, most authentic Mexican food is found in the most inconspicuous of settings. And lucky Queen Anne folks have caught on to the "small place, big taste" axiom in a hurry. Arrive late and you'll likely be assigned to the take-out line, as there are only four small tables and a short three-stool counter at the window. Everything here is served no-frills style on Styrofoam plates with plastic utensils. The *carne asada* (a delicious marinated skirt steak), shredded pork, and fish tacos come highly recommended. Heartier appetites will be satisfied by combination plates, which include rice and beans. Besides tacos, you will find authentic burritos, tasty tostadas, and *tortas* (a Mexican take on the sandwich). Take-out options include pint containers of rice and beans plus a number of smaller sides, including jalapeños and carrots. *Lunch, dinner every day; no credit cards; checks OK; no alcohol.*

MALTBY CAFE

8809 Maltby Rd, Maltby
☎ (425) 483-3123
Maltby   ✕ *American*

Upstairs, the 1937 Maltby School gymnasium, a WPA project, remains
as it was. Downstairs, in what used to be the school cafeteria, the
Maltby Cafe dishes up outstanding country breakfasts and equally satisfying lunches. Finding the place the first time might be tough, but
you'll never forget the way. A Saturday morning repast can fill you for
the weekend. Unhurried, bountiful breakfasts feature delicious
omelets (the Maltby is a huge affair, stuffed with more than a cup of
assorted veggies, ham cubes, or even pieces of roast beef), good new
potatoes, old-fashioned oatmeal, and thick slices of French toast. If
you have to wait for a table (which is usually the case on weekends),
order one of the legendary giant cinnamon rolls and savor it on the
steps outside. Lunch brings great sandwiches and soups (try a Reuben,
made with the cafe's own corned beef). *Breakfast, lunch every day;
MC, V; checks OK; beer and wine.* ♿

MAMA'S MEXICAN KITCHEN

2234 Second Ave, Seattle (and branch)
☎ (206) 728-6262
Belltown/Downtown   ✕ *Mexican*

Here's an ancient (by Belltown standards) Mexican joint that has been
proudly serving up south-of-the-border favorites for not too many
pesos since 1974. The maze of rooms, each a den of sticky plastic
tablecloths, is full of happy customers just about any time of day. The
popular Elvis Room (you'll see why) sits 12 lucky diners. The outdoor
patio, despite the occasional visiting yellowjacket in summer, boasts
just enough of a view of the passing street scene to warrant enduring
whatever weather comes along. The food is basic and straightforward,
brightly sauced and cheesed, and comes in seemingly any
combination. In the long-standing tradition of what the
menu calls "authentic Southern California–style" fare,
you get to fill up on burritos, enchiladas, tostadas, and
numerous daily and house specials; just be aware that
these platters are sized to last for a couple of meals. If you
really want to warm Mama's heart (she's no longer with
us, but her grandson is carrying on), you'll visit her sister
enterprise, Mamacita's, a one-room cafeteria-style luncheonette a few
blocks away that offers an equally tasty à la carte menu (216 Stewart

St, (206) 374-8876). *Lunch, dinner every day (Mama's), lunch Mon–Sat (Mamacita's); AE, DC, DIS, MC, V; no checks; full bar (Mama's only).*

MAPLE LEAF GRILL

8909 Roosevelt Way NE, Seattle
☎ *(206) 523-8449*
Maple Leaf   ✕ **Inventive Ethnic**

The popular Maple Leaf Grill has the feel of a bona fide tavern—a long bar, booths, and great wood paneling—with a kitchen that turns out fusion food with Cajun sparks. Want an artichoke heart, roasted garlic, and pine nut sandwich with your pint of Alaskan Amber? This is the place to find it, as well as a great turkey sandwich with smoked Gouda cheese and homemade chutney, red-pepper fettuccine with chicken and roasted poblanos, and lots of other dishes featuring chiles, homemade chutneys and apple slaws, tapenades, and garlic. The prices and flavors are a little rich for those who have other visions of what a neighborhood joint should be (sandwiches are around $7, and entrees go up to $11.95), and the experimentation results in misses from time to time, but nothing seems to deter the Maple Leaf's solid fan base. Perhaps it's the fact that you can always count on their burgers and crispy mountains of fries. Plus, the atmosphere is convivial without being too rowdy, and the deck is a great place to quaff a few pints when the days are long. *Lunch Mon–Fri, dinner every day; MC, V; checks OK; beer and wine.* ♿

MASHIKO

4725 California Ave SW, Seattle
☎ *(206) 935-4339*
West Seattle   ✕ **Japanese**

Neighborhood sushi may sound like an oxymoron, but this is exactly what the popular Mashiko delivers, in generous-to-a-fault portions and in a setting that's all crisp blond wood and bright halogen area lights. The folks of West Seattle crowd into this small space because the sushi really does look as if it's on steroids—it will make you fat without turning your wallet skinny. There are a few creatively flavored (and very popular) handrolls, such as the spicy salmon skin, that you won't find anywhere else in town. The bento dinner is a daily-changing assortment that usually includes some combination of tempura, sushi, and teriyaki, along with rice and miso soup, for a ridiculously low price. There's something on the long menu here for everyone in the family, from easy-to-eat ramen and udon dishes to kid-friendly rice bowls. *Lunch, dinner Mon–Sat; AE, MC, V; local checks only; beer, wine, and sake.* &

MATT'S FAMOUS CHILI DOGS

6615 E Marginal Way S, Seattle (and branch)
☎ *(206) 768-0418*
SoDo/Bellevue   ✕ *Hot Dogs/Sausage*

Expatriate Midwesterners head here when they get the urge for a Midwestern-style chili dog (lots of meat, no beans). Matt Jones's 450-square-foot sandwich stand near the First Avenue Bridge sports only a few stools, but there's plenty of counter space. Jones also cooks up Italian beef sandwiches with thinly sliced beef, sweet peppers, and sauce, and serves 'em on a French roll. He'll gladly make a chicken sandwich for those who don't do red meat. The Marginal Way branch is the beloved original, but Jones also has a much larger Bellevue location (699 110th Ave NE, (425) 637-2858) with a full dining room, if you want to relax while you chow your dog. *Lunch, early dinner Mon–Fri (Mon–Sat at Bellevue); no credit cards; checks OK; no alcohol.* & *(Bellevue only)*

MAYA'S

9447 Rainier Ave S, Seattle
☎ *(206) 725-5510*
Rainier Beach   ✕ *Mexican*

All roads, if taken far enough south, lead to Maya's, the Mexican institution in Rainier Beach. We don't know how they manage to fit the entire neighborhood into one building, but every night they pull it off. Families sit next to necking couples, and you may witness a group of teenagers shrinking in embarrassment as one of their teachers walks in. Everyone's there for the food, which is plentiful, affordable, and good—in a refried beans, rice, and shredded lettuce kind of way. Your meal will arrive mere seconds, it seems, after you order it—not necessarily a good thing, as tortillas can be soggy and chewy, enchiladas not heated all the way through, quesadillas not quite crispy. But the price is right, the meat dishes are savory and spicy, and the neighborhood atmosphere is festive and warm. *Lunch Mon–Fri, dinner every day; AE, DC, MC, V; no checks; full bar.* &

MCSORLEY'S

307 Madison St, Seattle
☎ (206) 233-9690
Downtown   ✕ *Soup/Salad/Sandwich*

Few assembly lines work as well as the one at this modest luncheonette on the slope of Madison above Third Avenue. McSorley's is a
bring-'em-in, send-'em-out kind of place that thrives on efficiency. The
staff stands in formation—from the person who takes orders to the
guy who stuffs your food into a brown bag—and confronts their daily
queue. The line (which almost always winds down the hill from the
entrance) is handled with simultaneous speed and congeniality, so
that most orders are ready for the taking as soon as you get past the
cashier. The service is not the only reward here: Lunch specials, in particular the Sandwich Special, are a steal for a measly four bucks—and
that's for a whole lotta sandwich (the meat loaf—with red onions,
mayo, lettuce, and, if you're feeling perky, jalapeños—is particularly
satisfying), a cup of soup, and a mammoth drink of your choice. This
is just the kind of comfort food Mom made when you stayed home
from school with the flu. Once you've got your order, take it to go or
sit at the counter facing the window—if there's a seat to spare. *Lunch
Mon–Thurs; no credit cards; checks OK; no alcohol.*

MECCA CAFE

526 Queen Anne Ave N, Seattle
☎ (206) 285-9728
Queen Anne   ✕ *Diner*

Located in the same spot for more than 65 years, the Mecca is one of
Seattle's oldest continuously operating eateries. On a busy Friday or
Saturday night, expect a mixture of folks united in a common aspira-
tion: strong, honest drinks in a humble setting. While the crowd com-
prises both young and old (and is mostly regulars), anyone into loud
music, alcohol, and smoke will feel right at home. The food is standard cafe fare: burgers, soups, salads, sandwiches, and the like. This is
the sort of place where eating is a mere necessity, a requirement
before getting on with more important things. While many
bars strive for an unpretentious, friendly atmosphere,
the Mecca succeeds without trying. *Breakfast, lunch,
dinner every day; AE, MC, V; no checks; full bar.*

MEDITERRANEAN KITCHEN

366 Roy St, Seattle (and branches)
☎ *(206) 285-6713*
Queen Anne/Bellevue/Capitol Hill   ✕ **Middle Eastern**

Queen Anne's beloved Mediterranean Kitchen has moved to newer, larger digs just north of Seattle Center. If the new, polished interior—burgundy carpet and Kermit-green walls and ceilings—leaves a little something to be desired, everything else is pretty much business as usual. The mostly Middle Eastern food is still delicious; the value, excellent. You won't be faced with the age-old soup-or-salad dilemma at dinner—because you get both, a bowl of the soup of the day plus a tomato, cucumber, and lettuce salad spruced up with a tangy house dressing. Adding to the bargain, dinners also come with velvety rice and a basket of pita bread. Most popular here is the Farmer's Dish ($10.50), a veritable mound of garlicky, long-marinated, charbroiled chicken wings drizzled with a lemon garlic sauce so good it's available in 12-ounce to-go bottles (as is the house salad dressing). The chicken or beef *shawarma* ($9.50), a scrumptious stewlike creation in a red wine vinegar base with spices, onions, tomato, and red cabbage, is another heavy-duty crowd-pleaser, and there's also a wide selection of fine vegetarian meals. Lunches, which include rice, salad, and pita bread, are about half the price of their dinner  counterparts. There's a second Kitchen in Bellevue (103 Bellevue Way NE, (425) 462-9422), and an offshoot to-go spot, Mediterranean Kitchen Express, in a Capitol Hill QFC/Bartell's megaplex (1417 Broadway, (206) 860-3989). The Express offers the same food as the Kitchen but for even less (sandwiches and full plates, beef and lamb kabobs). One caveat: If your next stop after dinner is the Opera House, a flick at the Broadway Market, or any other close quarters, don't forget your Altoids, as garlic is the mainstay of most of these Lebanese masterpieces. *Lunch Mon–Sat, dinner every day; AE, MC, V; checks OK; beer and wine (all info varies at Express).* ♿

MEE SUM PASTRY

1533 Pike Pl, Seattle
☎ *(206) 682-6780*
Pike Place Market   ✕ **Bakery**

Located in the Triangle Building on the market's central cobbled street, Mee Sum Pastry is more of a dent than a hole in the wall. You order from the sidewalk before a warmed glass case full of curious golden brown globes called humbao (think Chinese potpie), a tasty pastry stuffed with chicken, pork, or curried beef along with minced mushrooms, onions, and a delicious sweet and savory sauce. Toss in a creamy, melt-in-your-mouth Crab Rangoon, a vegetarian egg roll, or a barbecued pork skewer, and you've got a complete lunch for just over $3. For dessert, try a Chinese sweet roll, a mixed-nut or almond cake, or a red bean cake cookie. *Breakfast, lunch, dinner every day; MC, V; no checks; no alcohol.*

MERCHANTS CAFE
109 Yesler Way, Seattle
☎ *(206) 624-1515*
Pioneer Square ✕*Pub Grub*

A fixture in Seattle's history for over a century, Merchants Cafe is actually the oldest restaurant in its original location on the West Coast. The restaurant first opened as Gallagher Chambers Company in 1890, and customers could drink beer downstairs before enjoying a little company in the brothel upstairs. Things have changed since then, and the place has gone through a series of different names, including the Merchants Exchange Salon in 1892, the inspiration for the current name. Merchants Cafe features a beautiful 30-foot bar that traveled around the Horn on a schooner in the late 1800s and an intriguing and history-filled underground level, now a private dining room. Today, this is a good place to grab a meal before a ballgame or an evening gallery walk. Start your meal with the smoked salmon chowder, and then try one of  the tasty sandwiches. The hot, juicy Reuben, the unique portobello melt, and the Merchant lamb burger are all good. Merchants Cafe also serves fresh seafood entrees and a popular pepper steak. *Breakfast, lunch every day, dinner Tues–Sun; MC, V; no checks; full bar.*

MEZE
935 6th St S, Kirkland
☎ *(425) 828-3923*
Kirkland ✕*Middle Eastern*

It's no wonder Meze does boffo business in catering for Eastside parties large and small. The word *meze* means "small dish," but it has come to mean "party food," at least to Americans. Meze makes creamy, tangy hummus that is bold with garlic; fresh, robust baba ghanouj; delicious *karnibahar* (batter-fried cauliflower); and great green dolmathes with a sweet-spiced rice stuffing given texture by pine nuts. We could go on but we won't, not to tout the tabbouleh or try to tell you you'll never feel awful about the falafel. Warm Mediterranean winds have blown Ibrahim Pekin to this sunny spot in Houghton Plaza, where he chats up the clientele while grilling great panini (such as the one with hummus, roasted eggplant and red pepper, feta, and parsley), assembling a vegetarian platter, and serving up three (count 'em!) versions of flaky baklava. Fewer than a dozen tables inside (plus a couple outside in nice weather) and a few decent wines by the glass will tempt you to linger. *Light breakfast, lunch, dinner Mon–Sat; MC, V; checks OK; beer and wine.* &

MIKE'S CHILI PARLOR

1447 NW Ballard Way, Seattle
☎ *(206) 782-2808*
Ballard   ✕ *Chili*

Tucked away at the north end of the Ballard Bridge (not far from that neighborhood's famous neon sign advising you to "Add . . . Bardahl . . . Oil") lies a Seattle legend. Using the same recipe at the same location for over 75 years, Mike's Chili is one of Seattle's undisputed culinary legacies. And for good reason: The chili's great. Mike's grandson runs the place now, but he serves up the family recipe with pride. Take your pick from the chili burger, chili dog, chili steak, chili pasta, chili fries, or, of course, simply chili. You can't go wrong on this menu. Wash it down with a Rainier, take in the M's game, and color yourself native. *Lunch, dinner Mon–Sat; no credit cards; local checks only; beer and wine.*

MOGHUL PALACE

10303 NE 10th St, Bellevue
☎ *(425) 451-1909*
Bellevue   ✕ *Indian*

You've gotta like a place that makes its own mango ice cream, all fruity and chunked up with pistachios and almonds. It's a fine way to top off a beautifully spiced meal that comes rich in saffron, exotic as Marco Polo, and warming to the core with clove, cumin, and coriander. Owner Shah Kahn added this second Eastside Indian eatery following the success of India Gate in nearby Eastgate. The servers here may not know much about the food, but don't worry: Chef Salah Uddin certainly does. Mussels swim in a barely hot sweet-kissed curry, for which an order of naan—particularly the onion-cilantro version—is a must for dipping. Among the dinner entrees, the kormas are particularly good, the tandoori specialties are quite adequate, and you can't go wrong with curry. You can, however, go wrong with mango ribs—nice sauce, paltry bones. The lunch buffet offers an opportunity for sampling the old favorites and some spicy salads. *Lunch Mon—Sat, dinner every day; AE, DC, MC, V; local checks only; full bar.* &

MONA'S BISTRO & LOUNGE

6421 Latona Ave NE, Seattle
☎ *(206) 526-1188*
Green Lake   ✕ ***Inventive Ethnic***

Go to Mona's in midwinter, when you and the person you're trying to impress are parched for a little color. The owners, a couple from Puerto Rico by way of New York, have decorated the dining room and lounge in shades of yellow, peach, and purple, with high ceilings and artistic touches such as curved mirrors, red curtains, and huge, colorful paintings. Most of the menu is priced beyond budget eaters, but you'll find bargains in the lounge, where a Mediterranean menu of $4-$7 tapas is served until 11pm most nights, and until midnight on nights when live jazz is featured. Pony up to the ultrasleek bar and order a lovely plate or two, which are as artful as the surroundings: hand-tied marinated mozzarella served on grilled Como bread; clams steamed in an orange-and-lime-sparked sauce; kabobs of garlicky tiger prawns; roasted potatoes drizzled with a creamy aioli sauce; and the pasta of the day, which might be wild-mushroom-stuffed fresh ravioli or lemon pepper fettuccine. There are bargains to be found on the dinner menu next  door too, such as the duck confit, pan-seared and served with crispy potatoes ($8), or the entree-size plate of organic mixed greens. (Note: If you're feeling spendy, order the outstanding house paella for $16.) This is the perfect place to chase away the gray or to sip and nibble before heading off into the night. *Dinner, late-night tapas every day; AE, MC, V; checks OK; full bar.* &

MONDO BURRITO

2121 First Ave, Seattle

☎ *(206) 728-9697*

Belltown ✕ *Inventive Ethnic*

At this hip wrapped-food joint, the Americanized burrito (now a fast-food classic) tackles international flavors. There's Thai, with spicy coconut rice, bean sprouts, carrots, and Indonesian sweet-and-hot sauce. There's Greek, with kalamata olive tapenade, couscous, eggplant, spinach, feta, and tzatziki. There's even Korean, with rice, pickled ginger salsa, tomatoes, kimchi, and bean sprouts. These and other options are either intriguing or upsetting, depending on your ethnic roots and culinary conscience. The tortillas have a twist, too; some are made with Roma-tomato flour, others with spinach flour. If you feel that culinary borders exist only to be crossed, you'll find that dining here is always titillating (if not always perfect), especially when downed with a cerveza or a glass of vino. This Belltown hot spot is open until 3am on weekend nights. *Lunch, dinner every day; MC, V; local checks only; beer and wine.* ♿

MS. HELEN'S SOUL FOOD

1133 23rd Ave, Seattle

☎ *(206) 322-6310*

Central District ✕ *Southern*

Make no mistake about it, no one is standing in Ms. Helen's kitchen counting calories. This is soul food, after all. Located between a vacant lot and a beat-up red-brick building, Ms. Helen's is the place to come when you want Flavorful (with a capital "F") down-home cookin' with a Southern flair. The setting is homey and comfortable, with carved-wood tables and high-backed benches, lounge chairs, jelly-jar glasses, colorful rubber placemats, and a few pudgy table lamps here and there. Mint green walls are crowded with posters of art festivals, theater and gallery events, and photographs of satisfied customers, including a number of local sports heroes. And this is certainly no surprise, as Ms. Helen's keeps 'em coming back for more. You've never tasted chicken and dumplings this good. All dinners— including such favorites as the short ribs, pork chops, catfish, oxtails, and shrimp Creole—come with a giant, pancake-size hunk of corn bread lathered up with butter, and a choice of two side dishes. The yams and okra-and-corn sides come highly recommended. Other tasty sides include greens, cabbage, red beans, black-eyed peas, mashed potatoes, macaroni and cheese, and potato salad. The sandwich list is limited to fish or ham plus several burgers, including a Super Burger that's piled high with both beef and hot links and comes with a side of fries—all for $5.50. Mornings, Ms. Helen lays down a mighty fine breakfast spread, too. Parking is available across the street. *Breakfast, lunch, dinner Mon–Sat; no credit cards; no checks; full bar.*

MUSASHI'S SUSHI AND GRILL

1400 N 45th, Seattle
☎ *(206) 633-0212*
Wallingford ✕*Japanese*

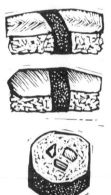

If you think that a crowded room is part of the fun of dining, and if you're a sushi lover, you're probably reading this as you stand in line at Musashi's. There is almost always a wait at dinnertime, and once you're seated, you'll be near enough to your fellow diner to closely observe all their sushi-eating rituals, such as whittling chopsticks down or mixing just the right amount of wasabe in soy sauce. It's all part of the experience at this small, unpretentious-yet-stylish Japanese eatery that has legions of followers. The sushi is indeed excellent—fresh, well-prepared, generously served, and very reasonably priced (salmon egg is the most expensive at $1.60). A $4.50 California roll, loaded with crab meat, bits of sweet omelet, and avocado, could be an entire meal in its own. They also have a nice selection of grilled veggie skewers, teriyaki plates, and bento. Tea is complimentary, and miso soup is brought right away. Tips for those who hate queuing up: Order takeout, go at lunch, or go alone, so that you can score a seat at the small sushi bar. *Lunch, dinner Tues–Fri, dinner only Sat; no credit cards; local checks only; beer and wine.*

NEELAM'S AUTHENTIC INDIAN CUISINE

4735 University Way NE, Seattle
☎ *(206) 523-5275*
University District ✕*Indian*

Up on the Ave—a strip chockablock with ethnic restaurants vying for the dining dollars of starving students—delightfully officious and prettily costumed Neelam Jain is not above rushing to the doorway of her dimly lit East Indian restaurant to convince hesitant passersby to come in and try her bargain-priced dinner specials. And we're convinced. Those specials include, among other offerings, 14 chicken- or lamb-based curries, and for a 10-spot you'll get a hubcap-size plate with a choice of entree, cooling raita, fragrant dal, cumin-scented basmati rice, feathery-light naan, appetizer (potato samosas or chicken pakoras), beverage, and dessert. Forget the à la carte stuff. And show restraint when asked how hot you like your curry, or youuuu'll be sorrrrry. *Lunch, dinner every day; AE, DC, DIS, MC, V; checks OK; beer and wine.* ♿

NEW HONG KONG MALAYSIAN RESTAURANT
212 12th Ave S, Seattle
☎ *(206) 324-4091*
International District   ✕ *Malaysian*

Don't know a thing about Malaysian food? Don't worry—just order from the thick photo album filled with photographs of the most popular dishes at this restaurant. Located in a small strip mall at the intersection of Jackson Street and 12th Avenue, NHK Malaysia is filled with Malaysian university students because of its authentic *nonya* style of cooking, a creolized approach that blends the influences of three cuisines: Indian, Chinese, and Malaysian. As familiar as those cuisines may be separately, they fuse unexpectedly in this cooking—in a manner that's better suited to the more adventurous palate. Everyone will love the *roti-canai*, an "Indian pancake" that resembles a paper-thin flour tortilla—fried up with enough grease to make it translucent. The Malay Lobak is a combination platter offering pork rolls, two shrimp toast, tofu, shaved ginger, and two halves of a "thousand-year-old" egg—a venerable Chinese delicacy. One of the most popular vegetable dishes is *kang kung belachan*—a vibrant green platter of lightly fried watercress flavored with shrimp paste. Noodle dishes—such as *malay chow kueh teow* (wide rice noodles, shrimp, and squid flavored with oyster sauce and thick sweet soy sauce) and Singapore noodles (vermicelli-style rice noodles and pieces of swordfish and shrimp)—are pleasantly flavored but greasy; maybe that's to be expected from dishes that are popular as street food back in Malaysia. Familiar-tasting and familiar in appearance, these noodle dishes, along with the satay sticks (beef or chicken), are the items to order if you're dining with squeamish friends. Desserts consist of shaved ice flavored with sweet red beans and green gelatinous squiggles—again, strictly for the adventurous palate. *Lunch, dinner every day; MC, V; no checks; beer and wine.* ♿

NIKOLAS PIZZA AND PASTA

1924 N 45th St, Seattle
☎ *(206) 545-9090*
Wallingford ✕ *American*

This is the ultimate place to visit when you can't decide what you want to eat. A homey sit-down restaurant in the heart of Wallingford, Nikolas boasts a massive menu that starts with Greek cuisine and adds pizza and pasta. And breakfasts. And burgers. And microbrews. Even with this range of offerings, the fare is well prepared and reasonably priced. Plus, whatever your hungry heart desires is available for the asking until well into the evening—and there's something ya gotta love about that. The airy, light-filled dining room has cozy booths by the front windows, plus an open seating area up a few steps with space for a large group. Park out back, but don't forget to give the hostess your license number. Nikolas is a good bet if you want to grab a bite before catching a movie playing at the Guild across the street. Two final words of advice: meatball grinder. *Breakfast, lunch, dinner every day; AE, MC, V; checks OK; full bar.* ♿

NOBLE COURT SEAFOOD RESTAURANT

1644 140th Ave NE, Bellevue
☎ *(425) 641-6011*
Bellevue ✕ *Chinese*

This seafood restaurant is a favorite with the Eastside's many Chinese residents, who show up on weekends for what most consider to be the best dim sum on either side of the Lake Washington bridges. But what many folks don't know is that Noble Court serves dim sum lunches *every* day of the week. The space is huge and great for large parties who can gather around a table for ten. The menu ranges from standard kung pao and fried rice to the more exotic shark's fin soup, stewed abalone, and bird's-nest-with-crabmeat soup. Live tanks at the entrance display fish and crustaceans ready for a little black bean sauce. Though some items creep above our cheap cost standards, stick with the obvious choices and you'll do fine. Noble Court also has live music in the lounge Wednesdays through Sundays. *Lunch, dinner every day; AE, MC, V; no checks; full bar.* ♿

NOBLE PALACE

4214A University Way NE, Seattle
☎ (206) 632-7248
University District   ✕ Chinese

Formerly the Proud Bird, this Chinese restaurant changed its name a few years back and moved a block down the Ave. Luckily for us, they brought their excellent food with them. Featuring Cantonese and Mandarin cuisine, Noble Palace's menu doesn't pack a lot of surprises: You'll quickly recognize all the usual suspects, like almond chicken, sweet-and-sour pork, and General Tso's chicken. But everything the Palace does, it does well—this place is packed every day at lunch for a reason. (Cheap and generous specials draw students and professors alike from the nearby UW; show up before or after the lunch rush if you don't want to wait for a table.) The kung pao chicken and broccoli with prawns are both excellent choices, but the real showpiece on the menu is the Mongolian beef, a faithful mainstay that's as good the 50th time you have it as it is the first. *Lunch, dinner every day; MC, V; checks OK; beer and wine.* ♿

NOODLE RANCH

2228 Second Ave, Seattle
☎ (206) 728-0463
Belltown   ✕ Pan-Asian

You *will* wait outside in the rain to eat here, but it *will* be worth it. The Noodle Ranch is a neighborhood hangout that welcomes all: married hipsters with babies, condo owners wearing Brooks Brothers and Anne Taylor, extended Asian families, bookish students with piercings, and lots of creatively paired couples. The menu is long and rectangular like the room, diverse and appealing like the crowd inside. Appetizers that deserve leisurely investigation include gyoza (pot-stickers) filled with savory pork and lightly fried; finger-lickin' bites of fish marinated and grilled in grape leaves; and a refreshing Asian salad composed of cabbage, carrot, and green onion slivers tossed with herbs and *nuoc cham* (a tangy, clear Vietnamese sauce resembling vinegar). Cool, fragrant herbs like mint, dill, lemongrass, and cilantro reach their highest expression in the wonderful *cha ca,* which features a modest portion of marinated, grilled fish atop a saladlike composition of mild noodles, refreshing greens, and tangy sauce. Avoid the hour between 6 and

7pm; everyone in the neighborhood drops in around that time, and service can slow down considerably. On the other hand, it's a great time to drape yourself provocatively over a chair while you wait for someone worth sharing your table with. *Lunch, dinner Mon–Sat; AE, MC, V; no checks; no alcohol.* &

NOODLE STUDIO
209 Broadway E, Seattle
☎ *(206) 325-6277*
Capitol Hill   ✕ *Thai*

The Noodle Studio does what we wish more of Seattle's many non-Western restaurants would do: reach beyond the standard to offer interesting regional dishes. The extensive Thai and Thai-Chinese menu tantalizes taste buds with curried soup from northern Thailand, marinated and flambéed game hen from the northwest, and Muslim-style rice with chicken from the south, as well as uncommon seafood, noodle, and rice dishes. All are prepared with a love of food, a flair for cooking, and youthful energy. The willingness to cater to special dietary requests, the friendly service, and the informal setting create a congenial atmosphere. Graceful, old-style Buddha images augment the restaurant's trendy black-and-peach interior. *Lunch, dinner every day; AE, MC, V; no checks; beer and wine.* &

OK CORRAL BBQ PIT-STOP AND SANDWICH SLINGERS
8733 Greenwood Ave N, Seattle
☎ *(206) 784-9795*
Greenwood   ✕ *Barbecue*

Talk about smokin'! After a fire chased it down the street for a spell, the OK Corral moved back into its original location in the bottom floor of owner Otis Austin's house. Long a secret mecca for barbecue devotees, the OK locale was, for a long time, betrayed only by the heavenly smells drifting down Greenwood Avenue from the steel-barrel grills in his front yard; now, there's a brand-new barnyard fence to mark this spot. The post-fire digs are revamped, but still retain their original charm—a roll of paper towels at every table, the soft chatter from the TV hanging from the ceiling, and the kind of service you'd expect from your dad—but the real reason to go, of course, is the food. Even if you're not from the South, you'll quickly realize that this is the genuine article: huge, mouth-watering piles of barbecued ribs (pork, of course), chicken, and hot links, served alongside beans cooked with sweet potatoes, white rice, melt-in-your-mouth corn bread, potato salad, and greens (for you Yankees, that's mustard, collard, turnip, or cabbage). If you can pace yourself, sample the dee-lish sweet-potato pie. On your second visit (trust me—you'll be back), forgo the barbecue just this once and try the equally delicious fried chicken or fried catfish. Otis started serving sandwiches post-move—the same great BBQ'd fixins slung between two pieces of bread, with a seafood sandwich thrown in for variety. The OK recently extended its hours on Saturday and Sunday nights until 5am for late-night munching. *Lunch, dinner every day; AE, DC, DIS, MC, V; local checks only; no alcohol.* &

OLYMPIA PIZZA AND SPAGHETTI HOUSE II
4501 Interlake Ave N, Seattle
☎ *(206) 633-3655*
Wallingford   ✗ *Pizza*

On the walls are paintings of tiny stone monasteries on high rocky cliffs that teeter over a landscape resembling an ancient, twisted Montana: Greece. Other than the artwork, only the proliferation of olives and feta cheese on a few specialty pizzas and a decent Greek salad are clues to the influence behind this small pizza and pasta place. Decor is casual and modest (vinyl booths, simple tables), and the pizza is solid. The menu offers various pasta items, a few chicken entrees, and an infinite variety of 'za combinations, with 26 possible toppings to mix and match any way you like. The crust is doughy, the sauce plentiful and sweet. The Veggie is especially well done, with its mushrooms,

olives, green peppers, onions, and cooked or fresh tomatoes, but you can always get more creative with items like peperoncini, pineapple, smoked oysters, or pesto. Pastas are pricier and decent but nothing special. The young waitstaff is efficient, and the clientele is a family affair: lots of kids, a few couples, and the occasional cell-phone addict. Local microbrews will wet your whistle; ambience is all up to you. Contrary to popular belief, the "branches" on Queen Anne and Capitol Hill are not at all related—except by name. At press time, the Queen Anne spot was still under construction after a fire. *Lunch Mon—Fri, dinner every day; MC, V; local checks only; beer and wine.* &

OMAR AL KHYAM

354 Sunset Blvd N, Renton
☎ *(425) 271-8300*
Renton   ✕ **Middle Eastern**

Rumor has it that two of this restaurant's regulars have showed up faithfully every weekday since this friendly Middle Eastern eatery opened 22 years ago. That's quite a tale, but such loyalty isn't hard to imagine once you sample the food. A longtime favorite of both native Rentonites and Boeing employees out for a quick bite, Omar Al Khyam has earned its reputation. This family-owned and family-run restaurant serves up tradition with every plateful: Lebanese-style favorites like kabobs and *shish tawouk* (chicken roasted in lemon, garlic, and onions) are prepared with love and pride. The chicken *shawarma* (chicken thigh strips marinated with spices and red wine vinegar and grilled with onions and green peppers) is heavenly. Even items on the menu that shouldn't have to work hard to impress—like hummus—do. To top it all off, the prices are reasonable and the service more than attentive. After a meal here, you may find yourself coming back the next day. And maybe the day after that . . . and the day after that. . . .
Lunch, dinner every day; MC, V; checks OK; no alcohol.

THE ORIGINAL PANCAKE HOUSE

130 Park Place Center, Kirkland
☎ *(425) 827-7575*
Kirkland   ✕ **Breakfast**

Smack-dab in the middle of a suburban shopping center sits a pancake house the likes of which you'd expect to find in Elgin, Illinois, not upscale Kirkland. (And, yes, Virginia, it is part of a chain, but not *that* chain.) The decor is country-cozy, with light wood, questionable ferns, and a comfortable mix of older folks, business types, and families. The moment you relax into a comfy booth or hunker down at a table, one of the kindly, efficient servers hustles you coffee while you decide among at least 13 different types of pancakes. The coffee is their own blend, and a laudable (and bottomless) cup 'o Joe it  is. As for the flapjacks, well, the options seem endless: Georgia Pecan Pancakes? Barney's Banana Pancakes? The rest of the menu consists of various waffles, crepes, cereals, and other egg dishes, and there is a separate lunch menu with the standard sandwiches and burgers, but, as one would expect, pancakes are the star here. Go for the standards, especially the delish Yeasty, Old-Fashioned Buckwheat Pancakes. The fresh-squeezed OJ is another must-do; it's amazingly sweet and fortifying. But the mammoth, oven-baked Dutch Baby, served with whipped butter, lemon, and powdered sugar, will blow your socks off. And take note: A short stack of any variety will be plenty for most folks. *Breakfast every day, lunch Mon–Fri; AE, DIS, MC, V; checks OK; no alcohol.* ♿

OWL 'N THISTLE

808 Post Ave, Seattle
☎ *(206) 621-7777*
Pioneer Square   ✕ *Irish*

This Irish pub near the walk-on ramp for the Bainbridge ferry enjoys a loyal following and a high-energy weekend scene, complete with live music and a game room (darts and pool). Blessed with real Irish owners and an in-house band, the "scene" can sometimes overshadow the fact that there's a full-service restaurant ready to take your order. Simply contrived and with a nod to the Emerald Isle, the menu relies on fresh garden salads, soups, sandwiches, and a tender-fried fish 'n' chips platter (yes, they do provide vinegar). The shepherd's pie is quite good, a hearty meal for a rainy afternoon—as is the Irish stew, chock-full of everything Dinty Moore himself would recommend. For those inclined to arrive near the popular happy hour, choose from among several items for a mere $2 (fish 'n' chips, hummus plate, or fries). If you like to wash fried taters down with your Guinness, take heart: Their fries come near-perfect, salted and greasy, with the skins on. *Lunch, dinner every day; MC, V; no checks; full bar.* ♿

PAGLIACCI PIZZA

426 Broadway E, Seattle (and branches)
☎ *(206) 324-0730*
Capitol Hill/Queen Anne/University District   ✕ *Pizza*

All three Pagliacci pizzerias offer the same simple yet eternal lure: excellent thin-and-tangy cheese pizzas. The true test of the exceptional crust is the original cheese pizza, which is unadorned except for a light, fresh tomato sauce and good mozzarella. Hot from the oven, it's hard to beat. The Pagliaccio salad is usually soaked with dressing, and—though it's far from healthy—we like it, if only to dip our crusts in the sauce. Otherwise, skip the salads (mostly blah) and go straight for the pies; this place is about pizza. You can take out or eat in, get it by the slice or order whole. Comfortable, echoing, and sometimes hectic, all the Pagliaccis—Capitol Hill, Queen Anne (552 Queen Anne Ave N, (206) 285-1232), and University District (4529 University Way NE, (206) 632-0421)—are fine places for a quick solo meal. A phone call to their primo central delivery service, (206) 726-1717, will get you service from one of their fast-growing number of neighborhood pizza kitchens. (And if you're a regular delivery customer, you may even get a free pizza at Christmas!) *Lunch, dinner every day; AE, MC, V; local checks only; beer and wine.* &

PANDASIA

1625 W Dravus St, Seattle
☎ *(206) 283-9030*
Magnolia   ✕ *Pan-Asian*

The next time you make your way to Magnolia, take note of this stylish little restaurant in Interbay. It was originally opened as one of two Panda's restaurants; now it is its own kingdom, run by a husband-and-wife team who renamed it and expanded the already long menu to reflect the "pan" part of the name. Thus the superb mu-shus, kung pao chicken, and homemade noodles are joined by Thai satays, Malaysian curries, and a small supermarket of "Asian tortillas." We like some of the recent additions, such as the elegant game-fish tortilla, laden with swordfish, tuna, mahi-mahi, and jasmine rice, and flavored with curry and mango chutney. But it's hard to avoid backsliding into ordering old favorites that still ring true, such as the veggie chow mein, which stars those wonderful thick noodles; or the sesame orange beef, a crispy, extra-sesamed, deep-fried concoction that is as decadent as ever. Pandasia's take-out is extremely efficient. They specialize in large group orders and can put together a "flash buffet" at a moment's notice. Delivery is free within a certain area. Note that dishes are a little pricier than those at other Chinese restaurants, but they're well worth the extra coin. Plus, servings are very large. *Lunch Mon—Sat, dinner every day; AE, MC, V; checks OK; beer and wine.*

PANOS KLEFTIKO

815 Fifth Ave N, Seattle
☎ *(206) 301-0393*
Queen Anne   ✕ **Greek**

Panos Marinos is the heart and soul (and host/chef) of this traditional Greek taverna in a small, cozy storefront a few blocks north of Seattle Center. Come with a fistful of friends and cram your table with *mezedhes*, or "little dishes" (there are 25 choices, priced from $1.50 to $5.25), several servings of warm pita bread (the best we've had anywhere), and a glass or three of retsina. There are full-blown entrees as well, including several selections of lamb and chicken. Everything's tasty, but we especially love the *melitzanasalata* (a cold salad of roasted eggplant, tomatoes, and herbs) and the spicy meatballs. Arrive early if you have tickets to a show; Panos encourages lingering and doesn't take reservations. *Dinner Mon–Sat; MC, V; local checks only; beer and wine.*

PASEO CARIBBEAN RESTAURANT

4225 Fremont Ave N, Seattle
☎ *(206) 545-7440*
Fremont   ✕ **Caribbean**

Here's voluntary simplicity for you: a Caribbean eatery that has nine choices on the menu (none over $7.50), a space that seats seven, and a Cuban owner named Lorenzo Lorenzo (formerly of Islabelle). You still might have trouble deciding, though. Should it be the scallops with fresh cilantro sautéed in olive oil and garlic; the grilled, marinated pork; the oven-roasted chicken; or the garlic-sautéed prawns in red sauce? Vegetarians have it easiest: There's just one choice, Tofu con Gusto, with the white stuff dressed in the same red sauce that gives the prawns and scallops their kick. If the sauce—the recipe's a house secret—is not hot enough for you already, you can ask for a side of habañero salsa. The heaping plates are made even more gorgeous with a bright house salad, a pile of rice, a cup of black bean stew, and half an ear of corn. It's worth a drive-by at lunchtime for one of their sandwiches, especially the marinated pork. Served with sautéed onions, it just might be—as the menu says—the best in town. No Cuba Libres here; just soft drinks and juices. *Lunch, dinner Mon–Sat, dinner only Sun; no credit cards; checks OK; no alcohol.* ♿

PASTA & CO.

2109 Queen Anne Ave N, Seattle (and branches)
☎ (206) 283-1182
Queen Anne/Bellevue/Capitol Hill/
Downtown/University District   ✗ *Soup/Salad/Sandwich*

Pasta to go is an elegant, simple concept—especially when it's inter-
preted by Pasta & Co. founder Marcella Rosene. Everything in this
small chain of airy, light-filled storefronts is ready to be packed and
trundled home (or to the beach, or to the game), from the legendary
sesame-scented Chinese vermicelli to a hearty
meat-filled lasagna. The choices and assortment of fresh pastas and deli foodstuffs vary at
each location but you'll always find a flavorful
little something to suit you. This is the perfect
place to stop for a gourmet picnic—all you need
supply is the blanket, a special outdoor place,
and a friend to share it all with. Sauces, olive
oils, and other accompaniments (such as gorgeous lemon dessert
tartlets) can be purchased here as well. Only the downtown Seattle
store offers adequate seating, but most of the other branches have a
handful of chairs or stools for those who can't wait to get home to
indulge. *Lunch, dinner every day; AE, DC, MC, V; checks OK; no alcohol
(bottled wine is sold at downtown and Queen Anne locations).* &

PASTA YA GOTCHA

123 Lake St S, Kirkland (and branches)
☎ (425) 889-1511
Kirkland/Bellevue/Downtown/Issaquah   ✗ *Italian*

Despite a name that clunks like a dropped stockpot, this homegrown
chain has continued to expand. It may have received the imprimatur of
success when it was selected to locate an outlet on the hallowed
ground of the Microsoft campus in Redmond, thus opening rare windows of opportunity. The original in downtown Bellevue sits below a
Red Robin; the Issaquah entry, in one of the town's many strip malls.
There's one in downtown Seattle too, but our favorite continues to be
the Kirkland location, with a wall of windows that open onto the heart
of the Lake Street scene. The very idea of quickie, precooked pasta may
offend purists, but who are we to get snooty? Besides, we like a plate
of radiatore doused with bourbon-based barbecue sauce every now
and then—not to mention pasta inspired by Thai peanut sauce or

teriyaki stir-fry. In a more conservative mood, we pick the four-cheese fettucine alfredo, which suits our fancy, if not our cholesterol count. *Lunch, dinner every day; AE, MC, V; checks OK; no alcohol.* &

PAZZO'S

2307 Eastlake Ave E, Seattle
☎ *(206) 329-6558*
Eastlake **Pizza**

The ultimate neighborhood hangout, Pazzo's is Eastlake's living room with good food, beer, and a full bar to enhance the hang factor. There's a thriving dinner crowd, but it's still a good place to nurse a brew (eight Northwest microbrews are on tap), chat with friends, or watch a game (four TVs hang in the corners). There's a full menu of pizzas, calzones, and Italian sandwiches with toppings (and fillings) both with and without meat. If you don't like the designated combinations (some are a tad bizarre), make up your own. A big, undivided space with brick walls, exposed beams, and huge windows streetside, Pazzo's at Saturday-night full tilt is as warm a room as you'll find in the city. *Lunch, dinner every day; AE, DC, DIS, MC, V; checks OK; full bar.* &

PECOS PIT BARBECUE

2260 First Ave S, Seattle
☎ *(206) 623-0629*
SoDo **Barbecue**

Just south of the new baseball stadium, you'll find one of Seattle's oldest, most successful barbecue joints. For almost 20 years, Pecos Pit has built a reputation and a following with its tasty Texas-style barbecue. Catering exclusively to the lunch-hour crowd (they're only open from 11am to 3pm on weekdays), Pecos packs 'em in from all over south of town, including a few office workers who've sneaked away from their downtown highrises for this messy delicacy. The menu is simple, with one of the highest pork-to-menu-item ratios in the city: big, sloppy barbecue sandwiches, made with your choice of sliced beef brisket, pork, Pecos beef, or ham, and served with beans and soda. The only other item on the menu is the hot links, but don't make the mistake of ordering these solo. Pecos pros know to get the links *in* their sandwich—ask them to "spike it" and you'll get a link tucked into your already meat-filled treasure. Choose from mild, medium, or hot sauce, but be warned: Hot means "Whoo, hot!" *Lunch Mon–Fri; no credit cards; no checks; no alcohol.*

PEGASUS PIZZA

2758 Alki Ave SW, Seattle (and branch)
☎ *(206) 932-4849*
West Seattle/Kirkland   ✕ *Pizza*

Here's a sure-bet scenario: Put a Greek-style pizzeria right next to Alki Beach, make it family-friendly, fast, and cheap, and make sure there's outdoor seating. It ain't rocket science, but it works like a charm. On warm summer nights, especially on weekends, it's pretty near impossible to get a table here without a wait: The families of West Seattle, it seems, are addicted to these pizzas. Savory marinara touches up the perfect, crisp crust with just the right amount of flavor and moisture. This decorous restraint is evident in the way the cheese is apportioned as well. In a town where the pies usually arrive drowning in sauce, Pegasus is a rare bird indeed. If you're a sauce addict, order one of the pastas, which come the way most folks seem to want 'em: with way too much red stuff. The huge Greek salad (big enough for four) will make driving across the West Seattle Freeway and braving the long summer lines seem a tiny price to pay for such pleasure. If you still aren't convinced, sit outside, order a pitcher of beer, and sip slowly while you watch the sun sink into the water. There's a Pegasus in Kirkland, too (12669 NE 85th, (425) 822-7400), that is a bit more spacious—try the soup and half-pizza offered at lunchtime. *Lunch, dinner every day; AE, DIS, MC, V; checks OK; beer and wine (full bar in Kirkland).* ♿

PHILADELPHIA FEVRE STEAK & HOAGIE SHOP

2332 E Madison St, Seattle
☎ *(206) 323-1000*
Central District   ✕ *American*

Ask any expat Philadelphian and they'll tell you: It's not Pat's Steaks, but, as they say in the City of Brotherly Love, "What's it to yez?" The cheesesteaks and hoagies at this luncheonette are the closest thing to the real McCoy around here. And if you sit at the counter listening to wisecracking grillmeister Renee LeFevre's David Brenneresque accent while reading *Philadelphia* magazine, you'll get more Philly flavor than you bargained for. Renee will grill up a pile of thinly sliced rib-eye steak with onions, add some white American cheese and hot cherry peppers if you like, and serve it on an Italian roll. Eat it as you should, with a basket of french fries and a TastyKake, and you'll learn the real reason Rocky Balboa had to run up and down the steps at the Philadelphia Art Museum. *Lunch, early dinner Mon–Fri; AE, MC, V; no checks; beer only.* &

PHO BAC

1314 S Jackson St, Seattle
☎ (206) 323-4387
International District   ✕ *Vietnamese*

This spot, little more than an oversize shack and smack in the middle of a busy intersection, is funky and crowded and serves nothing but pho—the everyday dish of Vietnam. You won't need a menu, and you won't wait long for a bowl of the fragrant, herb-infused beef stock, which is topped with paper-thin slices of raw beef that cook through as you slurp up the rice noodles nesting in the bottom. For an extra 50 cents, splurge on the large bowl and garnish it from a plate of fresh basil, bean sprouts, jalapeño, and lime that arrives alongside the steaming bowls. Customize your soup to suit your fancy with fish sauce, chile sauce, and hoisin sauce, all kept in squeeze bottles on the table. *Lunch, dinner every day; no credit cards; no checks; no alcohol.*

PIECORA'S PIZZA

1401 E Madison St, Seattle (and branch)
☎ (206) 322-9411
Capitol Hill/Kirkland   ✕ *Pizza*

Pie-tossing is an art form at Piecora's, where passersby can stand out-side the window and watch one of the gifted take well-kneaded dough and toss it upward as though his or her life depended on it. The dough spreads out, spins, and falls back into waiting fists like a wet towel and the pie-tosser keeps it spinning and sends it ceilingward again before placing it on a circular tin, smothering it with myriad toppings, adding cheese, and sliding it into an oven. After a brief while, it's ready—a pie for the taking. But not just any pie: Piecora's. This pizzeria features roomy booths and tables—two levels, in fact—where loyal fans of this New York–style delicacy can gorge. The pizzas themselves are worth it; for a large, which feeds at least three hungry grown-ups, you'll pay no more than $17. Slices can be had for a dollar or two, and, unlike many other places, Piecora's actually takes orders for half pizzas (God bless 'em). Oh yeah, there's also pasta and calzone on the menu—but it may take hundreds of visits before you tire of the pie. There's another Piecora's in Kirkland, too (6501 132nd Ave NE, (425) 861-7000). *Lunch, dinner every day; MC, V; local checks only; full bar.* &

PIG 'N WHISTLE BAR AND GRILL

8412 Greenwood Ave N, Seattle
☎ *(206) 782-6044*
Greenwood   ✕ *Barbecue*

Though its name derives from a string of pubs in England, this place is as American as down-home, sticky-fingers barbecue. Pig 'n Whistle puts a clean and classy spin on the hallowed barbecue "joint," with warm walls, a grand piano, and original paintings done in rich colors and thick textures by Mexican-born artist Luis Merino. The assortment of slow-cooked barbecue specialties, basted with P 'n W's trade-marked barbecue sauce, features applewood-smoked pork spare ribs and baby back ribs (both as tender as you please). Other items from the 'cue include a basted half chicken, a sloppy, barbecue-sauced burger called the Longbranch, and, for those looking to put the "pig" in Pig 'n Whistle, a combination plate of chicken and spare ribs. If your preference is something a little less messy or red-meaty, you won't go wrong with the po'boy sandwich, a halibut fillet marinated in Louisiana spices, quick-fried, and served with a tasty homemade tartar sauce. Vegetarians can take refuge in a veggie burger or an open-faced sandwich of roasted eggplant, bell peppers, red onions, and mush-rooms on grilled focaccia topped with melted feta and provolone. The Appaloosa chili is a house specialty: a slow-simmered concoction of white beans, onion, celery, leeks, house spices, pork, and Italian-syle chicken sausage in a rich broth; and the dinner menu features several pastas and more offerings from the grill. There's a late-night menu and live music and dancing after 11pm on weekends. *Breakfast Sat–Sun, lunch, dinner every day; AE, DIS, MC, V; local checks only; beer and wine.*

PIROSHKY PIROSHKY

1908 Pike Pl, Seattle (and branch)
☎ *(206) 441-6068*
Pike Place Market/Bellevue   ✕ *Russian*

To Market, to Market, to buy a hot roll. But these aren't rolls, they're piroshkis: Russian turnovers made of warm ground meat and cheese (or cabbage, or potatoes, or mushrooms) and swaddled in flaky pastry. Linger outside the tiny storefront to watch capable hands kneading dough into strips, folding in apples, and sprinkling cinnamon. Begin lunch with a beef-and-cabbage piroshki or a smoked salmon paté, and order an apple roll for dessert. Then park yourself in Victor Steinbrueck Park, look out at the Olympics, and imagine yourself a guest at the czarina's summer home. Eastsiders can revel in the delightful yeasty aroma of piroshkis at the Bellevue location in Crossroads Mall (15600 NE Eighth St, (425) 401-9870). *Breakfast, lunch, dinner every day; no credit cards; local checks only; no alcohol.* &

PIZZUTO'S ITALIAN CAFE

5032 Wilson Ave S, Seattle
☎ *(206) 722-6395*
Seward Park ✗ *Italian*

Pizzuto's is a classic neighborhood Italian restaurant: red-and-white-checked tablecloths, red linen napkins, and Pavarotti in the background—but with acoustics that make it possible to converse without raising your voice. Food is piping hot, service friendly and fast. Pastas, made fresh and topped with rich sauces, are excellent (this is not a place for the cholesterol- or weight-conscious). A plate of meat-filled tortellini alla Romano with marinated artichoke hearts and wild mushrooms is enough for two meals, and you can expect the highly seasoned veal piccata to disappear from your plate at astonishing speed. Best is the superb pizza: A crisp but still chewy crust covered with the freshest ingredients—including tomatoes seemingly just out of the garden—is light enough to make this a fine appetizer for two. *Dinner Tues–Sat; MC, V; local checks only; beer and wine.* &

PLENTY FINE FOODS

1404 34th Ave, Seattle
☎ *(206) 324-1214*
Madrona ✗ *Bistro*

This delightful spot seems to have organically evolved to fit its locale so seamlessly that it's hard to imagine anything else being there. Owner Jim Watkins originally intended Plenty to be a neighborhood grocery store, but people kept standing around to eat his food. So he plunked down a few chairs and kept adding more until suddenly— voilà!—a restaurant was born. Folks here flock to this whimsically decorated storefront because they want what it offers: fresh, elegant food that happens to be good for you. Beautifully arranged groceries line the shelves of the center room, and refrigerator cases dominate the main dining area, as if to stress that Plenty is a space devoted to fine eating. The eclectic menu, which favors vegetarians, changes weekly but usually features Watkins's signature red beans and rice as well as a meat, pasta, and seafood entree. You might also find something like a barbecued duck breast or a wild mushroom casserole. The crowning glory of the resplendent dessert case is the chocolate cake—huge, moist, and frosted just right. *Lunch every day, dinner Mon–Sat; AE, MC, V; local checks only; beer and wine.* ♿

PON PROEM

3039 78th Ave SE, Mercer Island
☎ *(206) 236-8424*
Mercer Island   ✕ *Thai*

At last count, the Big Rock boasted three Thai restaurants; happily, the competition has only sharpened the slight edge Pon Proem enjoys over the other two. Service is as crisp as the stir-fried pea pods. The square dining room feels a little old, thanks in part to the dull white paint on its flat walls, but there are appealing homey touches, such as the seat covers hand-sewn by the owner and changed seasonally. We like the little things here, such as the sweet-mustard salad dressing, the cup of homemade chicken soup at lunch, and the rice and bread puddings. Phad Thai carries a load of tofu and is free of any strong aroma of fish sauce. Stir-fries such as *gai phad met ma muang* possess better balance than a gymnastics team thanks to the three kinds of soy sauce, along with chile paste, that accompany the veggies and chicken. The *sam sahai* appetizer plate, deep-fried tempura style, presents an assortment of chicken wings, calamari, and shrimp. At the start of the lunch hour, the staff light incense for the Buddha; they then proceed to honor him with their work until closing. *Lunch Mon–Fri, dinner every day; AE, DIS, MC, V; Mercer Island checks only; beer and wine.* ♿

POST ALLEY PIZZA

1123 Post Alley, Seattle
☎ *(206) 382-8475*
Downtown   ✕ *Pizza*

Just a few paces south of the Harbor Steps is a little pizzeria hidden in the shadows of the viaduct off-ramp. Despite this somewhat obscure location, Post Alley Pizza has been a popular place to grab a quick bite since it opened, and the word has spread—during a weekday lunch break, don't plan on getting one of the 10 or so seats in this tiny corner establishment. (Of course, you can always grab a few slices and take them out to the Steps or the waterfront.) Even when the place is packed, though, the service is quick and friendly. Solid choices are the spicy extra pepperoni or the flavorful four-cheese/pesto. All the pies feature a zingy homemade sauce whose recipe is a five-generation family secret brought over from Naples (ask about taking home some sauce). In addition to pizzas, Post Alley also makes hearty hero sandwiches, including a delicious meatball parmigiana. *Lunch, dinner Mon—Fri; no credit cards; checks OK; no alcohol.* &

PROVINCES ASIAN RESTAURANT & BAR
201 Fifth Ave S, Edmonds
☎ *(425) 744-0288*
Edmonds   ✕ *Pan-Asian*

Today the idea of a pan-Asian restaurant is accepted even in the quiet hamlet of Edmonds—where a serene and decidedly older crowd enjoys a range of Asian cuisine in an attractive, oversize dining room set in Old Mill Town Mall. Favorite menu items include the Vietnamese salad rolls and the Bangkok hot and sour soup—served in a clay pot brimming with shellfish and straw mushrooms, fragrant with lemongrass, and large enough to feed four. The Cantonese-style seafood lobster sauce is dense with shellfish and vegetables and flavored with Chinese black beans. Mongolian ginger beef is a touch sweet but pleasantly potent with ginger and garlic. An abbreviated lunch menu—including humongous bowls of udon with various meats, vegetables, and seafood—is a bargain and a half considering the quality of the ingredients. Service is swift and efficient. In the adjoining cocktail lounge, folks meet to bend an elbow, smoke a cigarette, and make merry. The owners of Provinces opened Shallots in 1997, a downtown Seattle eatery with a slightly different menu (see separate review). *Lunch Mon—Sat, dinner every day; AE, DC, DIS, MC, V; local checks only; full bar.* & *(dining room only)*

PYRAMID ALEHOUSE
1201 First Ave S, Seattle
☎ *(206) 682-3377*
SoDo   ✕ *Pub Grub*

Even finicky diners will appreciate this nosh-and-sloshery (formerly known as Hart Brewery and Pub, and still operated by the same people). Walk into the huge two-deck warehouse dining space and catch the acrid-sweet scent of fermenting barley and wheat from the brewery next door. Straightforward bar fare complements (and often is cooked with) the robust Pyramid ales and Thomas Kemper lagers. There's a smattering of trendy stuff (hummus in pita, bland focaccia) and some successful attempts at Americanizing gluey British pub fare. Stick to such basics as baby beef ribs in a slurpy beer-barbecue sauce, beer-battered halibut and chips, chunky burgers, and sausages with garlic mashed potatoes. Before and after Kingdome games, the line outside is a block long and service can be glacial. Big-screen televisions abound, kids are allowed inside, and tours are available. *Lunch, dinner every day; AE, MC, V; checks OK; beer and wine.* &

QUEEN MARY

2912 NE 55th St, Seattle
☎ *(206) 527-2770*
Ravenna   ✗ *Teahouse*

Hail to the Queen! With its red walls, flowery chintz, and bric-a-brac, Queen Mary is just the sort of proper place to take your mother, great-aunt, or passionate Anglophile friend. Though breakfast and lunch are served (menu items include egg dishes, quiches, sandwiches, and English offerings such as bangers and steak-and-kidney pie), the tea's the thing here. All the usual dainty suspects are available in the Formal Afternoon Tea (served every day from 2pm to 5pm): crustless sandwiches of cucumber, tomato, and chicken pâté; crumpets and currant scones served with jam, butter, and whipped cream; lemon curd tartlets; tiny cookies; and slices of a typical English chocolate cake. Embellishments include large, individual pots of your tea of choice; a wide variety of sliced fresh fruits; and, as an opener, three tiny balls of sorbet—maybe pear, raspberry, or tropical punch—with a sliver of buttery shortbread. Naturally, it's all served on flowered china with linen napkins and tablecloths. So civilized! *Breakfast, lunch, tea every day; MC, V; checks OK; wine only.* &

RACHA NOODLES

537 First Ave N, Seattle
☎ *(206) 281-8883*
Queen Anne   ✗ *Thai*

Racha, opened in 1998, is a lovely addition to the Seattle Center area: tea-green walls, murals, fresh flowers, paper lanterns, and an open kitchen that offers views into a world of exotic ingredients. Noodles, as one might expect, are Racha's raison d'être, but it also serves a full Thai menu as well as a selection of exotic teas worthy of a fully dedicated teahouse. The noodle dishes, generously served and priced at around $7, are probably the best bargain on the menu. There are four types: *sen lek*, a thin egg noodle that stars in phad Thai and beef noodle soup; *sen mee*, a thin rice noodle served in lighter dishes of grilled meats and chile vinaigrettes; *ba mee*, a thin egg noodle; and *sen yai*, a wide rice noodle that figures

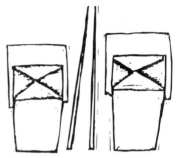

in dishes that are the Thai equivalent of comfort food. Try the excellent ba mee duck, layers of steamed duck, noodles, and black mushrooms; or the *pud kee mao*, sen yai noodles mixed with Chinese broccoli, Thai basil, peppers, onions, and tomatoes. Other hits are *moo yang*, a tangy appetizer of grilled pork served with cucumber and a lime juice–chile sauce; and a kicky papaya salad. Dishes are occasionally underspiced and oversauced (such as the Racha Special Noodles, awash in a bland peanut sauce), but most are on target. If you can't find something to eat on the extensive menu, you can always linger over a bottomless pot of fresh-brewed jasmine or chai tea that will set you back only $2. *Lunch, dinner every day; AE, MC, V; checks OK; beer and wine.* &

RAIN DANCER: A RESTAURANT & BAR

4217 University Way, Seattle
☎ *(206) 634-2433*
University District   ✕ *Soup/Salad/Sandwich*

In 1998, Rain Dancer closed its doors on Brooklyn, pulled up stakes, and set them down again just around the corner on the more heavily trafficked University Way. Squeezed in between a tattoo parlor and an old barbershop, Rain Dancer nevertheless injects a splash of class onto the predominately mangy Ave. The menu and mood at Rain Dancer's new locale remain much the same as before: This is a place for those looking to *not* scarf their sandwiches standing up at a lunch counter or scrunched around Formica tables between packs of multipierced teens. The Signature sandwiches are around $7 and include such tasty and slightly upscale favorites as blackened salmon with Cajun spices, jerk chicken dressed up with a spunky mango and cilantro salsa, and a sautéed vegetable sandwich on bruschetta. Lunch also features such mainstays as ham and cheese and turkey with cranberry sauce. Dinner entrees are tempting, but pricey. The biggest differences at the new spot are the full bar and larger dining area (it's three times bigger). Other nice touches include the massive, exposed wood beams overhead, the walls washed the color of Spanish olives, and full views of the open kitchen. *Lunch, dinner Mon–Sat; AE, DIS, MC, V; checks OK; full bar.* &

RED MILL BURGERS
312 N 67th St, Seattle (and branch)
☎ *(206) 783-6362*
Phinney Ridge/Magnolia   ✕ **Burgers**

In 1994, siblings Babe and John Shepherd opened Red Mill in a little corner shop in the Phinney Ridge neighborhood, immediately attracting crowds of worshipers who came for one of their 18 varieties of the all-American favorite. Within months, they expanded into an adjoining space to accommodate the hordes. Now they own the building. This is not a fast-food joint, but the wait is worth it, as you'll see when you sink your teeth into a burger topped with thick slices of pepper bacon, anointed with smoky homemade mayo, and sandwiched between a big, warm bun with the freshest of lettuce and tomatoes. Those who don't do red meat will find a terrific array of veggie and chicken burgers. Don't miss the killer onion rings, and knock 'em back with a milk shake. Magnolians can now enjoy Red Mill's cheap eats too—a second burger joint opened in Interbay in 1998 (1613 W Dravus St, (206) 284-6363). *Lunch, dinner Tues–Sun; no credit cards; local checks only; no alcohol.* &

RIALTO PASTA BAR & GRILL
1400 N 80th St, Seattle
☎ *(206) 522-6635*
Green Lake   ✕ *Italian*

Rialto, offering fresh, unpretentious pasta dinners, is a calm spot in the storm of the often-frenzied north Green Lake scene. The space is simple and airy and the scent of garlic wafts out from the small open kitchen. Tables are scattered about; several line the front windows—perfect for dining alone or watching the world go by. Four or more basic pasta dinners are featured, such as primavera, but the real deal here is the Pasta Plate Special—which asks you to choose your pasta variety and match it to one of four homemade sauces. Rudy's Red is a

classic, tomato-based sauce, and, while it's a
bit too mild to comfortably wear the tag of
"mama's own," the light meaty flavor tastes
good clinging to thick penne and two big
homemade meatballs. There are also usually three or four interesting blackboard spe-

cials, which might be something like the BLT Pasta, a mix
of bacon, escarole, and fresh tomatoes over spaghetti. All dinners
include a fresh garden salad, warm garlic bread, and big portions for
around $8.95 and under. And where else in Seattle can you get a
drinkable red wine for only three bucks? Finish with cheesecake—either
the lemon mousse (a creamy wedge of lip-tightening tartness) or the
chocolate pecan. At press time, plans for lunch service were uncer-
tain—call ahead. Service is pleasantly low-key. *Dinner every day; DIS,
MC, V; checks OK; beer and wine.* &

RICO'S SALVADORAN COCINA
7821 Aurora Ave N, Seattle
☎ *(206) 297-2449*
Green Lake   ✕ **Central American**

Rico's, a modest restaurant that sits an illegal U-turn across from
Chubby & Tubby on Aurora, has a small but potent claim to fame: It's
the Seattle home of the Salvadoran delicacy known as *pupusa*, a handmade corn tortilla stuffed with beans, cheese, or pork, fried just until
crisp, and served with a side of pickled cabbage. *Pupusas* are humble
and filling, cost $1.50 each, and will make you very, very happy. While
you're there admiring the soccer paraphernalia and Christmas lights,
try another Central American specialty, such as a platter of fried plan-
tains, beans, and cream; a heaping dish of fried cassava (called yucca
in Spanish) and pork; or a sweet corn tamale, wrapped in a banana
leaf and steamed. That will do for dessert, especially when washed
down with a large iced glass of *horchata*, a sweet rice drink that barely
hints of cinnamon. Rico's menu also features a couple of serious main
dishes such as marinated flank steak, plus a number of Mexican
dishes. Just don't ask about Rico, the Salvadoran who started the
restaurant. Current waitstaff have never heard of him. *Lunch, dinner
Thurs–Tues; DIS, MC, V; local checks only; no alcohol.* &

ROANOKE INN

1825 72nd Ave SE, Mercer Island
☎ *(206) 232-0800*
Mercer Island   ✕ **Pub Grub**

"This is the perfect place to hide and have a few beers," muses the guy at a table near us in the Roanoke Inn, Mercer Island's oldest business establishment. Our thoughts precisely, subtracting half the beers and adding a French dip sandwich or a plate of nachos. How could anyone find us here when hardly anyone in the world knows that here is even here? The Roanoke is tucked into a residential area, right up the street from the dock for the ferry that Seattleites used to take back when the deer hunting here wasn't half bad, Prohibition-era hooch was the beverage of choice, and gambling competed for consumer dollars right alongside ladies of the night. The fine old tavern is still a classic hideaway—a great place to munch a burger out on the deck, with its peekaboo view through the rhodies of Lake Washington, downtown Bellevue, and even the Cascades on a clear day. Inside it's dark and a bit smoky, with poster-size paintings dating back past your great-grandfather's time. And it's always as friendly as the dickens. Recent kitchen renovation has bolstered the lunch and dinner trade. *Lunch, dinner every day; AE, MC, V; Mercer Island checks only; beer and wine.* ♿

ROASTED PEPPER CAFE & DELI

3701 NE 45th, Seattle
☎ *(206) 525-6500*
Laurelhurst   ✕ **Inventive Ethnic**

Bright and spacious, this Mediterranean-influenced restaurant located near University Village has become popular with its mix of Northwest-cum-American-cum-Mediterranean dishes. Housed in a large space that could easily have the feel of a cafeteria but doesn't—thanks to tastefully designed booths and a unique nutmeg-color ceiling—Roasted Pepper serves a very capable menu of personal-size pizzas prepared in an applewood-fired brick oven  and entrees such as a traditionally seasoned lamb tagine, a competently baked salmon, and generously portioned salads with fresh and diverse ingredients. The pizzas offer the standard combinations plus some original inventions (roasted chicken, roasted peppers, garlic, and orange) that, in most cases, work just fine, and the children's menu offers real food at bargain prices for wee ones, from basic pizza to grilled chicken breast. Despite the wood floors and the open kitchen, you can easily converse with dinner mates without fighting a wall of noise. The breakfast menu includes standard eggs and waffles, plus frittatas. The food here won't stun you with excitement, but it won't leave you disappointed either, and families are always made to feel welcome. *Breakfast, lunch, dinner every day; AE, MC, V; checks OK; beer and wine.* ♿

ROMIO'S PIZZA & PASTA

3242 Eastlake Ave E, Seattle (and branches)
☎ *(206) 322-4453*
Eastlake/Downtown/Greenwood/Lake City/Magnolia ✗ **Pizza**

With five Seattle locations, Romio's now qualifies as a bona fide homegrown chain. Some visitors find the original Magnolia location (on Dravus) to be the liveliest, but Romio's Eastlake "headquarters" is spacious, well appointed, and family-friendly. Romio's pizza is built on a soft, slightly biscuit-flavored crust, with a moderate application of sweet marinara, a stunning abundance of toppings, and a thick layer of cheese on top. The pizza is always good, and the menu features several interesting Greek-influenced topping combinations such as the zesty Zorba, with its traditional lamb, tomatoes, onions, feta, mozzarella, Greek olives, and tzatziki sauce. One of our favorites (and perhaps the most popular) is the pungent and filling G.A.S.P. pie, with its toppings of garlic, artichoke hearts, sun-dried tomatoes, and pesto layered between slabs of thick mozzarella. Those not in the mood for pizza can try pasta dishes, salads, or Romio's unusually large and delicious specialty sandwiches. The company also has a thriving home-delivery business. *Lunch, dinner every day; AE, DC, DIS, MC, V; checks OK; beer and wine.* ♿

ROSITA'S MEXICAN GRILL

7210 Woodlawn Ave NE, Seattle
☎ *(206) 523-3031*
Green Lake/Greenwood ✗ **Mexican**

You won't be fooled by the decor at this popular Mexican restaurant, not with its walls of cool Southwest pastels and murals of saguaros and beaver-tail cacti. This place fairly shouts in your ear: "Hola, I am a Mexican restaurant!" Still, sometimes the familiar is just what you want, and Rosita's serves up large plates of reliable, recognizable Mexican standards to the constant satisfaction of neighborhood residents

and visitors. It's a good thing the food
arrives at your table in a blink of an
eye, or you might already be filled
to capacity on the complimentary
homemade corn tortillas that are
grilled before your eyes in the cantina and rolled up with a touch of
butter and a spoonful of salsa. Two of

the local favorites are the arroz con pollo, a saucy chicken specialty
served over Spanish rice, and the Expresso Burrito, a bulging
conflation of meat (beef, chicken, or pork), Spanish rice, and refried
beans topped with a red sauce, Jack cheese, sour cream, guacamole,
onions, and tomatoes. One of Seattle's great happy-hour deals takes
place in the cantina between 4 and 6pm daily—when the house margaritas are cheaper and Rosita's excellent appetizers are half-price.
There's a second Rosita's in Greenwood (9747 Fourth Ave NW, (206)
784-4132). *Lunch Mon–Sat, dinner every day; AE, DIS, MC, V; checks
OK; full bar.* &

RUBY

4241 University Way NE, Seattle
☎ *(206) 675-1770*
University District   ✕ *Inventive Ethnic*

Though just two doors down the Ave from its sister establishment
(Flowers), Ruby feels a world apart in atmosphere. If the floor-to-
ceiling windows didn't give away your location, you might imagine
you'd just stumbled off the Sahara into an old cantina in Casablanca.
Moving across the scuffed, rusty-red floor past walls with a sand-dune
complexion, you step under a giant half-circle arch to reach the raised
main dining room, whose hodgepodge of tables and chairs has been
cobbled together, it would seem, from innumerable flea markets. Oriental tapestries and gold-trimmed mirrors hang on the walls, while
ceiling fans spin silently above your head: an entirely pleasant sensation. What makes it even more enjoyable is that nothing on the menu
is over $9. The soup, rice, and grain bowls are an excellent value
($6–$9) and feature inspired couplings of flavorful pan-Asian ingredients. Try a rice bowl of chicken marinated in gingered sour cream
served over jasmine rice with a red curry. Thrifty college kids come for
a large rice bowl at lunch and leave with enough grub for dinner. There
are a half-dozen well-conceived sandwiches to choose from, including
a tasty grilled salmon fillet with fresh spinach on toasted sourdough
bread with dill tartar sauce. The sandwiches come with a spinach

salad lightly sprinkled with a forgettably bland dressing. *Lunch, dinner Mon–Sat; MC, V; checks OK; beer and wine.*

SAIGON BISTRO

1032 S Jackson St, Seattle
☎ *(206) 329-4939*
International District   🍴 *Vietnamese*

The light, airy Saigon Bistro is a cut above the many other cafes found along Jackson Street's Little Saigon. The open kitchen lends the room life. The menu's many options reflect the South Vietnamese style of cookery, and everything here is prepared with care. A signature dish is *bun mang vit*, the glorification of soup and salad: a light soup of noodles in duck stock on one side, and a duck and cabbage salad with sweet, pungent ginger sauce on the other. Many dishes can be ordered in cold- and hot-weather versions: with dry noodles, fragrant broth, or roll-your-own rice pancakes served with an array of fresh herbs. *Lunch, dinner every day; MC, V; checks OK; beer and wine.* ♿

SAIGON CITY

15045 Bellevue-Redmond Rd, Bellevue
☎ *(425) 401-0823*
Bellevue   🍴 *Vietnamese*

Saigon City is a cheerful place to visit. What for? What pho! Its specialty, the Vietnamese noodle soup, pho, is excellent: generously portioned, dark, fragrant, and steaming, carrying a surprising note of sweetness. Though the Eastside is becoming home to ever more Vietnamese joints, this is currently the best spot to order some pho and start tossing in bunches of crisp sprouts, sprigs of fresh basil, a wedge of lime, and rounds of jalapeño. Down in the shadows lurk thin strips of beef, meatballs, or beef tendon on a bed of long, thin rice noodles. The two best non-pho dishes are *ga xao gung* (chicken stir-fried with threads of ginger in a thickened chicken-stock sauce) and *ga xao sa ot* (chicken with lemongrass). Everything is super cheap, and the family who owns and runs the place seems to enjoy themselves immensely. *Lunch, dinner every day; MC, V; checks OK; no alcohol.* ♿

SALMON BAY CAFE

5109 Shilshole Ave NW, Seattle
☎ *(206) 782-5539*
Ballard ✕ *Breakfast*

Salmon Bay is a real-life reminder that Ballard was once a fishing village. Local denizens in commercial fishing gear fill the place most weekdays (but the kind, no-nonsense waitresses aren't above serving their diner-style fare to the Patagonia crowd or to multipierced types). You can get lunch, but breakfast is what you should aim for here. In the tradition of great coffee shops, the larger-than-life breakfasts come with bottomless cups of coffee. The omelets, named after local neighborhoods, could satisfy a starving angler. Expect to wait in line for weekend breakfasts. *Breakfast, lunch every day; MC, V; checks OK; beer and mimosas.* &

SANTORINI GREEK GRILL

106 Central Way, Kirkland
☎ *(425) 822-0555*
Kirkland ✕ *Greek*

A fiver gets you a world-class gyro and change at this storefront gem. The pillowy pita will not stretch all the way around the many chunks of meat and feta, tzatziki and veggies. A wax-paper wrap can hold it together enough for one-handed eaters, and even the occasional inadvertent bite of paper can't spoil this Greek treat. Better still is the souvlaki sandwich, with freshly seasoned meat chunks. Many choose to order to go, but why rush off when you can command one of a handful of tables in the heart of Kirkland and gawk at the street scene, or simply admire a wallful of colorful Greek pictures? Or stare at a display case of spanakopita, hummus, skordalia, baklava, and other Greek specialties that tempt you to take home a batch of nibbles or even dinner? All of it is reasonably priced, and the ever-present owners, Elsa Arehart and Stavros Ioannou, aim to please. *Lunch, dinner Mon–Sat; no credit cards; local checks only; no alcohol.*

SEA THAI

2313 N 45th St, Seattle
☎ *(206) 547-1961*
Wallingford   ✕ *Thai*

Residents here have long known about Sea Thai, an easily overlooked sliver of a restaurant where the curries are eye-wateringly hot and the prices are reasonable even by Asian-restaurant standards. The food can be uneven; best bets are the saucier dishes, which show off Sea Thai's flair (and occasionally heavy hand) with the spices. These include the *gai pud pet* (sautéed chicken with red curry sauce, basil, bamboo shoots, and vegetables); the *tom kah gai* (a spicy soup of chicken, coconut milk, lemongrass, and lime); and the Jumping Squid (sautéed squid with chile sauce, onions, bell peppers, and basil). The most expensive thing on the menu is the *goong Siam* (sautéed prawns with garlic, pepper, coriander, and scallions) for $7.95; most dishes are $5.95. It's a welcoming spot, with burnt umber walls, Christmas lights hung all year round, and a huge aquarium in the back. The dinner music fluctuates between traditional Thai and the likes of Sarah McLachlan. A limited selection of beer and wine is available. *Lunch, dinner every day; AE, MC, V; checks OK; beer and wine.* ♿

SEATTLE BAGEL BAKERY

1302 Western Ave, Seattle (and branch)
☎ *(206) 624-2187*
Downtown   ✕ *Bagels*

Seattleites rarely match Manhattanites in their lust for the doughy rings, but this spot comes close to inspiring the same passion. (It does differ from a New York bagelry, though, in that it's clean, airy, non-smoking, and full of sunlight.) Sometimes warm, always fresh, these little wonders with raisins, cheese, garlic (gotta be a garlic lover, for the cooks are generous), or poppy seed can be eaten alone or split open and heaped with cream cheese and lox or—oy!—turkey and sprouts without smothering the taste of the bagel. At press time, the main branch at the Harbor Steps has plans to move into a nearby space—call for details. There's another downtown location located near the Greyhound bus station (804 Howell St, (206) 667-9327). *Breakfast, lunch every day; no credit cards; checks OK; no alcohol.* ♿

SEATTLE CATCH SEAFOOD BISTRO

460 N 36th Ave, Seattle
☎ *(206) 632-6110*
Fremont   ✕ *Seafood*

Seattle Catch lures you in with the promise of affordable seafood, and, on most counts, it delivers. Inspired by the legendary Daily Catch in Boston, Seattle Catch serves Sicilian-style pasta and seafood. Inside, there's an imposing mahogany bar, lots of tables and booths, and an open kitchen with a huge hood and overhanging rack of pans. Pastas, which come straight from the stove to the table in said pans, include the perfect-for-two *linguini fra diavlo* (linguine, mussels, clams, and calamari in a spicy marinara sauce). Grilled fish options are restrained, almost to the point of blandness, but you can't argue with the healthy portions. Most entrees come with a choice of salad and vegetable or linguine with sauce. Salads are squeaky clean and very satisfying. The house mix of baby greens, red onion, and shaved ricotta is gently dressed with a crisp balsamic vinaigrette. For a dollar extra you can substitute the caesar: hearts of romaine sliced into neat mouthfuls, light on the authentic caesar dressing (anchovies by request only). No creamy white goo here—this is the best caesar in town, and it's also available with rock shrimp and scallops for a dinner-size portion. *Brunch Sun, lunch Mon–Sat, dinner every day; MC, V; local checks only; full bar.* &

74TH STREET ALE HOUSE

7401 Greenwood Ave N, Seattle
☎ *(206) 784-2955*
Phinney Ridge   ✕ *Pub Grub*

The 74th Street Ale House is a rarity. The atmosphere is satisfyingly publike—a bit dark, with a long bar, two TVs going, wooden tables, even green linoleum—but its cuisine borders on the innovative. For instance, they don't serve nachos; instead, you can munch on pecans roasted with ancho chiles, or shallot bread, or salsa verde and chips. Oh, you can get a super burger here, but you can also dine on a teriyaki mahi-mahi sandwich, organic mixed greens salad, spicy-savory gumbo soup, or a towering pastrami sandwich. There are five specials every week, such as a roasted corn and red chile ravioli salad. At another bar, these touches might seem like bowing to trends, but not at the 74th (hey, they haven't even started serving espresso here). The hordes agree; this spot is always crowded, but in an amiable sort of way. The Hilltop Ale House on Queen Anne (2129 Queen Anne Ave N,

(206) 285-3877) is owned by the same folks and serves a similar menu. *Lunch, dinner every day; MC, V; checks OK; beer and wine.* &

SHALLOTS ASIAN BISTRO

2525 Fourth Ave, Seattle
☎ *(206) 728-1888*
Belltown   ✕ *Pan-Asian*

There are a lot of pan-Asian options in town, but none so likable as this intimate little bistro. Inside, the booths are done up in dark sleek wood, napkins are folded with elaborate flair, and walls are accented with spot lighting and tastefully arrayed Asian art; when the weather's warm enough, you can sit on the patio outside. Shallots serves mostly Chinese with an intriguing mix of Thai, Vietnamese, Cambodian, Japanese, and Korean dishes thrown in—all in generous, well-priced portions. The satays and satay rolls, for example, are meal-size appetizers that arrive with a tiny fragrant bowl of rice and a miniature salad. If you're not adventurous, you can order Szechuan garlic pork—but why not try the saté-pepper coconut prawns, the rock-candy gingered rabbit, or the French-Cambodian New York steak salad (our favorite). Shallots also serves wonderful dishes made in a Lu pot—a stovetop slow cooker. And make every effort to sample the duck—they know how to treat that bird well. *Lunch Mon–Fri, dinner Mon–Sat; AE, DIS, JCB, MC, V; no checks; beer and wine.* &

SHAMIANA

10724 NE 68th St, Kirkland
☎ *(425) 827-4902*
Kirkland   ✕ *Indian*

Dinner entrees here top out in the mid-teens, but we nonetheless consider Shamiana to be a great source of cheap eats. A fine meal can be made simply of bread and soup—that is, when the bread is heavenly naan, especially the garlic variety with its brush of garlic-coriander butter and dipping sauce of cumin-flavored raita, and the soup is an out-of-this-world mulligatawny—a warmly spiced, rich red brew with chicken and lentils. The lunch buffet special is a best buy at this local institution, winner of scads of Eastside "best of" polls. It gets its "India and Beyond" subheading from influences that range from Bangladesh to Kenya, all areas where the brother-sister team of Tracy Larson-DeVaan and Eric Larson grew up as foreign service brats. Vegetarians have choices aplenty, and the menu marks dishes made sans dairy products. Spicing of various curries and other entrees is bold; if you order hot, you'd better be prepared for hot. Desserts deserve mention too, especially a cool mango yogurt mousse topped with a golden crown of mango purée. *Lunch, dinner Mon–Fri; AE, DC, MC, V; checks OK; beer and wine.* &

SHANGHAI GARDEN

524 Sixth Ave S, Seattle (and branches)
☎ *(206) 625-1689*
International District/Bellevue/Issaquah ✕ *Chinese*

We are witnessing the creation of an empire based on the hand-shaven noodle—Shanghai's original specialty sliced fresh from a block of handmade dough. First in the International District and then in Issaquah (80 Front St N, (425) 313-3188), Chef Hua Te Su popularized his specialty. Brother Ping Fu Su followed suit, opening a smaller cafe (called, appropriately, Shanghai Cafe) with the same great noodles in the Factoria area of Bellevue (12708 SE 38th St, (425) 603-1689). In any of the three locations, the wonderfully chewy shards also assume a green guise called barleygreen and star in various dishes, including the dandiest house-special chow mein you've ever tried, along with calamari, prawns, eggs, and scallops. Also spreading is the popularity of pea vines, which sauté to a spinachlike consistency and have a fresh, buttery taste. Try them with shrimp or black mushrooms. Crispy fried shrimp prove sweetly addictive, too. While it is possible to blow out the cheap-eats budget—especially at the ID and Issaquah branches, with their more extensive menus that include ostrich, sautéed hog maw, and fish-head casserole—even a budget-minded customer can dine grandly and feel pretty darn Imperial. *Lunch, dinner every day; MC, V; no checks; beer and wine (full bar in Issaquah, beer only in Bellevue).* &

SHILLA RESTAURANT

2300 Eighth Ave, Seattle (and branch)
☎ *(206) 623-9996*
Queen Anne/Redmond ✕ *Korean*

Regina and Sam Koh opened this Korean restaurant near Seattle Center almost two decades ago, and every year it gets better and more popular—despite, to put it gently, the shabby gentility of the interior. Regulars have long delighted in the pleasures of Shilla's expertly seasoned *bulgogi*, thinly sliced beef that's grilled to order on a tabletop gas grill. Some helpful hints if you haven't eaten Korean food before: When all those little plates of spiced, marinated veggies arrive in front of you, *wait*. Don't dive in with your chopsticks until your rice and meat have arrived. First take a mouthful of rice and then some pepper-hot kimchi (pickled, fermented cabbage). Next, pop in a slice of beef. Chew contemplatively. Pick up some lettuce, put a dollop of rice and meat on it, slather a bit of pepper-bean paste on top, and voilà, it's your own handroll! If you can't stand the heat, try the soothing *duk man du guk*, an expertly rendered beef soup with dumplings and rice cake, or the ever-popular *bebim bop*, which, true to its name ("mixed-up rice"), is a bowl of rice combined with all sorts of goodies. Note: Various celebrity rockers have been sighted eating in the back room, where you *have* to take off your shoes and sit on the floor. It's an un-written rule that dessert after a Korean meal means eating ice cream or chain-smoking. Guess which one applies here? Both! There's now an Eastside Shilla, in Redmond Town Center (16330 Cleveland St, (425) 882-3272). *Lunch, dinner every day; AE, MC, V; no checks; full bar.* &

SHORTY'S CONEY ISLAND

2222 Second Ave, Seattle
☎ *(206) 441-5449*
Belltown   ✕ *Hot Dogs/Sausage*

In describing a common apocalyptic vision, prophets often speak of a dark, somewhat narrow, and very smoky chamber. If you add to that chamber a spooky circus big-top motif dominated by unsettling images of clowns and hundreds of clown-dolls dangling from the ceiling like so many corpses, plus a dozen pinball machines blinking and pinging, and prehistoric video games (Asteroids, Defender, Donkey Kong) contributing mightily to the electronic mayhem, you'll have an accurate—and perhaps equally frightening—description of Shorty's Coney Island. Here, sullen, unkempt hipsters  and assorted derelicts sit languidly on stools before a long crimson counter, stuffing their faces with chili-oozing Coney dogs and drinking Lucky Lager from the bottle. The grub is exactly what you'd expect to find at the circus, a ball game, or a showing of the summer's blockbuster film about the end of the world. There are several hot dog choices: standard Coney, New York–style, German sausage, and Italian link. The chili-cheese nachos come drenched in that familiar, funky, orange liquid cheese. There's also a small, dingy tavern in the back room that serves draught beer and offers less of a circus-tent atmosphere than the front. *Lunch Mon–Sat, dinner every day; AE, MC, V; no checks; beer only.*

SHULTZY'S SAUSAGE

4142 University Way NE, Seattle
☎ *(206) 548-9461*
University District   ✗ *Hot Dogs/Sausage*

Cheap restaurants come and go, but a select few survive long enough to develop a history. Shultzy's Sausage is one of these places, a fact that won't be lost on you as you step off the Ave into this cramped restaurant. The walls are literally covered with photos of Shultzy's fans over the years, prominently sporting their Shultzy's T-shirts as they travel around the world, from Trafalgar Square to the Panama Canal. (A few photos even show such luminaries as former Seattle mayor Norm Rice and American Gladiators Emeritus "Hawk" and "Lazer" weighing in as Shultzy's supporters.) Don't take all these endorsements lightly—try a sausage (or a burger), and you'll be convinced too. If you're feeling indecisive, the sweet garlic andouille and Ragin' Cajun are particularly good. If you're feeling guilty—or find sausage a nutritionally suspect food—have the excellent black bean burger or the Chicken Turkey Select sausage. If you do become a convert but aren't planning on traveling the world anytime soon, you can still find a place for yourself on the wall: Certificates list the names of Shultzy's hun-

griest customers, and how many sausages each of them put away in a single sitting. The current record is nine. *Lunch, dinner every day; no credit cards; no checks; no alcohol.*

SI SENOR

2115 Bellevue-Redmond Rd, Redmond
☎ *(425) 865-8938*
Redmond   ✗ *Mexican*

The cuisines of Peru and the northeastern Mexican city of Monterrey account for much of this menu's originality. And while you can order the usual south-of-the-border standbys, why miss out on exotica? *Lomo de almendra* is marinated pork loin in a deliciously dark and almond-flavored sauce. *Seco*, a Peruvian lamb dish, comes sauced with a blend of cilantro, onions, and tomatoes. *Camarones à la diablo* are devilishly hot and spicy prawns sautéed with mushrooms in a complex red sauce. A dinner-size appetizer, *anticuchos*, will astound those frustrated by skimpy little sticks of Thai satay; here you get a platter with baked potatoes flanking skewers laden with flat slabs of tender,

marinated, charred beef heart (don't balk: if you
didn't know it, you'd never guess). The staff is
lively and lighthearted, occasionally barreling
into the dining room with a platter and hol-
lering, "Cheeseburger!" Live mariachi or Andean music
accompanies dinner on weekends. *Lunch, dinner every day; AE, DIS,
MC, V; local checks only; full bar.* &

SIAM ON BROADWAY

616 Broadway E, Seattle (and branch)
☎ *(206) 324-0892*
Capitol Hill/Eastlake   ✕ *Thai*

Among Seattle's multitude of Thai restaurants, tiny Siam wins the
popularity contest, hands down. Working the woks and burners in a
tiny open kitchen fronted by counter seating, a quartet of women
moves with the utmost grace, portioning meats and vegetables and
dipping them into salty potions. They produce, among other flavorful
dishes, the city's best *tom kah gai*—the chicken soup spicy with chiles,
sour with lemongrass, and soothed with coconut milk. The menu
doesn't stray far from the Bangkok standards, but the dishes created
by the deft hands in the kitchen are distinctive. Sit at the counter and
enjoy the show, or wait for one of the (too few) tables in back. The
sister establishment in Eastlake (1880 Fairview Ave E, (206) 323-
8101) is much bigger, with karaoke, a full bar, a slightly different
menu, and less consistent results. *Lunch Mon–Fri, dinner every day;
AE, DC, MC, V; checks OK; beer and wine.* &

SICHUANESE CUISINE RESTAURANT

1048 S Jackson St, Seattle
☎ *(206) 720-1690*
International District   ✕ *Chinese*

Don't let the generic name dissuade you. A step-above-a-take-out on
the western edge of the International District, this place is about
food—and some of the tastiest Szechuan food in Seattle at that. Portions are big and sauces are authentic, meaning they are simply spicy,
not heavy in oil and starch. Good choices are the
deep-fried crispy prawns ($7.50), seductively light
and crunchy; the Szechuan eggplant ($5.50); and
the seafood wonton soup. Plus there's a variety of
hot pots, each big enough for the family. Fresh

jaozi and pot-stickers are on sale—take 'em home and stick 'em in your freezer for your own recipes. To top off the dining experience, smoking is OK, and you can bring your own six-pack of Tsing Tao. Cheers! *Lunch, dinner every day; MC, V; checks OK; no alcohol.* &

SILENCE-HEART-NEST VEGETARIAN RESTAURANT

5247 University Way NE, Seattle
☎ *(206) 524-4008*
University District   ✕ *Vegetarian*

If being relaxed aids the digestive process, then dining at Silence-Heart-Nest—a name derived from a poem by the spiritualist poet Sri Chinmoy—may be the next best thing to being fed intravenously while totally unconscious. Whether your mood is induced by the quiet East Indian music on the stereo, the soothing pastel tabletops, the gentle mantralike aspect of the restaurant's name, or the simple pleasures of a wholesome vegetarian meal, you can't help but feel relaxed and tranquil, speak softly, and eat unhurriedly, with measured movements. Many of the compelling vegetarian and vegan dishes here are Indian influenced: There are three "Curries of the Day," spicy or not, and successful East Indian takes on the Italian calzone and Mexican burrito. Those jonesing for a faux-meat-and-potatoes meal should try the Neat Loaf, a hearty conflation of wheat cereals, ricotta, rice, and herbs served with airy mashed potatoes and a light mushroom gravy. On each table you will find the newsletter of the Sri Chinmoy Centre, a meditation group, and dispersed throughout the restaurant are snippets of Sri Chinmoy's wisdom. *Lunch, dinner every day except Wed and Sun; no credit cards; checks OK; no alcohol.* &

SISTERS EUROPEAN SNACKS

1530 Post Alley, Seattle
☎ *(206) 623-6723*
Pike Place Market   ✕ *Soup/Salad/Sandwich*

The sisters referred to are German, and there are three of them—which takes care of the first two words in this eatery's name. The "Snacks" part begs for more careful elaboration, because the food served up at this colorful lunch counter is more than just finger food—it's soul-satisfying sustenance. Study the board for different sandwich combinations—say a bit of mozzarella, basil, roasted eggplant, and red pepper—and watch as one of the charming sisters or a helper piles it all

together between two pieces of focaccia before grilling the whole in a European sandwich press. Each sandwich is served with a very simple half salad. Businesspeople and Market cognoscenti love the daily vegetarian-leaning soups and the salads composed of greens and grains, and you'll definitely appreciate the apple-mint tea, which is as wildly refreshing as it sounds and is served only in the summertime. In warm weather, there are a few outdoor tables for dining on the cobblestones of Post Alley. *Breakfast, lunch every day; no credit cards; local checks only; no alcohol.*

SIT & SPIN

2219 Fourth Ave, Seattle
☎ *(206) 441-9484*
Belltown   ✗ *Soup/Salad/Sandwich*

This eatery/club/laundromat/coffeehouse is a good place to take visitors who want a taste of the real "grunge Seattle." The vast cavelike space is packed with retro-Jetsons decor—red booths, Formica tables, tubelike lamps—and slackerlike folks who look as if they were born to sit on amoeba-shaped furniture and look cool.

There are so many activities at Sit & Spin that very little slacking actually goes on, though. First there's eating: The grub is decent and cheap, including panini, burritos, soups, nachos, and salads. There's also a full juice bar, lots of caffeine and herb drinks, and beer and wine. Then there's the king's ransom of board games such as chess, Monopoly, Trivial Pursuit, Scrabble, Risk—even the ones from the '70s you'd prefer to forget, such as Life. Sit & Spin is also one of Belltown's most happening nightlife spots, with bands playing several nights a week. Finally, there's the full-service laundromat in the side room. Your quarters will also get you handfuls from the candy machines that line the entrance. *Lunch, dinner every day; no credit cards; no checks; beer and wine.* ♿

SIX ARMS PUB & BREWERY

300 E Pike St, Seattle
☎ *(206) 223-1698*
Capitol Hill   ✕ *Pub Grub*

The Portland-based McMenamins chain of brewpubs has so far made three encroachments into Seattle: McMenamins on lower Queen Anne, Dad Watson's in Fremont, and Six Arms on Capitol Hill. Located in a prime corner storefront among the antique shops and coffeehouses on not yet completely gentrified East Pike Street, Six Arms still feels like a comfortable neighborhood hangout—unlike its local siblings, which cater to the upscale urban set and scream "chain, chain, chain." Inside, piled-high burgers and sandwiches with mondo platters of hand-cut fries accompany a good selection of microbrews (try the Hammerhead Ale or Troll Porter) and a lively atmosphere. Pewlike benches surround a number of booths under huge windows that stretch to the high ceiling. The floors are concrete with a few well-worn Oriental rugs thrown here and there. Service can be relaxed to the nth degree—and may prove positively aggravating if you're sitting upstairs in the cozy balcony. A small, viewable beermaking operation in back gives the place that freshly brewed aroma. *Lunch, dinner every day; AE, MC, V; no checks; beer and wine.* ♿

SIX DEGREES

7900 E Greenlake Dr N, Seattle (and branch)
☎ *(206) 523-1600*
Green Lake/Kirkland   ✕ *Bistro*

Six Degrees wants nothing more than to be that place where everybody knows your name. It's not a restaurant, it's a self-styled "Spirited Neighborhood Kitchen" that's often packed to the gills with good-lookin' folks eatin' and imbibin' and generally havin' a great time. You'll find this relentlessly cheerful place either a welcome tonic or just too darn eager. Food, in keeping with the neighborhood tavern atmosphere, stays comfortably below 10 bucks. Expect a twist on the usual pub grub treats: Instead of plain ol' ribs, the menu offers wild boar ribs. In addition to beef burgers, there are buffalo and salmon burgers. The caesar salad with prawns makes for a generous meal; other notable dishes on the constantly evolving menu include New York steak sandwiches and chicken rotisseried in various guises. Note: The Kirkland branch opened in late 1998 (121 Park Lane,

(425) 803-1766), and owners of Six Degrees plan to roll out other sites using the same menu and general game plan. *Lunch, dinner every day; AE, DC, DIS, MC, V; checks OK; beer and wine.* &

THE SLIP

80 Kirkland Ave, Kirkland
☎ *(425) 739-0033*
Kirkland
🍴 *Bistro*

The Slip boasts of being the smallest full-service restaurant in Washington; we say it's a darling slip of a place. When it's nice enough to dine on the patio, though, there's room for more than your average basketball team. Out there non-cheapsters can fire up one of the Slip's fine cigars and sip a choice single malt or sour mash. Just a few steps up from the Kirkland Marina, the place is aptly named. Creative burgers include a homemade veggie version chock-full of mushrooms and bulgur. The shrimp burger, our favorite, gets swabbed with a wasabe-touched mayo. Black bean chili never tasted so good—thanks to the fresh salsa, yes, but thanks even more to the Jack Daniels in the mix. Creole prawns make their own fat statement—first-rate finger food—and the fries are roasted, not fried, so you can toast your health as you dip fistfuls into the Slip's own smoky ketchup. *Lunch, dinner every day; AE, DC, DIS, MC, V; checks OK; full bar.* &

SNAPPY DRAGON

8917 Roosevelt Way NE, Seattle
☎ *(206) 528-5575*
Maple Leaf
🍴 *Chinese*

Some say that this modest pink-and-white house disguised as a restaurant serves up the best Chinese food in Seattle. One slurp of chef Judy Fu's homemade, hand-cut noodles—which star in the various chow mein dishes and several soups—and you might agree. The long, chewy-tender curlicues are a challenge to maneuver gracefully into your mouth, but have become justifiably famous in recent years. Fu's devotees also rave about the clay pot stews, the mu-shu dishes, the Mongolian beef, and the fantastic "crispy eggplant"—sauced perfectly with a slightly spicy glaze. But be warned: Snappy is almost always crowded, so on Friday and Saturday nights, it's best to do the take- out thing. Prices aren't the cheapest around—most dishes run $8–$10—but the portions are extremely generous. *Lunch Mon–Sat, dinner every day; AE, DC, MC, V; checks OK; beer and wine.* &

SOUP DADDY SOUPS

106 Occidental Ave, Seattle
☎ *(206) 682-7202*
Pioneer Square   ✕ *Soup/Salad/Sandwich*

Anytime is a good time to duck into Soup Daddy Soups. But hot soup truly tastes best on cool, drizzly afternoons, so reserve your rainy-day pennies for a trip to this bright little storefront off Occidental Park. Choose from one of five fresh soups made daily, like the "Popeye," a thick, filling cream of mushroom with spinach; the chicken noodle; the Southwest corn chowder; or other inventive combinations. (The exception is the spicy gazpacho, which is oddly not puréed and loaded down with too many vegetables and conflicting flavors.) The soup in a bread bowl is a good option, too; you can pull apart your bowl and dunk it in the broth as you go. One of the most pleasant surprises this soup-cafeteria offers, however, is its sandwiches, reason enough to drop by. At $3.40, the sandwiches-on-a-bagel are a hunky deal; try the fabulous, bacon-heavy BLT, with its sweet, runny combination of mayo and homemade honey-mustard sauce. (Vegetarians will find plenty of options, including a wide range of salads all made with crisp romaine lettuce.) Order at the counter and eat in, or take your lunch over to the park and munch beneath the totem poles. Service is friendly but a bit spacey. *Breakfast, lunch Mon–Fri; no credit cards; checks OK; no alcohol.* ♿

SPEAKEASY

2304 Second Ave, Seattle
☎ *(206) 728-9770*
Belltown   ✕ *Coffeehouse*

Where else but at the Speakeasy can you check your email, sip a latte, watch an art film or spoken-word performance, listen to live music, and munch on vegetarian lasagne, all on the same evening? The space in this converted warehouse remains wide-open, with the massive wooden beams and concrete floors left in place and some two dozen computer terminals plopped down on tables and counters throughout the room. Spooky techno music contributes nicely to the cyberscene, while assorted potted plants provide a bit of greenery and a welcome counterpoint to the overall industrial look. Pastries and bagels complement espresso in the morning, while "comfort food" like turkey or tuna salad sandwiches and homemade soup keeps the computer-literate tapping at the terminals in the afternoon and evenings. You won't find bathtub gin at the Speakeasy, but wine and microbrews are available by the glass, pint, or pitcher—and after 9pm Thursdays through Saturdays, minors are given the heave-ho and IDs are checked at the door. Films and performances are usually held in the back room. *Light breakfast, lunch, dinner every day; AE, MC, V; checks OK; beer and wine.*

SPUD FISH 'N' CHIPS

2666 Alki Ave SW, Seattle
☎ *(206) 938-0606*
West Seattle   ✕ *Fish 'n' Chips*

If you're longing for the battered and deep-fried, then head west to Alki Beach, where Spud is celebrating 60 years of serving fish 'n' chip specials over the same counter and under the same ownership. There's nothing exalted or different about the fish 'n' chips here: They're pure grease, baby. As if in testimony to that fact, the whole interior, which is always jam-packed, is dulled by a thin film. But this doesn't stop anyone from waiting in line, placing their order at the counter, and standing around till their cardboard crate of chips is ready. Most intelligent folk try to escape the din and hot air inside by taking their greasy treasure across the street to a bench on the beach. If you stay inside, just remember to douse the fish with garlic vinegar, drown the chips in tartar sauce, and tell your heart to hold on for the ride. As a palate cleanser, try one of Spud's wonderfully briny barrel pickles or the perfectly mayonnaisey coleslaw. The Spuds in Green Lake and Juanita are separately-owned ventures; stick with the real deal on Alki. *Lunch, dinner every day; MC, V; no checks; no alcohol.* &

STEAMERS SEAFOOD CAFE

Pier 59, 1500 Alaskan Way, Seattle (and branches)
☎ *(206) 624-0312*
Downtown/Queen Anne   ✕ *Seafood*

The fish 'n' chips biz is thriving on the Seattle waterfront. How else to explain two Steamers Seafood Cafes in a three-block stretch? The Pier 56 location (1200 Alaskan Way, (206) 623-2066) earns the cafe label with wood tables and counters inside (or plastic chairs and tables out on the pier on sunny days). Three blocks to the north, the Pier 59 Steamers is a big, noisy family joint, with burgers and a thriving summer ice cream business to placate youthful tastes. The fish fillets can be replaced by clams or prawns if you wish, the chowder is tasty, and the food quality is quite consistent for a large-scale operation with a touristy clientele. Steamers also has a restaurant at the Seattle Center in lower Queen Anne (313 Harrison St, (206) 728-2228). *Lunch, dinner every day; DIS, MC, V; no checks; beer and wine.* ♿

STILL LIFE IN FREMONT

709 N 35th St, Seattle
☏ *(206) 547-9850*
Fremont   ⚜ *Soup/Salad/Sandwich*

Fremont's favorite coffeehouse is a Seattle classic: a big, steamy, well-lit space with a wall of windows, mismatched wooden furniture, and a big '40s radio. Add to these good art, occasional live entertainment, and—remember these?—good vibes. Still Life smacks of the '60s, when all hanging out required was a good book and a bowl of soup. Indeed, the soups are stunning: thick purée of curried split pea and sweet potato, or perhaps parsnip and celery root. The short sandwich menu is now overshadowed by the specials: perhaps a wild-rice rosemary salad studded with smoked turkey, green beans, mushrooms, crunchy carrots, and hazelnuts; a hefty square of polenta topped with tomato, red pepper, olives, and pepper Jack; or a quiche packed with artichokes, red peppers, and smoked mozzarella. (There's a heavy, but not strict, emphasis on vegetarian choices here.) Or you may choose to sip a good beer or a cup of steaming chai and nosh on a sweet. You'll leave reflecting on your good fortune that there is, in fact, still life in Fremont. Service is your own. *Breakfast, lunch, dinner every day; no credit cards; local checks only; beer and wine.* ♿

STONE WAY CAFE

3620 Stone Way N, Seattle
☏ *(206) 547-9958*
Wallingford   ⚜ *Diner*

A luncheonette should always have counter seating, stools with chrome bases, and, most importantly, Blue Plate Specials. These criteria are met and surpassed at this unassuming diner near the bottom of Stone Way, where the plates are bluer than blue, the stools and surrounding tables are usually filled at noontime, and the low prices make it easy for you to stuff yourself to the gills with all-American food you *wish* your Mom used to make. Every day there's a special soup/sandwich combo ($4.25) and entree, and between the sandwiches and burgers you'll probably end up ordering a chocolate malt ($2.50) to wash it all down. Sandwiches are served on fresh multigrain bread with all the fixins (the meat loaf was a winner), and the malt comes in a huge metal tumbler reminiscent of soda-fountain days. The cafe makes a mean caesar salad, a blackened chicken burger, and soup you almost forgot existed (navy bean). Watch out when you pay, though: A cradle-size wicker basket sits beside the register, brimming over with homemade chocolate chip  cookies. Stone Way does breakfast too, and everything but the pancakes continues on into lunch hour, so it could be very easy to bring a book and an appetite and stay happily for hours. *Breakfast, lunch every day; no credit cards; checks OK; no alcohol.*

STREAMLINER DINER

397 Winslow Way NE, Bainbridge
☎ *(206) 842-8595*
Bainbridge Island   ✕ *Diner*

A breezy 30-minute ferry ride from downtown is all that separates most of us from this beloved throwback to small-town Americana on Bainbridge Island. You almost expect to see a young George Bailey scooping up ice cream sundaes and flirting with the girls. Once off the ferry, the Streamliner Diner rests a few walkable blocks from the terminal in a low-key stripmall. The room is pretty and light—two walls are mostly windows—and both the floral tablecloths and the cast-iron pans hanging behind the long wooden counter give it a homey feel, with a slight hippy aura thrown in. Island natives and Seattle daytrippers mingle at tables and perch happily on the shiny chrome and vinyl bar stools; a display of fruit pies tempts incomers near the front door. Breakfasts are renowned, featuring a funky mixture of hearty omelets, fresh baked goods, and various scrambles, and a ridiculously rich quiche-of-the-day is served, it seems, by the quarter-pie. At lunch, homemade soup  comes with a small, flaky biscuit and sandwiches are filling. Try the grilled chicken club with havarti, avocado, and pesto mayo. Service is no-nonsense. Come early, before the crusty, fruity wedges of pie are all snatched up. There's a little park down the street where you can walk off your slice. *Breakfast, lunch every day; no credit cards; checks OK; no alcohol.* ♿

SUNFISH

2800 Alki Ave SW, Seattle
☏ *(206) 938-4112*
West Seattle ✕ *Fish 'n' Chips*

Fish 'n' chips aficionados swear by the food here—and those who come here don't ever go to the other one down the road, whose name we won't mention right now (Spud's). It's a matter of philosophy as to which is better—do you prefer your batter shiny with grease, as it is there, or deceptively dry and crackly, as it is here? Bite into a Sunfish chip and you'll be startled by the pure molten heat of the flesh within. Cod is the most popular fish that gets battered here, but Sunfish also turns out wonderfully crispy versions of halibut, oysters, clams, squid, and shrimp. In the battle for the best fish joint on the beach, Sunfish has one thing going for it that no one else has: Fishkebabs, glorious skewers of perfectly grilled halibut and veggies, all sans batter and all very good for you. It's worth knowing that Sunfish is far enough away from the frenzied action on Alki Beach that you might be able to find parking nearby *and* you might actually be able to get a table and eat like civilized folk (which explains the preponderance of older couples and families with itty-bitty kids here). Afterward, walk it all off by taking an after-dinner stroll along the water. *Lunch, dinner every day; no credit cards; no checks; no alcohol.* ♿

SUNLIGHT CAFE

6403 Roosevelt Way NE, Seattle
☏ *(206) 522-9060*
Roosevelt ✕ *Vegetarian*

The Sunlight's reputation for being a '60s kind of place is not surprising, considering that the cuisine is vegetarian and the waitperson who serves your garlic-ginger tofu sauté is likely to be bearded and Birkenstocked. There's also a bit of pure Norman Rockwell here, though, with regular customers sitting at the lunch counter, showing off pictures of their grandkids, and trading quips with the cooks. Either way, this wood-paneled, light-filled restaurant is as sunny and laid-back as you'd expect from its name. Brunch, served on Saturday and Sunday, is a big deal, with a menu dedicated to easy-on-the-arteries items such as vegetarian tofu scramble, sesame crunch waffles, and wonderful fruit salads. (Luckily, they don't forgo touches such as serving Vermont maple syrup with the soy-milk French toast.) The lunch and dinner menus are a bit less exciting—stir-fries, rollups, black bean burritos, and salads at lunch, with pasta and several tofu-vegetarian stir-fries added at dinner—but items are reliable and very reasonably priced. Try one of the salads, the nutburger, or the rich veg-etarian lasagne. Even the beer and wine is additive-free. *Brunch Sat–Sun, breakfast, lunch Mon–Fri, dinner every day; MC, V; checks OK; beer and wine.* &

SUPER BOWL NOODLE HOUSE

814 NE 65th St, Seattle
☎ *(206) 526-1570*
Roosevelt ✕ **Pan-Asian**

The squiggly servings at Super Bowl come doused, dry, and more ways than you could probably imagine. Noodles in all their glory bob and tangle themselves in giant bowls filled with broth, spices, veggies, and (if you desire) meat. How many different ways could you possibly want to sample rice, egg, and cellophane? As many ways as there are options (28)! Since the dishes have all the heat and tangy sweetness of Thai flavoring, you can expect your taste buds to run their paces. The

menu, for example, warns that the "HOT" M-80 Noodles require photo ID before ordering. The Super Bowl Noodles are an explosive pleasure, packed with spices, chicken, squid, celery, spinach, clear noo-dles, and green onions. Wow. With names as inviting as the combinations of ingredi-ents (Donald Duck, Green Lake, Sahara

Desert, Turbo, Old Faithful, Hobo), Super Bowl's dishes have attracted a small but steady stream of devotees, all of whom seem per-fectly calm about plunging their spoons and chopsticks into the mas-sive, steaming white bowls. Whether you're sitting in the main room, at the take-out counter, or out on the patio, Super Bowl takes noodles past the end zone. *Lunch, dinner every day; DIS, MC, V; local checks only; beer, wine, and sake.*

SUPER CHINA

8460 164th Ave NE, Redmond
☎ *(425) 869-7478*
Redmond ✕ **Chinese**

Strip malls are never intriguing propositions to begin with, and Super China is housed in one of those really small ones, the kind that are so easy to zip past when you're driving toward Redmond Town Center. Take care to not zip by—instead, drop in to this brightly scrubbed, nondescript storefront for cheap, fast, and really, really fine Hunan and Mandarin-style Chinese food. (If you're from New York City, this is the kind of Chinese food you grew up eating.) Anything on the chef's special lineup—say General Tso's chicken, Happy Family, or orange flavored beef—is intense with vivid flavors. Have a hankering for East Coast-style shrimp with lobster sauce? It's here, and it rocks. Mandarin and Hunan classics are organized into their own section; if you want to set your tongue a-buzzin', look here first. This is one of those menus with over 100 items; we recommend picking up a copy of the tablemat/menu so you can order take-out to enjoy in the comfort of your own home. Lunch is the best time to explore the riches of the vast menu—for under five bucks you get an entree, fried or steamed rice, and a choice of soup: egg drop, hot and sour, or wonton. *Lunch, dinner every day; MC, V; checks OK; no alcohol.* ⅄

SWINGSIDE CAFE

4212 Fremont Ave N, Seattle
☎ *(206) 633-4057*
Fremont ✕ *Inventive Ethnic*

Owner/chef Brad Inserra (he's the guy working his buns off in the absurdly small kitchen) produces a world of big flavors and an always inventive menu. There are hearty stews and sautés and pasta dishes spiced with unpredictable North African, Creole, and nouvelle American accents. The brown Moroccan sauce caresses the mouth; tangy seafood dishes sing of the sea; the gumbo is extraordinary, and spicy enough to cure what ails you. Everything's rich, delicious, and amply portioned; don't overorder, or you may have to be carried home. As for atmosphere, you've probably forgotten that eating out could be as simple, casual, and friendly as this. Dinner in the "fish room"—a tiny aquarium-like atrium attached to the back of the house—is an experience  all its own. At press time, Inserra had recently begun serving lunch and weekend brunch. *Brunch Sat–Sun, lunch Tues–Fri, dinner Tues–Sun; MC, V; local checks only; beer and wine.* ⅄

TACO DEL MAR

1336 First Ave, Seattle (and branches)

☎ *(206) 623-8741*

Downtown/Ballard/Bellevue/Capitol Hill/First Hill/
Fremont/Greenwood/Kirkland/Lake City/Pioneer Square/
Queen Anne/Redmond/Renton/Roosevelt/University
District/SoDo/Wallingford   ✕ *Mexican*

Target a fast-food idea that's hot in another part of the country, and import it: That's what the Taco del Mar folks did with the San Francisco–born "Mission-style burrito," and 25 or so Puget Sound eateries later, they're flying high. Their satisfying burritos stick fairly close to the original model: a steamed flour tortilla foil-wrapped tightly around chicken, roasted pork in mole sauce, or beef; long-grain rice; refried or whole beans; and salsa; with optional additions of cheese, guacamole, and sour cream.

(Vegetarian versions are available, too.) They come in two sizes: jumbo ($3.60), which would feed your average construction worker; and super ($4.58), which would feed your average nuclear family.

For smaller appetites, there are several kinds of tacos as well as a taco salad. The best buy here is their specialty, the fish taco. For under $2, you get a wonderfully messy and filling rendition of the classic: tender Alaskan cod, shredded cabbage, salsa, a "mystery white sauce," and a squirt of lime—all spilling out of two fresh flour tortillas. (They also have a fish burrito.) All meats are lean and skinless, and the whole beans are fat-free, but—unfortunately for some—the fish is fried. One last note: Unless you're unusually graceful, we recommend eating all Taco del Mar items outside. *Lunch, dinner every day; no credit cards (branches vary); checks OK; no alcohol (select branches serve beer only).* ♿

TAKOHACHI

610 S Jackson St, Seattle

☎ *(206) 682-1828*

International District   ✕ *Japanese*

Some restaurants are so charming that all you want to do is keep them a jealously guarded secret. Takohachi is one of those rare birds: It's a small, family-run business that has survived almost a decade in Seattle's quicksilver restaurant scene through the devoted patronage of Japanese students. And it serves food so simply good, at such affordable prices, that you will want to—and be able to—make it a weekly habit. Owner Chozaburo Kobayashi has been cooking for 50 years, starting at his father's restaurant, also called Takohachi, on the island of Shikoku, Japan. Outside, the only eye-catching feature on the plain storefront is a bright red octopus waving its tentacles. The main dining room is bare-bones and cleanly scrubbed, with a few booths and tables. To Japanese students, Takohachi is just the cure for a homesick palate because of the "American-style" Japanese cooking that's served here: combination meals ($6.95–$8.45) of "hamburg steak," potato cro-quettes, fried pork cutlets, tempura, or fish, served with rice, salad, miso soup, and a tiny platter of *tsukemono*. Daily specials are posted on the walls with hand-painted portraits: You may get *yasai* ramen, a very slurpable mix of spicy stir-fried vegetables, sweet carrots, and gratify-ingly chewy noodles, or a bento box of egg, grilled salmon, shrimp tem-pura, and a fried piece of chicken. Especially popular during lunch are the different ramen combinations, in soup or stir-fried form. The best meal here is the most traditionally Japanese: black cod kasazuke ($8.45), a slice of cod brushed with a special miso paste and broiled until the skin crisps. No dessert—but you won't need it. *Lunch Mon–Fri, dinner Mon–Sat; MC, V; no checks; beer and wine.* &

TANDOOR

5024 University Way NE, Seattle
☎ *(206) 523-7477*
University District   ✕ *Indian*

This small, popular U-District storefront looks a bit unassuming when you first peek in, but don't be fooled. A second room is festooned with pillows, reminiscent of a pasha's hangout, and a true feeling of deca-dence sets in when your meal arrives. Tandoor serves excellent, reliable Indian food—some of the most reasonably priced in the city—with an emphasis on tandoori-style cooking. A good introduction is chicken tikka masala, tender and delicious. Also recommended is the eggplant bhatta: eggplant is roasted, mashed, then sautéed with onions—it melts in your mouth like some exotic dish from a fantasy banquet. The side dishes here are tasty as well: basil and garlic naan is chewy with a hint of oil, and the rice pulao is fragrant and perfectly prepared. Family-owned and operated, Tandoor has kindly service fit for a raj. *Lunch, dinner every day; AE, DIS, MC, V; local checks only; beer and wine.* &

TAQUERIA DEL RIO

10230 16th Ave SW, Seattle
☎ *(206) 767-9102*
White Center   ✕ *Mexican*

If you've ever been to Tijuana, the store that fronts this taqueria might prompt a reminiscence about the Avenida de la Revolución. You see the same mixture of native tradition, Catholic iconography, and Western pop culture lining every wall—from the mural-size paintings of ancient women making bread to multiple crucifixes and statues of La Guadalupana to ceramic Winnie the Poohs and piggy banks. But this store is a functional one and not a tourist trap, and interested shoppers can pick up jars of mole, pickled pigs feet, star-shaped piñatas, Latino CDs, and even movies here. On busy weekend afternoons, there's plenty of time to shop while your order is being prepared. Once inside the front door, turn to the right and head straight back to the taqueria. (You might want to brush up on your Spanish before you go— there's no fooling around with translation in this authentic place.) Menu items are available while supplies last,  but don't be daunted if your first choice has run out. The food is simple and well prepared, and anything you choose will be tasty and cheap. Taqueria del Rio's cuisine tends toward the spicy side, but even if you're a spice wimp, the payoff is in the extra flavor that's usually missing from most taqueria menus. Combination dishes are available with choice of meat, and come with beans and rice and tortillas, or you can opt for the standard burrito, tacos, or nachos. *Lunch, dinner every day; no credit cards; no checks; beer only.* ♿

TAQUERIA GUAYMAS

1622 SW Roxbury St, Seattle (and branches)
☎ *(206) 767-4026*
White Center/Capitol Hill/Green Lake/Lynnwood/
Renton/West Seattle   ✕ *Mexican*

When we look back at the food fads of the 1990s, one thing will be obvious: Burritos were one of the hottest trends. Everyone reinterpreted this classic Mexican meal (and many folks got rich doing it). But when we crave the real thing, what we want is a big, fat barbecue pork burrito from Taqueria Guaymas, a well-loved local chain of Mexican food joints. Used to be there was only one TG, the original one in

White Center; now there are three more, in West Seattle, Renton, and Lynnwood, as well as two hipper, yuppier Tacos Guaymas—one in Green Lake, the other on Capitol Hill. We say the more people realize how very tasty the food is here, the better. Besides the barbecued pork, other burrito fillers include chicken, beef, and more exotic options such as *lengua* (beef tongue) and shrimp. You can get other familiar dishes like enchiladas, fish tacos, and quesadillas, but why not opt for a daily chalkboard special—say a tostada smothered in a piquant tomatillo sauce? Decor is bare-bones—wooden tables and chairs—and the walls feature paintings of sleepy señors and señoritas. The salsa bar, with its fantastic selection of pickled carrots, peppers, and fresh salsas, is too good for your own good—you'll be enticed into eating way too many chips. *Lunch, dinner every day; AE, MC, V (Renton branch only); checks OK; beer only (beer and wine at West Seattle branch, no alcohol at Capitol Hill branch).* ᯢ

TEAHOUSE KUAN YIN

1911 N 45th St, Seattle
☎ *(206) 632-2055*
Wallingford   ✕ *Teahouse*

You can peruse the latest guide to India while sipping a Darjeeling or study a map of Japan while warming your hands on a bowl of matcha. It wasn't by chance that this teahouse—"Seattle's first"— was located beside Wide World Books. Started by two former travel agents with a longtime interest in Asia, Kuan Yin is now owned by one of the original owners, Miranda Pirzada. Complementing the full spectrum of teas, including plenty of blacks and greens, a few oolongs, and some herbals, is a multiethnic and reasonably priced assortment of quiches, piroshkis, curried veggies, and some pan-Asian dishes such as humbao and pot-stickers. Also offered are desserts such as green tea ice cream, pies, and scones. The mood is meditative but worldly; customers are invited to sit in leisurely and lengthy contemplation. Instruction in the ways of tea drinking is dispensed generously and with a philosophical air. *Lunch, dinner every day; MC, V; local checks only; no alcohol.* ᯢ

TERIYAKI 1ST

5201B University Way NE, Seattle
☎ *(206) 526-1661*
University District   ✕ *Teriyaki*

Psst . . . this teriyaki joint is run by a Korean brother-and-sister team and offers a Korean menu (written in Korean). Down-home Korean dishes like *duk-bok-i* (thick rice cakes and veggies sautéed in hot chile paste) and *yuk-ae-jang* (beef stew in chile broth), which can be hard to find at other teriyaki joints, are both larger and hotter than anything you're likely to find outside of Seoul. It's not much of a sit-down place—so pack up the food and head over to nearby Ravenna Park or, if you don't mind undergrads, the UW campus. A word of warning: The spice scale here is the highest we've encountered in this city. If your taste buds are tame, ask for mild versions of the Korean dishes, or stick to the various teriyaki or fried Korean *mandu* (pot-stickers). Don't miss the homemade kimchi; you can get a monthly supply to take home, too. Teriyaki 1st is open until 3am in summer. *Lunch, dinner every day; AE, MC, V; no checks; no alcohol.*

TEXAS SMOKEHOUSE BAR-B-Q

14455 Woodinville-Redmond Rd, Woodinville
☎ *(425) 486-1957*
Woodinville   ✕ *Barbecue*

Out past Yuppie Pawn and Yuppy Puppy Day Care and down the road from a sod farm, you can follow a steady stream of shiny new SUVs and rusty old pickups as they lead the way to some of the Eastside's best barbecue. Such is the egalitarian nature of good food (especially good barbecue), and the smoky-sweet fare that Texas Smokehouse serves up is no exception. Unabashedly Texas national-  ists, the proprietors greet their guests with a decor dominated by all things Lone Star: license plates, maps, flags, cow skulls, and various "Texas-size" accoutrements. Just as it should, the menu doesn't pack any surprises. All the barbecue food groups are faithfully represented, from beef brisket to sliced pork to sausage to chicken to ribs (spare and back, beef and pork), and most everything you order comes in Texas-size portions. Make sure you sample the sides, particularly the authentic corn bread with actual corn bits. *Lunch, dinner every day; AE, MC, V; checks OK; beer and wine.* ♿

THAI GINGER

3717 128th Ave SE, Bellevue
☎ *(425) 641-4008*
Bellevue/Redmond   ✕ *Thai*

On finishing the namesake entree at the original branch of this Thai eatery, a little charmer wedged in the heart of Factoria, you'll likely say, "Man, that was a lot of ginger! Good, though!" Considerable energy was spent converting a former sub sandwich shop into a cozy, comfortable place where rattan-frame, faux-leather-clad cushioned chairs invite lingering. So too does the kitchen counter, where books on Thailand compete for your attention with the chattering conclave of cooks (the place is staffed almost exclusively by women) kicking out simply wonderful dishes practically before they are ordered. That means if you want pacing, you must order incrementally. Choice bites include good old red curry, with its vermilion coconut sauce sopped up by forkfuls of fragrant jasmine rice, and cashew chicken, whose chile paste–spiked sauce adds wonderful piquancy to the veggie-nut-chicken sauté. *Tod mun* fish cakes can be marred by excess grease, and the pedestrian peanut sauce does not complement the excellent satays. But black rice pudding will end any meal on a sweet note. There's a second Thai Ginger in the Redmond Town Center (16480 NE 74th St, (425) 558-4044). *Lunch, dinner every day; DIS, MC, V; checks OK; beer and wine.* &

THAI KITCHEN
7811 SE 27th St, Mercer Island
☎ *(206) 232-2570*
Mercer Island ✕ *Thai*

The first piece of good news about this busy little Mercer Island spot is that owners/chefs Sandy and Sam Pongauksira haven't dumbed down any of the Thai spices for the suburban crowd. The curries are complex and have plenty of kick; the *tom yu koong*, hot and sour chicken soup, abounds with lemongrass flavor; and the *larb*, chicken or pork salad, is as full of lime and chile flavor as it should be. Other good choices include *lard nar*, a satisfyingly rich combination of stir-fried soft noodles with beef and broccoli, and the Ginger Lover, meat or prawns with ginger, served with a host of al dente veggies. Ingredients are always fresh, and vegetables are always cooked until just crisp. Don't miss the satays or the angel wings, which in the Kitchen's hands become the world's most perfect appe- tizer: chicken wings stuffed to bursting with luscious pork and vermicelli noodles, sided by plum sauce and cucumber. Thai Kitchen also has good seasonal specials; be sure to stop by in the summer for a large helping of mango served on sticky rice with fresh coconut. The atmosphere is strip-mall stripped-down, but somehow the wonderful smells and sizzling sounds coming from the kitchen seem to distract you from the decor. Oh, glad you asked about the second piece of good news: Ninety percent of the dishes on the menu cost $5.95. *Lunch Mon–Fri, dinner every day; MC, V; checks OK; beer and wine.* &

THAI RESTAURANT

101 John St, Seattle
☎ *(206) 285-9000*
Queen Anne   ✕ *Thai*

One of Seattle's first noteworthy Thai restaurants remains a local favorite. The staff are incredibly efficient; they swirl by in their cool, bright shirts, trailing essences of coconut, peanut, and orange. Start with the *mee krob*, a nest of crunchy noodles fried with a tangy citrus flavor and topped with red pepper, a sweet plum sauce, bean sprouts, shreds of red cabbage, and tofu. The spring rolls, filled with lettuce and surimi, are wrapped in a tender rice pancake; they're good dipped in plum sauce and dabbed in chopped peanuts. The tender squid sautéed with garlic and pepper sauce is outstanding. Hotness is not quite dependable here: Someone in the kitchen likes playing with fire. Note: At press time, rumors of a remodel and menu changes were afoot. But the same ownership and management should keep this spot at fave. *Lunch Mon–Fri, dinner Mon–Sat; AE, MC, V; local checks only; beer and wine.*

THAI THAI

11205 16th Ave SW, Seattle
☎ *(206) 246-2246*
White Center   ✕ *Thai*

Smack-dab in the middle of no-man's-land—between White Center and Burien—stands the whitewashed building of Thai Thai. This popular restaurant has been holding forth for over a decade, serving the same great food at amazing prices. The decor is perfunctory at best, but regulars come from as far away as Issaquah to treat themselves to the best phad Thai and Panang curry in the Puget Sound area. Go there more than a couple of times, and owner Sam Sudthaya will start greeting you by name. Perennial customer favorites include the intense soups, *larb gai, yum neau*, and anything made with peanut sauce, one of the few such sauces in town  that's actually pounded out from scratch. There are precious few places that don't use prefab sauces and powders; Thai Thai is one of those places, and you can taste the difference. Chances are you'll be overwhelmed by the 100-plus items on the menu, so treat yourself to a combination dinner, a multicourse option that's a steal at around 10 bucks a head. If you go this route, make sure you nab one of the two massive teakwood dining sets—enormous and intricately carved, these behemoths are downright primeval. Dining at them will make you feel like presiding Thai royalty. *Lunch Mon–Fri, dinner Mon–Sat; MC, V; no checks; beer and wine.*

THAN BROTHERS RESTAURANT

7714 Aurora Ave N, Seattle
☎ *(206) 527-5973*
Green Lake   ✕ *Vietnamese*

Don't go unless you want pho, because Than Brothers, a funky little Vietnamese place on Aurora, does nothing but. And not surprisingly, they do those steaming bowls of rice noodle soup very well: They're fragrant, delicately flavored, very cheap, and very, very filling (the menu tops out at $4.95 for an extra-large, which you will not be able to finish). You can choose from several varieties, including pho topped with chicken (*pho ga*), with meatballs (*pho bo vien*), or with several kinds of beef, from paper-thin slices of "well-done flank" to tripe. Each bowl comes sided by a lovely plate of add-your-own garnishes such as mint leaves, bean sprouts, and sliced jalapeño. Plus, there are the usual condiments—hoisin, fish sauce, and chile sauce—that you can also add at your discretion. Slurp it down with sweet, strong Thai iced tea or "young coconut drink." There is one dessert on the menu, custard puffs, which are also served as a pre-pho complimentary appetizer. *Lunch, dinner every day; no credit cards; checks OK; no alcohol.* ♿

THAT'S AMORE ITALIAN CAFE

1425 31st Ave S, Seattle
☎ *(206) 322-3677*
Mount Baker   ✕ *Italian*

Locals flock to this cheery, urbane cafe on the Mount Baker/Leschi ridge as if it were their private club. The cooking style reflects owners Celester and Salina Gray's take on Italian, with generous family-style portions. Folks show up for plates of creamy lemon fettuccine or a nicely crusted pizza with artichokes and what-have-you. A fresh, thin focaccia appetizer, crisp and warm, arrives with a wedge of creamy, blue-veined Cambozola cheese to spread like butter over each slice: a little bit of heaven. This informal city cafe is great for families (there's a children's menu) and has plenty of vegetarian selections. The view of downtown Seattle from the back windows is worth a trip in itself. *Lunch, dinner every day; MC, V; local checks only; beer and wine.* ♿

THOMPSON'S POINT OF VIEW

2308 E Union St, Seattle
☎ *(206) 329-2512*
Central District   ✕ *Southern*

By the time you finish your meal, the warmth of a satisfied tummy will transform your view of this rather plain room. Excellent long-simmered red beans and rice accompany the star entree, a lightly breaded and moist catfish with a crisp skin. The side dishes are often the best part of the meal. Thompson's gives you two with each dinner, so you may find yourself agonizing over whether to have potato salad, black-eyed peas, sweetened yams, creamy baked macaroni and cheese, green beans with ham hocks, or Southern-style greens that take you straight to Georgia. The sheer size of these meals is a challenge: The Thompson Burger is a massive soul-food sandwich with sliced hot links, crisp bacon, a grilled beef patty, cheese, and condiments on an egg bun (yes, you *can* hear your arteries slamming shut); meat loaf comes in two hearty slabs. The corn bread is shaped like a pancake, crisp around the edges and bathed in butter. Late-night dining is an option every night. *Lunch, dinner every day; MC, V; no checks; full bar.* ♿

THREE GIRLS BAKERY

Pike Place Market, Seattle
☎ *(206) 622-1045*
Pike Place Market   ✕ *Bakery*

Stop by any day around noon, and the crowd around Three Girls' L-shaped lunch counter will likely be three hungry locals and a couple of displaced New Yorkers deep. Sandwiches don't get a whole lot better than this, and "whole" is the operative word here, 'cause there ain't no halves, as these wisecracking architects of meat and cheese will gladly tell  you. There's soup—nothing fancy, but filling and hot—and a meat loaf sandwich just like Mother used to make. Order bakery fixings at the take-out window. *Breakfast, lunch every day; MC, V; checks OK; no alcohol.*

TOP GUN SEAFOOD RESTAURANT

668 S King St, Seattle
☎ *(206) 623-6606*
International District   ✕ **Chinese**

Cantonese seafood restaurants come and go like the wind, but this latest addition will stay around for a long, long time if the weekend crowds have any sway. Everything that's served in this bright and shiny space is as good as it is cheap. While the dim sum here is practically a local legend, it's the swell seafood served at dinner that secures Top Gun's place in the local pantheon of great eats. There are literally hundreds of items: Forgo the usual sweet and sour and try abalone with sea cucumber, deep-fried squab, or crab in black bean and chile sauce. You won't find the usual assortment of *gwailo* (white folks) here—it's so authentic that you might as well be back on Lamma Island, Hong Kong. A recommendation for those who feel overwhelmed by the menu: Opt for the combination dinners, or peek at neighboring tables to see what they're enjoying. If you like what you see, just point to it— this method is especially useful if you get a server who doesn't speak English. The daring should simply point to anything on the menu written in Chinese—it will be good. Another plus: Dinner's served until 3am on Friday and until 2am on other nights. *Lunch (dim sum only), dinner every day; MC, V; no checks; beer only.* ♿

TOYODA SUSHI

12543 Lake City Way NE
☎ *(206) 367-7972*
Lake City   ✕ **Japanese**

A caveat: To qualify Toyoda as a cheap eat requires a bit of strategic ordering. But the splendid array of homey Japanese specialties is worth the effort. The restaurant's noisy, casual atmosphere is comparable to that of Japan's *izakaya* establishments, which offer wide varieties of cuisine and copious alcohol at reasonable prices.

Toyoda's food pleases right from the start: a hot bowl of fresh miso that should convert the most ardent of bean-paste skeptics. From there, the options are unmatched in Seattle, and available here at a much more reasonable price than at several other overrated sushi spots downtown. The à la carte sushi and sashimi menu is conducive to 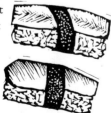 bold experimentation. Enthusiasts of *uni* (sea urchin) will be delighted to find it at a fraction of Tokyo prices. The loyal customer base and high volume served assure that the tuna is melt-in-your-mouth fresh. Toyoda also offers the rare treat of hand-sushi, a hearty style of sushi wrapped in a cone of nori. A number of hot food selections, including basic teriyaki, tempura, and a variety of grilled fish, will please the sushi-squeamish. *Dinner Wed–Mon; MC, V; checks OK; beer and wine.* ♿

TRATTORIA MITCHELLI

84 Yesler Way, Seattle
☎ *(206) 623-3885*
Pioneer Square ✕ *Italian*

Mediocrity has never had a more appealing backdrop than this, the original "Trat" in Pioneer Square. Owner Dany Mitchell (the self-proclaimed "Papa Mitchelli") has earnestly built himself an empire of restaurants that serve good-enough Italian food. The other branches are Angelina's Trattoria in West Seattle (see separate review) and

Stella's Trattoria in the U-District, the best feature of which is that it's open 24 hours. Trattoria Mitchelli continues to outshine them all. Yes, the fare is often mediocre, but it's dependable, and this is a place where you can host an impromptu party in the bar or restaurant at almost any time of night (it's open till 4am Tuesday through Saturday). Some dishes are even quite good—say, the ravioli in garlic, the pizzas, anything made with veal, the Italian frittatas, and the cheesy omelets. In summer, this is a nice, casual spot for a beer at one of the outdoor tables. *Breakfast, lunch, dinner every day; AE, DIS, MC, V; checks OK; full bar.* ♿

TRES HERMANOS FAMILY MEXICAN RESTAURANT

12821 NE 85th St, Kirkland (and branch)
☎ *(425) 827-4422*
Kirkland/Bellevue ✕ *Mexican*

There are more than three brothers behind this highly successful independent Mexican operation, which recently opened an authentic-though-too-bright branch in Bellevue Square (180 Bellevue Square, (425) 452-1456). It's run by the whole family, whose members started by serving an apprenticeship in the Las Margaritas group before breaking out on their own. The Kirkland version, with wrought-iron-

and-amber-glass light fixtures and bird-of-paradise-pattern carpet, feels more comfortable than its Bellevue sibling, like a broken-in shoe rather than something just out of a Nordstrom box. So what if there's a scuff or two? One margarita and a bowl of warm tortilla chips will blur the distinction between broken-in and tired. Focus on an appetizer platter (pretty much everything arrives on wide platters) of *camarones*, a half pound of prawns in a surprisingly lively (à la diablo) sauce that may overpower sensitive palates. In fact, heat—both temperature and spiciness—appears to be a common theme here: All platters, not just the sizzling fajita skillets, arrive hot. All dinners also arrive with enough beans and rice to ensure that lunch tomorrow will be *no problemo*. Kids love the place, and family units are the norm, happy throngs ending meals with deep-fried ice cream or *chimichanga de manzana*, with apples, cinnamon, ice cream, and strawberry sauce. *Lunch, dinner every day; AE, DIS, MC, V; checks OK; full bar.* ♿

TRIANGLE LOUNGE

3507 Fremont Pl N, Seattle
☏ *(206) 632-0880*
Fremont   ⚜ *Bistro*

The Triangle Tavern, the laid-back hipster haven at the center of the Center of the Universe, underwent an upgrade in 1998, during which time it officially graduated to Lounge status. Don't worry, though; as high school geometry taught us, you can mess with the size and shape of a triangle, and even change its name, but it's always gonna have three sides. Likewise, at the Triangle Lounge, there's no doubt that certain features will always be the same. The menu has expanded, but it still features satisfying $7 sandwiches (such as the charbroiled lamb burger and the grilled chicken and hummus pita) and $8 pasta entrees (spinach lasagne) of consistently good quality, plus a selection of pizzas and daily seafood specials. The triangular dining room, decorated with artwork of a conspicuously three-sided theme, still enters onto a narrow, festively lit patio in the shape of . . . a triangle. At the opposite end of the dining room is the retro lounge (expanded to more than a mere tavern) with a long, well-stocked bar dominated by large pier pilings and an overhanging red neon sign proclaiming "Prescriptions." The new lounge may be the real attraction here. Though

it's painted in dark, moody tones, large windows let the light shine in on late summer evenings and offer a fine vantage point for people-watching. *Lunch, dinner every day; AE, MC, V; no checks; full bar.*

TRIPLE J CAFE

101 Central Way, Kirkland
☎ *(425) 822-7319*
Kirkland ✕ *Soup/Salad/Sandwich*

Situated on the corner of Central Way and Lake Street, the Triple J literally anchors downtown Kirkland's crossroads. Within about 200 yards in any direction, there are basically three things one can do: look at art, eat, or watch people on their way to look at art or eat. Triple J may be the best place in town for this third pastime. Comfy couches huddle 'round the fireplace. Tables line the windows and walls. The ceiling's about a mile up, with artsy light fixtures a little lower; the walls that aren't windows are hung with art. Belly up to the counter, resist the fresh-baked goodies if you can, order a sandwich, salad, or maybe a pasta plate, add a decent cup of soup, and then fight for a seat (folks tend to linger) and wait for your number to be called—or hollered, to be precise. Hang out awhile, and we guarantee that you too will begin to feel artistic. *Breakfast, lunch, dinner every day; MC, V; local checks only; no alcohol.* ♿

TUP TIM THAI

118 W Mercer, Seattle
☎ *(206) 281-8833*
Queen Anne ✕ *Thai*

Tup Tim Thai is almost always bustling. Yet, somehow, there never seems to be much of a wait and, once you're seated, it doesn't take long for food to arrive on the table. This clean, light, and airy restaurant offers traditional Thai food that is consistently good and sometimes excellent. With a menu boasting close to 100 choices (lunch entrees average $5 and dinner entrees, $6), Tup Tim Thai has a dish to satisfy almost any palate. Mainstays, such as *phad Thai goong* and *rard nah* (big, soft, almost doughy noodles pan-fried with tender broccoli in the house special sauce) never disappoint. *Tod mun pla*, small deep- fried, fish cakes (the fish is mixed with curry paste and green beans) is served with a spicy-hot cucumber sauce and makes an excellent appetizer, and the spicy Dancing Calamari salad, tossed with tart lime juice, mint, lemongrass and red onion, is a zesty addition to any meal.

The *larb gai* (tender, minced chicken cooked with chiles, mint, and other spices and wrapped in leaves of lettuce) is a dish the menu claims is especially good with beer—and it is. Most dishes feature a succulent blend of spicy-hot, sweet, sour, and salty flavors, all delicately balanced so that each flavor is distinguishable while complementing the others. Should your curiosity be piqued, friendly partners George Lertkantitham, Malika Coval, and Teerayuth Pramoulmetar have even been known to pull out their favorite Thai cookbook and generously share a recipe or two. *Lunch Mon–Fri, dinner Mon–Sat; MC, V; local checks only; beer and wine.*

TURKISH DELIGHT
1930 Pike Pl, Seattle
☎ *(206) 443-1387*
Pike Place Market   ✕ *Turkish*

It's easy to understand why out-of-town customers have Turkish Delight's delicacies shipped to them: The Yavuz family creates a welcome range of well-herbed, well-spiced Turkish treats in this plain, cafeteria-style cafe at the northern end of the market. The cafe is also a wonderful source of vegetable salads and savory pastries for an exotic picnic. Try one of the generous pita sandwiches stacked with grilled meat and vegetables in yogurt sauce. Red lentil and chicken soups pair well with the shepherd's salad of crunchy vegetables. Delightful! *Breakfast, lunch, early dinner every day; no credit cards; local checks only; no alcohol.* ♿

TWO BELLS TAVERN
2313 Fourth Ave, Seattle
☎ *(206) 441-3050*
Belltown   ✕ *Burgers*

Because many Two Bells staffers are involved in the musical or visual arts, this tavern is not only a place for excellent burgers but has also become a hangout of sorts for the artist community. Artwork often decorates the walls, while a tiny stage along the back wall hosts occasional performances by various acts. Most of the eclectic crowd that gathers here, though, does so in common worship of the burger. It's big and juicy, smothered in onions and cheese, served on a sourdough roll with your choice of side orders, including a rich, chunky potato salad. Another favorite is the hot beer-sausage sandwich. This food is so full of flavor and freshness and goes so well with the beer that you won't care about getting mustard all over your face. On Sundays, a limited-menu brunch is served (think challah French toast and omelets). *Brunch Sun, lunch, dinner every day; AE, DIS, MC, V; no checks; beer and wine.* ♿

THE UGLY MUG CAFE

1309 NE 43rd St, Seattle
☎ *(206) 547-3219*
University District ✂ **Soup/Salad/Sandwich**

The Mug is filling a much-needed niche in the University District: that of classy coffeehouse. The music is pleasant instead of jarring, the atmosphere (lamp-lit tables, slightly faded Oriental rugs, and velvet curtains) as suitable for a date as for a quick lunch, and the menu reasonably priced and creative. Breakfast offerings are espresso and baked goods such as cinnamon rolls, lemon-raspberry bread, and the Mug's own scones. The rest-of-the-day menu features excellent soups, good salads, and—the Mug's specialty—a selection of generously sized sandwiches. Recommended are the veggie focaccia, with roasted red peppers, grated carrots, Swiss cheese, and tapenade; the meat loaf; and the smoked turkey with Danish havarti and rosemary mayo. The cozy one-room space also stars a couch and a couple of recliners, where you can eavesdrop on students either pontificating about Chaucer or having conversations that begin, "That was the ninth party I've been to this week!" There's live music Thursday through Saturday night. *Breakfast, lunch, dinner Mon–Sat; no credit cards; checks OK; beer and wine.*

UPTOWN CHINA

200 Queen Anne Ave N, Seattle
☎ *(206) 285-7710*
Queen Anne ✂ **Chinese**

A traditional Chinese-American restaurant where stylish subtlety supplants kitschy decor, the Uptown features an array of Cantonese dishes. The menu includes excellent pot-stickers spiced with a little chile oil, and dry-sautéed string beans done to perfection. Some dishes, however, such as shrimp with vegetables, are occasionally marred by a glutinous cornstarch-heavy sauce that overwhelms any subtle flavors or otherwise well-cooked ingredients. The Uptown, located close to Seattle Center, offers prompt service for those attending nearby performances. *Lunch, dinner every day; AE, DC, MC, V; local checks only; full bar.* ♿

VARSITY INN RESTAURANT

1801 N 34th St, Seattle
☎ *(206) 547-2161*
Wallingford   ✕ *Breakfast*

Settled in its Gas Works Park base after being transplanted from the U-District, the Varsity jumps for breakfasts and early lunches. Amid the hanging plants and cheery yellow decor waft the scents of pancake batter, syrup, melted butter, and, of course, strong coffee. This is the home of the reasonable meal deal, where you can have a full-fledged breakfast plate with eggs any way you want 'em, pancakes, bacon or sausage, and hashbrowns; or you can order half a grapefruit and some Cream of Wheat. Or, depending on the time of day, have a tall soda to wash down a deli sandwich and a bowl of soup. It must be stressed that the pancakes here are second to none (sorry, Mom), and the cozy booths and service make you feel as if you just rolled out of bed and it's gonna be a good day. Biscuits and gravy, strawberry waffles, and the almost hair-raising (in terms of the spiciness) Taco Omelet beckon. Chances are you'll spend a good while traversing the menu and asking for whatever the people next to you are having. If so, take heart: You really can't go wrong. *Breakfast, lunch every day; AE, DIS, MC, V; checks OK; no alcohol.* ♿

VENTANA

4401 Fremont Ave N, Seattle
☎ *(206) 632-6825*
Fremont   ✕ *Inventive Ethnic*

Despite the no-frills interior, there is romance to be found in this Fremont hideaway: With a little candlelight, the strains of contemporary music, and plenty of affordable wine options, your heart will beat a bit faster. But Ventana's deceptively simple approaches to customer satisfaction don't end with the ambience; its global offerings—from Thai to Italian to Caribbean to Korean—are top-notch and change with the season. The salads, made with organic add-ins and fresh-snipped greens, are divine, particularly one recent special with roasted baby beets and Gorgonzola (a deal for five bucks). We've had a mean Mediterranean tomato soup with saffron for less than that, and a tangy tart of onions and Stilton cheese—a creamy, crusty $7 starter course. The main courses require a bit more cash; in fact, "cheap eats" *almost* doesn't apply here, but hey, you won't mind shelling out a bit more once your taste buds are at the wheel. Ventana's no-sauce pizza comes soft, cheesy, and loaded with roasted garlic and cherry tomatoes, and the most recent crowning glory was the Cuban-style halibut, glazed with orange and rum and served with fried plantains and cumin-stoked black beans ($14). *Dinner Tues–Sun; AE, MC, V; checks OK; beer and wine.*

VIET CHI
710 Third Ave, Seattle
☎ *(206) 622-4180*
Pioneer Square   ✗ *Pan-Asian*

Viet Chi's quick, cheap eats appeal to downtown office workers, who come in with their oxford-cloth shirtsleeves rolled up to lunch on fresh Vietnamese and Chinese specialties. There's not much to look at in the dining room, set up cafeteria-style with one long counter and many small tables. But wait until you see the very visual menu, complete with photographs of what's to come, and featuring such selections as Chinese fried rolls, Vietnamese salad rolls, rice, curries, soups, and noodles with meats, poultry, seafood, or vegetables. The hardworking owners provide excellent combinations along with swift, friendly service. *Lunch, dinner Mon–Fri; no credit cards; no checks; no alcohol.* &

VIET MY
129 Prefontaine Pl S, Seattle
☎ *(206) 382-9923*
Pioneer Square   ✗ *Vietnamese*

Prefontaine Place is a very strange street that cuts diagonally, starting from nowhere and going nowhere. There's an abandoned feel to the block that would discourage all but the most intrepid of restaurateurs from setting up shop here—and all but the most devoted of foodies from looking for something to eat here. But if you go, you will stumble upon Viet My, surely one of the city's top purveyors of cheap, good Vietnamese food. This fortress, in fact, has been serving food for over a decade, and the only things preventing Viet My from taking over the world are the abominably slow service and the loud atmosphere. What diminishes the pain of sitting there: the best spring rolls ever, kick-ass black cod in black bean sauce, delicious lemongrass anything, soups that will soothe the most troubled beast, and noodle combinations that balance flavor with texture in surprisingly delightful ways. This spot is a Seattle classic—and waaay better than most of the overpriced fusion eateries uptown. *Lunch, dinner Mon–Fri; no credit cards; local checks only; no alcohol.*

VIETNAM'S PEARL

708 Rainier Ave S, Seattle
☎ *(206) 726-1581*
International District   ✕ *Vietnamese*

The cars are numerous on this stretch of Rainier, as are the Vietnamese restaurants (this is one of four in a close-knit row). But the Pearl has been around longer than most, and remains a favorite among Westerners since it features familiar ingredients and preparations in a number of Chinese- and Thai-influenced dishes. A large sky-lit dining room has a spacious, airy feel, all the better to enjoy any of the rock-bottom Vietnamese combinations, luncheon specials, or big bowls of pho. The level of authenticity isn't high, but the food is good and the service swift and competent. *Lunch, dinner every day; MC, V; checks OK; beer and wine.* ♿

VOLUNTEER PARK MARKET AND CAFE

1501 17th Ave E, Seattle
☎ *(206) 328-3155*
Capitol Hill   ✕ *Soup/Salad/Sandwich*

Every neighborhood needs a place like this. Tucked between the park and the shaded, cozy homes of one of Capitol Hill's quieter streets, Volunteer Park Market and Cafe is an urban oasis. Set up as a combination natural foods grocery, catering business, and sidewalk cafe, this homey establishment is a good neighbor to have. The well-worn building has rested comfortably on this corner for over 100 years and doesn't seem the least bit bothered by the constant activity: Families with small children take a break from playing in the park to grab fresh juice and water; young couples sitting outside lazily munch on  sandwiches and salads; harried commuters duck in on their way home for a bottle of wine and a bunch of flowers. The food is creatively prepared—if predictable—deli fare, with pasta salads, sandwiches, soups, and quiches, all fresh and ably made. The grocery isn't comprehensive, but stocks a versatile, aesthetically pleasing (and healthy) selection in a tight space. Visit on a sunny day if you can, and soak in the quiet of the neighborhood from a sidewalk table. *Breakfast, lunch, dinner every day; MC, V; checks OK; no alcohol.*

WALTER'S WAFFLES

106 James St, Seattle
☎ *(206) 382-2692*
Pioneer Square   ✕ *Waffles*

Have no doubt, Walter himself is ever-present behind the counter at Walter's Waffles, and regulars have a special affection for his Swiss-tinged, friendly "Hellooo!" Since a recent remodel, the dining space has tripled and now has more ambience: exposed brick, a photo gallery, and soft lighting on muted green walls. As you might have guessed, the specialty at Walter's is waffles. At any time of day you can have them any way imaginable: plain waffles, whole wheat waffles, pumpkin or chocolate chip waffles, waffles with toppings (syrup, fruit, whipped cream, or ice cream). Ask about Walter's special concoction, the waffle of the month. For a fiver and some change, you get one of Walter's filling grilled panini, your choice of chips or fruit, and the dessert of the day, picked out by Walter himself (a snack waffle, of course). The Roma sandwich, served on toasty (not oily) flat-bread with turkey, Roma tomatoes, basil, and fontina cheese, is a popular choice, as is its vegetarian counterpart. Not to be upstaged by the plentiful Pioneer Square competition, Walter's also serves espresso. *Breakfast, lunch every day; no credit cards; checks OK; no alcohol.* &

WEDGWOOD ALE HOUSE & CAFE

8515 35th Ave NE, Seattle
☎ *(206) 527-2676*
Wedgwood   ✕ *Pub Grub*

This slightly worn tavern has a congenial atmosphere geared toward neighborhood locals, but its menu is a step above typical pub grub. Sure, it's got burgers and fries, but this burger comes specially seasoned with onion, garlic, Worcestershire, and sage (unseasoned also available), and these fries are hand-cut and not dripping in grease. Wedgwood roasts its own turkey, too, making the hot turkey and swiss served on a thick baguette a good bet. All sandwiches include a choice of fries or coleslaw. Try the fresh, homemade slaw, a simple mix of green and purple cabbage with a mayo-ey sauce and poppy seeds. Entrees include a London broil and a few pasta options; the chicken fettucine is more like a bountiful primavera, full of fresh vegetables and tender sliced chicken in a cream sauce. Daily blackboard specials include a pasta, soup, appetizer, and dessert. This place looks like a re-vamped bar from the '50s—a sort of cleaned-up dive. But settle into one of the booths, at a table on the sidewalk patio, or on a stool at the classic U-shaped bar and you'll get over it. As the name implies, the Wedgwood features 18 Northwest brews on tap, as well as a decent selection of wines. Service is surprisingly attentive. *Breakfast Sat–Sun, lunch, dinner every day; MC, V; checks OK; beer and wine.*

WILDFIRE RANCH BBQ
317 NW Gilman Blvd, Issaquah
☎ *(425) 392-1334*
Issaquah   ✗ *Barbecue*

A gas-fired wood smoker turns out chicken and ribs seasoned with a wonderful spicy rub that renders barbecue sauce superfluous—Wildfire, as the name inplies. And if it's not spicy enough, a rack of hot sauces will give anything a mule kick to the head. The cook here once worked at what is now Relais, a fine French restaurant, so you can expect potato salad that's a little different, a spicy carrot slaw, or perhaps even blue corn bread spiked with jalapeño and sun-dried tomato. A special treat is the addictive roasted pumpkin seeds. But meats are the main attrac-tion—chewy ribs and bulky pork sandwiches you can't hold together however hard you may try. In nice weather, the walls literally roll up, garage door-style, for patio eating that's a bit like a rural Texas picnic right in the middle of quaint Gilman Village. *Lunch, dinner every day; MC, V; checks OK; beer and wine.* ♿

WORLD CLASS CHILI
93 Pike St, Seattle
☎ *(206) 623-3678*
Pike Place Market   ✗ *Chili*

Much of the stuff that passes for chili these days is either a tomato soup–like concoction sprinkled with a few handfuls of chili powder, or an oatmeal-like concoction weighed down with an excess of rice and beans. So head to World Class Chili for a heady bowl of the real stuff: Fragrant and brothy, its spices balanced, this stew is loaded with rich ingredients without being too thick. Our favorite is the Cincinnati (ground beef and pork, flavored with chocolate and cinnamon), but the other three are not to be sneezed at. The Texas-style features beef and five kinds of chiles; the California-style stars chicken; and even the Vegetarian is a proud version, brimming with lentils, carrots, onions, and zucchini. The corn bread eats like cake, and this is a good thing. This is an informal little spot, down a few stairs in the Market's South Arcade and decorated with a neon sign, a TV set, and owner Joe Canavan's faded ribbons from decades of winning chili cook-offs. Canavan himself is a bit of a curmudgeon, which seems to go with the chili-making profession. You can order your chili in one of three sizes—Texan (big), Alaskan (bigger), and a quart—for $4.26, $7.33, and $14.66, respectively. ("Straight" chili—without beans, rice, or pasta—is pricier.) Don't even try to ask if Canavan will put a smaller portion size on the menu; that's for wimps. *Lunch, dinner Mon–Sat; no credit cards; no checks; beer only.* &

WORLD WRAPPS
7900 E Greenlake Dr N, Seattle (and branches)
☎ *(206) 524-9727*
Green Lake/Capitol Hill/Downtown/
First Hill/Kirkland/Lake Union/Queen Anne/
University District ✕ *Inventive Ethnic*

This place is not trying to unite the world in peace and understanding through healthy, multicultural, fast-food burritos—it only seems that way. Begun in San Francisco in 1996, World Wrapps has expanded to include nine locations in and around Seattle alone. Each World Wrapps restaurant is a collage of colorful mosaics, brightly painted tables, and ceilings that are half blue and half green in symbolic tribute to land and sea. Queued up at the counter or seated in the hard-backed stools, you can expect to find a predominantly young, health-conscious crowd (and probably a former Peace Corps volunteer or two). And why not? You can easily get fueled up for under $5, and throw in a blended fruit smoothie for a few dollars more. The various burrito fillings, whose inspiration truly spans the globe, are wrapped up inside your choice of tortilla—low-fat flour, Roma tomato, or spinach. The one constant ingredient is rice (jasmine or Spanish), but beyond that lies a whole world of taste combinations ranging from the Thai chicken (with ginger slaw, cucumbers, scallions, and peanut sauce) to the Barcelona (essentially paella in a tortilla). Other wraps are inspired by Mexican, Caribbean, Japanese, Indian, and Italian cuisine.

Occasionally the combinations are a little bland, but for the most part this chain has scored a major hit against its fat-packing, burrito-peddling fast-food competitors. Other options here include rice bowls (basically, unwrapped wraps), salads and soups. The Downtown and First Hill locations serve Mornings (breakfast wraps) too. *Breakfast, lunch, early dinner every day (Downtown and First Hill branches); lunch, dinner every day (all other branches); MC, V; checks OK; beer only (limited locations in summer only).* &

YANNI'S GREEK RESTAURANT

7419 Greenwood Ave N, Seattle
☎ (206) 783-6945
Greenwood   ✕ Greek

One of the brightest spots in Seattle's neighborhood ethnic dining scene is one of its best Greek restaurants. The place exudes the humble comforts of a Greek taverna. The deep-fried calamari appetizer is meal-size, with tender, perfectly fried squid and a side of pungent skordalia for dipping. That and a horiatiki salad—a heaping mound of tomatoes, cucumbers, kalamata olives, peppers, romaine, and feta—can make a complete dinner for two, along with the good pita. The moussaka is especially good—each layer distinct, yet the whole a pillow of richly blended flavors—and we know people who swear by the spit-roasted chicken (which is also available for take-out). The music is appropriately manic, and Yanni's offers the largest selection of Greek wines in the city. *Dinner Mon–Sat; MC, V; checks OK; beer and wine.* &

YASUKO'S TERIYAKI

530 Broadway, Seattle (and branches)
☎ (206) 322-0123
First Hill/Green Lake/Magnolia/West Seattle   ✕ Teriyaki

Trust us, one chicken teriyaki dinner from Yasuko's stretches your stomach as far as your dollar. Besides a large piece of poultry, you get steamed rice soaked with a lovely sweet teriyaki sauce, and a mild shredded cabbage salad. This is take-out at its no-frills greatest: Order at the window inside, inhale the roast meats and sweet tangy sauces, and feel your mouth water on the drive home (warning: do not balance food on your lap when at the wheel—and it's

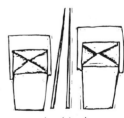

a good idea to keep the windows down all the way, to keep the aroma from making you tear through the plastic bag to get at the Styrofoam box). Besides the standard chicken, they have other versions of the bird, as well as temptingly tangy ribs. Don't forget to check the menu; sometimes you get quite a nice surprise when you go out on a limb. *Lunch, dinner every day; no credit cards; no checks; no alcohol.* &

ZAINA

108 Cherry St, Seattle
☎ *(206) 624-5687*
Pioneer Square   ✕ *Middle Eastern*

This Middle Eastern restaurant comes with a subtitle: Food, Drinks, and Friends. The broad, airy room in Pioneer Square is plastered with pictures and postcards from Jerusalem, Bethlehem, and much of the Middle East. On warm days, large windows swing open onto Cherry Street, giving the place a light, relaxing feel as the ceiling fans spin. A simple counter, stacked with baklava and honey cakes, separates the kitchen from the dining area, and the smell of lamb and beef hangs heavy in the air. Excellent gyros and falafel sandwiches and plates (add basmati rice and hummus) make up the core of the menu. There are also daily specials, and everything's served with (or on) fresh, warm pita bread. At lunchtime a line usually begins to snake toward the door, but the servers work quickly and the spicy, pungent food is well worth a short wait. A collection of wooden camels is displayed along the wall opposite the kitchen, and in the center of the camel procession sits a large, decorative hookah. Show up on Fridays for belly dancing performances; loud Arabic music plays most of the time, spilling out onto the street. *Lunch, early dinner Mon–Sat; DIS, MC, V; checks OK; beer and wine.*

ZEEK'S PIZZA

41 Dravus St, Seattle (and branches)
☎ *(206) 285-6046*
Queen Anne/Belltown/Phinney Ridge   ✕ *Pizza*

The original Zeek's—known for its absurd pizza toppings and too-nice-to-be-for-real staff of pizza-throwers, salad-makers, and money-takers—has moved one door down from its first location into a larger spot in the same stripmall between Seattle Pacific University and the Fremont Bridge. In 1995, young pizza impresarios Doug McClure and Tom Vial's busy pizza parlor gave rise to a second (much bigger) Zeek's on Phinney Ridge (6000 Phinney Ave N, (206) 789-0089), and now a third branch has opened in northern Belltown (419 Denny Way, (206) 448-6775). Regardless of which Zeek's you visit, you should not hesitate to order the Thai-One-On, a pizza doused with the makings of phad Thai: chunks of chicken, slivers of carrot, crunchy mung bean sprouts, and fresh cilantro atop a spicy hot peanut sauce that'd do a satay proud. Purists might lean toward the Frog Belly Green, with basil pesto, Roma tomatoes, and whole-milk mozzarella layered over a very white, slightly doughy crust with an olive oil glaze. Then there's the weird-but-wonderful Texas Leaguer (with barbecued chicken, red onion, and cilantro), and

the very popular Tree Hugger (with sun-dried and Roma tomatoes, spinach, mushrooms, artichoke hearts, broccoli, garlic, and olives). Meat-lovers will appreciate the Puget Pounder. Order by the slice or the pie, to eat in or take out (call 285-TOGO). Good, huge, inexpensive salads, too. *Lunch, dinner every day; MC, V; checks OK; beer and wine.* ♿

ZEENA'S

1320 Madison St, Seattle
☎ *(206) 328-3993*
First Hill   ✕ *American*

Located in the First Hill Plaza building, this spot functions as a modern diner, doing breakfast and lunch for the busy urban working crowd. Portions here are large and the service is swift, both aimed at keeping you fueled and on your way. Zeena's covers the breakfast standards, featuring six kinds of pancakes (including potato), frittatas, omelets, and the classic egg combos. It also gets a little fancy with croissant French toast, matzo brei (frittata-style with eggs), and kosher salami and eggs. Heavy lunch eaters should look to the daily lunch plate specials featuring such belt-busters as homemade meat loaf or beef brisket from Seattle's Market House. Grilled chicken, chopped beef, or teriyaki beef or chicken platters await the less ambitious. A number of kosher meats (knockwurst, beef hot dogs, pastrami, salami) are represented in the sandwich department, as is the usual assortment of burgers and chicken sandwiches. Salads and soups are also well accounted for. Choose your own seat in Zeena's split-level dining area, done up in gray-greens with large canvases of abstract paintings hanging from the walls and large windows opening up views to a tree-lined section of Madison Street. *Breakfast, lunch every day; MC, V; no checks; beer and wine.* &

ZEN JAPANESE RESTAURANT

10720 SE Carr Rd, Renton
☎ *(425) 254-1177*
Renton
✕*Japanese*

Take just a few steps into Zen Japanese Restaurant, and you'll know everything you need to about this orderly, inviting establishment just up from Valley Medical Center: The atmosphere is clean and bright, the decor thoughtful and arranged with care. Tables are spaced deliberately to be cozy yet private. The sushi bar cuts the restaurant exactly in half, proudly displaying the inner workings of the well-organized kitchen beyond. Those who argue for a benign order to the universe will find solace here. Not surprisingly, the food matches its surroundings perfectly: excellent Japanese standbys like teriyaki, katsu, tempura, and yakisoba are served up with precision, and standouts like the *saba shioyaki* (broiled mackerel) don't disappoint. The sushi is likewise skillfully prepared, and tempting specials abound on the menu; everything is fresh and reassuringly authentic. *Lunch, dinner every day; MC, V; checks OK; beer and wine.* &

ZOOPA

1071 Bellevue Square, Bellevue (and branches)
☎ *(425) 453-7887*
Bellevue/North End/South Seattle
✕ *Soup/Salad/Sandwich*

Fresh Choice Restaurants, the corporate parent of these flashy all-you-can-eateries, presents unlimited gut-slamming possibilities at ZOOPA. This is your diet-be-damned dream-come-true, and it's yours for the price of a movie ticket. Bewildered by the choices (and how to nab them properly)? You'll be greeted at the door and informed of the drill: Select your beverage, pay the cashier and head for the various food islands before taking a booth in the colorful dining area. There are a multitude of soup, salad, pasta, and fresh fruit options. The selection includes ethnic treats like sesame chicken stir-fry and pasta with kalamata olives, as well as comfort stuff like macaroni and cheese and chocolate pudding. Careen over to the baked goods for muffins or garlic bread. Hit the dessert area for a soft-freeze sundae or a slab of cake. Still hungry? Grab a clean plate and do it again . . . and again. ZOOPAs abound: in this area there's one in Southcenter (393 Strander Blvd, Tukwila; (206) 575-0500) and a branch in Northgate (463 Northgate Mall, (206) 440-8136). *Lunch, dinner every day; AE, DIS, MC, V; local checks only; beer and wine.* &

location index
seattle neighborhoods

BALLARD
Ballard Bait & Tackle Baithouse
  Coffee Shop
Bright Street Pub & Cafe
Cascioppo's
The Dish
Hale's Ales Brewery & Pub
Hattie's Hat
Hoki's Teriyaki Hut
Lockspot Cafe
Mike's Chili Parlor
Salmon Bay Cafe
Taco del Mar

BEACON HILL
King's Barbecue House

BELLTOWN
Afrikando
Belltown Billiards
Belltown Pub
CJ's Eatery
Macrina Bakery and Cafe
Mama's Mexican Kitchen
Mondo Burrito
Noodle Ranch
Shallots Asian Bistro
Shorty's Coney Island
Sit & Spin
Speakeasy
Two Bells Tavern
Zeek's Pizza

CAPITOL HILL
Angel's Thai Cuisine
Aoki Japanese Grill and Sushi Bar
Ayutthaya Thai Cuisine
B&O Espresso
Bacchus
Ballet Vietnamese and Chinese Cuisine
Bimbo's Bitchin' Burrito Kitchen
Cafe Septieme
Charlie's on Broadway
Coastal Kitchen
Deluxe Bar & Grill
Dick's Drive-In
Elysian Brewing Company
Gravity Bar

Green Cat
Jalisco
Kidd Valley
Kingfish Cafe
Kitto Japanese Noodle House
Mediterranean Kitchen
Noodle Studio
Pagliacci Pizza
Pasta & Co.
Piecora's Pizza
Siam on Broadway
Six Arms Pub & Brewery
Taco del Mar
Taqueria Guaymas
Volunteer Park Market and Cafe
World Wrapps

CENTRAL DISTRICT
Assimba
Catfish Corner
Ezell's Famous Fried Chicken
Judkin's BBQ & Restaurant
Ms. Helen's Soul Food
Philadelphia Fevre Steak
  & Hoagie Shop
Thompson's Point of View

COLUMBIA CITY
La Medusa

DOWNTOWN
  (see also BELLTOWN,
  PIKE PLACE MARKET,
  AND PIONEER SQUARE)
Blowfish
Botticelli Caffe
Briazz
FareStart
The Frankfurter
John's Wok
Mamacita's
  (see Mama's Mexican Kitchen)
McSorley's
Pasta & Co.
Pasta Ya Gotcha
Post Alley Pizza
Romio's Pizza & Pasta
Seattle Bagel Bakery

DOWNTOWN cont.
Steamers Seafood Cafe
Taco del Mar
World Wrapps

EASTLAKE
Daly's Drive-In
14 Carrot Cafe
Le Fournil
Pazzo's
Romio's Pizza & Pasta

FIRST HILL
Mad Pizza
Taco del Mar
Yasuko's Teriyaki
World Wrapps
Zeena's

FREMONT
Bagel Oasis
Bright Street Pub & Cafe
Costas Opa Greek Restaurant
The Dish
Fremont Classic Pizzeria and Trattoria
Fremont Noodle House
Hale's Ales Brewery & Pub
Hoki's Teriyaki Hut
Longshoreman's Daughter
Mad Pizza
Paseo Caribbean Restaurant
Seattle Catch Seafood Bistro
Swingside Cafe
Still Life in Fremont
Taco del Mar
Triangle Lounge
Ventana

GEORGETOWN
Jules Maes Saloon & Eatery

GREEN LAKE
Beth's Cafe
Kidd Valley
Krittika Noodles & Thai Cuisine
Mona's Bistro & Lounge
Rialto Pasta Bar & Grill
Rico's Salvadoran Cocina
Rosita's Mexican Grill
Six Degrees
Taqueria Guaymas
Than Brothers
World Wrapps
Yasuko's Teriyaki

GREENWOOD
Barbacoa Caribbean Grill
Bick's Broadview Grill
Burrito Loco
Dick's Drive-In
Georgia's Greek Deli
Gordito's Healthy Mexican Food
Greenwood Bakery
Maharaja Cuisine of India
OK Corral BBQ Pit-Stop and
    Sandwich Slingers
Pig 'n Whistle Bar and Grill
Romio's Pizza & Pasta
Rosita's Mexican Grill
Yanni's Greek Restaurant

INTERNATIONAL DISTRICT
Canton Wonton House
Hing Loon
Huong Binh
King's Barbecue House
New Hong Kong Malaysian Restaurant
Pho Bac
Saigon Bistro
Shanghai Garden
Sichuanese Cuisine Restaurant
Takohachi
Top Gun Seafood Restaurant
Saigon Bistro
Vietnam's Pearl

LAKE CITY
Dick's Drive-In
Jalisco
La Guadalupana Taqueria Mexicana
Romio's Pizza & Pasta
Taco del Mar
Toyoda Sushi

LAKE UNION
Buca di Beppo
Cucina! Cucina! Italian Cafe
World Wrapps

LAURELHURST
Roasted Pepper Cafe & Deli

LESCHI
Leschi Lakecafe

MADISON PARK
Madison Park Cafe
Mad Pizza

MADRONA
Cafe Soleil
Cool Hand Luke's
Hi-Spot Cafe
Plenty Fine Foods

MAGNOLIA
Pandasia
Red Mill Burgers
Romio's Pizza & Pasta

MAPLE LEAF
Gaspare's Ristorante Italiano
Maple Leaf Grill
Snappy Dragon

MOUNT BAKER
Baker's Beach
That's Amore Italian Cafe

NORTH END
The Frankfurter
Kidd Valley
Koryo Restaurant
Zoopa

PHINNEY RIDGE
Mae's on Phinney Ridge
Red Mill Burgers
74th Street Ale House
Zeek's Pizza

PIKE PLACE MARKET
Alibi Room
Athenian Inn
Chicken Valley
Delcambre's Ragin' Cajun
El Puerco Lloron
Emmett Watson's Oyster Bar
Gourmondo
The Incredible Link
Jack's Fish and Chip Spot
Kosher Delight
Mee Sum Pastry
Piroshky Piroshky
Sisters European Snacks
Three Girls Bakery
Turkish Delight
World Class Chili

PIONEER SQUARE
A La Francaise
Bakeman's
Grand Central Baking Company

King Street Bar & Oven
Mac's Smokehouse
Mae Phim Thai
Merchants Cafe
Owl 'n Thistle
Soup Daddy Soups
Taco del Mar
Trattoria Mitchelli
Viet Chi
Viet My
Walter's Waffles
Zaina

QUEEN ANNE
Bahn Thai
Banjara
Caffe Ladro
Chinoise Cafe
Dick's Drive-In
The 5 Spot
The Frankfurter
Jalisco
Kidd Valley
Maharaja Cuisine of India
Malena's Taco Shop
Mecca Cafe
Mediterranean Kitchen
Pagliacci Pizza
Panos Kleftiko
Pasta & Co.
Racha Noodles
Shilla Restaurant
Steamers Seafood Cafe
Taco del Mar
Thai Restaurant
Tup Tim Thai
Uptown China
World Wrapps
Zeek's Pizza

RAINIER BEACH
Maya's

RAVENNA
Bagel Oasis
Kidd Valley
Queen Mary

ROOSEVELT
Sunlight Cafe
Super Bowl Noodle House
Taco del Mar

SEWARD PARK
Pizzuto's Italian Cafe

SODO (south of Downtown)
The Frankfurter
Kolbeh Persian & Mediterranean
  Cuisine
Matt's Famous Chili Dogs
Pecos Pit Barbecue
Pyramid Alehouse
Taco del Mar

UNIVERSITY DISTRICT
A La Francaise
Asia Grille
Betty Sue's Urban Bar-B-Q
Big Time Brewery & Alehouse
Boat Street Cafe
Briazz
Continental Greek Restaurant
  and Pastry Shop
Kiku Tempura House
Neelam's Authentic Indian Cuisine
Noble Palace
Pagliacci Pizza
Pasta & Co.
Rain Dancer: A Restaurant & Bar
Ruby
Shultzy's Sausage
Silence-Heart-Nest Vegetarian
  Restaurant
Taco del Mar
Tandoor
Teriyaki First
The Ugly Mug Cafe
World Wrapps

WALLINGFORD
Ai Japanese Restaurant
Asteroid Cafe
Beso del Sol

Bizzarro Italian Cafe
Boulangerie
The Bungalow Wine Bar and Cafe
Dick's Drive-In
Eggs Cetera's Blue Star Cafe and Pub
Honey Bear Bakery
Jitterbug
Julia's in Wallingford
Kabul
Musashi's Sushi and Grill
Nikolas Pizza and Pasta
Olympia Pizza and Spaghetti House II
Sea Thai
Stone Way Cafe
Taco del Mar
Teahouse Kuan Yin
Varsity Inn Restaurant

WEDGEWOOD
Black Pearl
Fiddler's Inn
Wedgwood Ale House & Cafe

WEST SEATTLE
Admiral Way Cafe
Alki Bakery
Angelina's Trattoria
Cat's Eye Cafe
Jak's Grill
Liberty Deli
Luna Park Cafe
Madison's Cafe
Maharaja Cuisine of India
Mashiko
Pegasus Pizza
Spud Fish 'n' Chips
Sunfish
Taqueria Guaymas

seattle environs

BAINBRIDGE ISLAND
Blue Water Diner
Harbour Public House
Streamliner Diner

BELLEVUE
Acapulco Fresh
Briazz
Bulgogi
California Pizza Kitchen
Chace's Pancake Corral
City Thai
Coyote Creek Pizza
Cucina! Cucina! Italian Cafe
Dixie's BBQ
European Gourmet Cafe & Deli
The Frankfurter
Gilbert's on Main
Guiseppe's Italian Restaurant
  and Lounge
Kidd Valley
La Cocina del Puerco
Mediterranean Kitchen
Moghul Palace
Noble Court Seafood Restaurant
Pasta & Co.
Pasta Ya Gotcha
Piroshky Piroshky
Saigon City
Shanghai Cafe
Thai Ginger
Tres Hermanos Family Mexican
  Restaurant
Zoopa

BOTHELL
Alexa's on Main
Beth's Cafe
Black Sheep Cafe
Jalisco
Kidd Valley

EDMONDS
Anthony's Beach Cafe
Brusseau's
Provinces Asian Restaurant & Bar

ISSAQUAH
Acapulco Fresh
Cucina! Cucina! Italian Cafe
Issaquah Cafe
Jak's Grill
Pasta Ya Gotcha
Shanghai Cafe (see Shanghai Garden)
Wildfire Ranch BBQ

KENMORE
Acapulco Fresh

KIRKLAND
Cafe DaVinci's
Coyote Creek Pizza
Cucina! Cucina! Italian Cafe
Jalisco
Kidd Valley
Meze
The Original Pancake House
Pasta Ya Gotcha
Pegasus Pizza
Piecora's Pizza
Santorini Greek Grill
Shamiana
Six Degrees
The Slip
Taco del Mar
Tres Hermanos Family Mexican
  Restaurant
Triple J Cafe
World Wrapps

LYNNWOOD
A.P. Barbara's
Ezell's Famous Fried Chicken
Kidd Valley
Taqueria Guaymas

MALTBY
Maltby Cafe

MERCER ISLAND
Pon Proem
Roanoke Inn
Thai Kitchen

MONROE
Monroe Cafe (See Issaquah Cafe)

REDMOND
Acapulco Fresh
Banzai Japanese Restaurant
The Bento Box
Big Time Pizza
Caffe Infinito
Cucina! Cucina! Italian Cafe
Desert Fire
Shilla Restaurant
Si Señor
Super China
Taco del Mar
Village Square Cafe
  (see Issaquah Cafe)

RENTON
Hong's Garden
Omar Al Khyam
Taco del Mar

Taqueria Guaymas
Zen Japanese Restaurant

SOUTH SEATTLE
  (Sea-Tac and Tukwila)
Bai Tong
Mac's Smokehouse
Zoopa

WHITE CENTER
El Pargo Mexican Seafood
  Restaurant
Jalisco
Taqueria del Rio
Taqueria Guaymas
Thai Thai

WOODINVILLE
Armadillo Barbecue
at home cafe
Forecaster's Public House
Texas Smokehouse Bar-B-Q
Woodinville Cafe (see Issaquah Cafe)

food type index

CAJUN/CREOLE
(see also SOUTHERN)
Delcambre's Ragin' Cajun

CARIBBEAN
Barbacoa Caribbean Grill
Paseo Caribbean Restaurant

CENTRAL AMERICAN
Rico's Salvadoran Cocina

CHICKEN (see also SOUTHERN)
Chicken Valley
Ezell's Famous Fried Chicken

CHILI
Mike's Chili Parlor
World Class Chili

CHINESE (see also PAN-ASIAN)
Black Pearl
Canton Wonton House
Hing Loon
Hong's Garden
Noble Palace
Snappy Dragon
Shanghai Garden
Sichuanese Cuisine Restaurant
Super China
Top Gun Seafood Restaurant
Uptown China

COFFEEHOUSE (see also SOUP/SALAD/SANDWICH)
B&O Espresso
Caffe Ladro
Speakeasy

DELI
Cascioppo's
European Gourmet Cafe & Deli
Liberty Deli

DINER (see also AMERICAN, BREAKFAST)
Admiral Way Cafe
Blue Water Diner
Hattie's Hat
Jules Maes Saloon & Eatery
Luna Park Cafe
Mecca Cafe
Stone Way Cafe
Streamliner Diner

ETHIOPIAN
(see also AFRICAN, WEST)
Assimba
Cafe Soleil

FISH 'N' CHIPS
(see also SEAFOOD)
Jack's Fish and Chip Spot
Lockspot Cafe
Spud Fish 'n' Chips
Steamers Seafood Cafe
Sunfish

GREEK
Bacchus
Continental Greek Restaurant and
  Pastry Shop
Costas Opa Greek Restaurant
Georgia's Greek Deli
Panos Kleftiko
Santorini Greek Grill
Yanni's Greek Restaurant

HOT DOGS/SAUSAGE
The Frankfurter
The Incredible Link
Matt's Famous Chili Dogs
Shorty's Coney Island
Shultzy's Sausage

INDIAN
Banjara
Maharaja Cusine of India
Moghul Palace
Neelam's Authentic Indian Cuisine
Shamiana
Tandoor

INVENTIVE ETHNIC
(see also BISTRO)
A.P. Barbara's
Hi-Spot Cafe
Jitterbug
Maple Leaf Grill
Mona's Bistro & Lounge
Mondo Burrito
Roasted Pepper Cafe & Deli
Ruby
Swingside Cafe
Ventana
World Wrapps

IRISH
Owl 'n Thistle

ITALIAN (see also PIZZA)

Angelina's Trattoria
The Asteroid Cafe
Belltown Billiards
Bizzarro Italian Cafe
Buca di Beppo
Cafe DaVinci's
Cucina! Cucina! Italian Cafe
Gaspare's Ristorante Italiano
Guiseppe's Italian Restaurant
  and Lounge
La Medusa
Pasta Ya Gotcha
Pizzuto's Italian Cafe
Rialto Pasta Bar & Grill
Trattoria Mitchelli
That's Amore Italian Cafe

JAPANESE (see also PAN-ASIAN)

Ai Japanese Restaurant
Aoki Japanese Grill and Sushi Bar
Banzai Japanese Restaurant
The Bento Box
Kiku Tempura House
Kitto Japanese Noodle House
Mashiko
Musashi's Sushi and Grill
Takohachi
Toyoda Sushi
Zen Japanese Restaurant

KOREAN (see also PAN-ASIAN)

Bulgogi
Koryo Restaurant
Shilla Restaurant

KOSHER/Kosher Options

Kosher Delight
Zeena's

MALAYSIAN

New Hong Kong Malaysian
  Restaurant

MEXICAN (see also SOUTHWESTERN)

Acapulco Fresh
Beso del Sol
Bimbo's Bitchin' Burrito Kitchen
Burrito Loco
El Pargo Mexican Seafood Restaurant
El Puerco Lloron
Gordito's Healthy Mexican Food
Jalisco
La Cocina del Puerco
La Guadalupana Taqueria Mexicana
Malena's Taco Shop
Mama's Mexican Kitchen
Maya's
Rosita's Mexican Grill
Si Señor
Taco del Mar
Taqueria del Rio
Taqueria Guaymas
Tres Hermanos Family Mexican
  Restaurant

MIDDLE EASTERN

Kolbeh Persian & Mediterranean
  Cuisine
Mediterranean Kitchen
Meze
Omar Al Khyam
Zaina

PAN-ASIAN (see also CHINESE, JAPANESE, KOREAN, THAI, VIETNAMESE)

Asia Grille
Blowfish
Chinoise Cafe
Cool Hand Luke's
John's Wok
Noodle Ranch
Pandasia
Provinces Asian Restaurant & Bar
Shallots Asian Bistro
Super Bowl Noodle House
Viet Chi

PIZZA (see also ITALIAN)

Big Time Pizza
California Pizza Kitchen
Coyote Creek Pizza
Fremont Classic Pizzeria and Trattoria
Mad Pizza
Olympia Pizza and Spaghetti House II
Pagliacci Pizza
Pazzo's
Pegasus Pizza
Piecora's Pizza
Post Alley Pizza
Romio's Pizza & Pasta
Zeek's Pizza

PUB GRUB

Belltown Pub
Big Time Brewery & Alehouse
Elysian Brewing Company
Fiddler's Inn
Forecaster's Public House
Hale's Ales Brewery & Pub
Harbour Public House
King Street Bar & Oven
Leschi Lakecafe
Madison's Cafe
Merchants Cafe
Pyramid Alehouse
Roanoke Inn
74th Street Ale House
Six Arms Pub & Brewery
Wedgwood Ale House & Cafe

RUSSIAN

Piroshky Piroshky

SEAFOOD
(see also FISH 'N' CHIPS)

Anthony's Beach Cafe
El Pargo Mexican Seafood Restaurant
Emmett Watson's Oyster Bar
Leschi Lakecafe
Noble Court Seafood Restaurant
Seattle Catch Seafood Bistro
Steamers Seafood Cafe

SOUP/SALAD/SANDWICH
(see also AMERICAN, DELI, DINER, PUB GRUB)

Ballard Bait & Tackle Baithouse
  Coffee Shop
Black Sheep Cafe
Botticelli Caffe
Briazz
Brusseau's
Caffe Infinito
Cat's Eye Cafe
FareStart
Gilbert's on Main
Gourmondo
McSorley's
Pasta & Co.
Rain Dancer: A Restaurant and Bar
Sisters European Snacks
Sit & Spin
Soup Daddy Soups
Still Life in Fremont
Triple J Cafe

The Ugly Mug Cafe
Volunteer Park Market and Cafe
Walter's Waffles
Zoopa

SOUTHERN
(see also BARBECUE, CAJUN/CREOLE, CHICKEN)

Catfish Corner
Kingfish Cafe
Ms. Helen's Soul Food
Thompson's Point of View

SOUTHWESTERN
(see also MEXICAN)

Desert Fire

TEAHOUSES

Queen Mary
Racha Noodles
Teahouse Kuan Yin

TERIYAKI

Hoki's Teriyaki Hut
Teriyaki First
Yasuko's Teriyaki

THAI (see also PAN-ASIAN)

Angel's Thai Cuisine
Ayutthaya Thai Cuisine
Bahn Thai
Bai Tong
City Thai
Fremont Noodle House
Krittika Noodles & Thai Cuisine
Mae Phim Thai
Noodle Studio
Pon Proem
Racha Noodles
Sea Thai
Siam on Broadway
Thai Ginger
Thai Kitchen
Thai Restaurant
Thai Thai
Tup Tim Thai

TURKISH

Turkish Delight

VARIOUS

FareStart
Nikolas Pizza and Pasta

VEGETARIAN
Gravity Bar
Green Cat
Silence-Heart-Nest Vegetarian
    Restaurant
Sunlight Cafe

VIETNAMESE
  (see also PAN-ASIAN)
Ballet Vietnamese and Chinese
    Cuisine

Huong Binh
Pho Bac
Saigon Bistro
Saigon City
Than Brothers Restaurant
Viet My
Vietnam's Pearl

WAFFLES
  (see also BREAKFAST)
Walter's Waffles

seattle **cheap eats**
report form

Based on my personal experience, I wish to nominate the following restaurant as a "Cheap Eat"; or confirm/correct/disagree with the current review.

_____
_____
_____
_____

(Please include address and telephone number of establishment, if convenient.)

Report:

Please describe food, service, style, comfort, value, date of visit, and other aspects of your experience; continue on other side if necessary.

_____
_____
_____
_____
_____
_____

I am not concerned, directly or indirectly, with the management or ownership of this establishment.

Signed _____
Address _____
_____
Phone _____
Date _____

Please address to *Seattle Cheap Eats* and send to:

Sasquatch Books
615 Second Avenue, Suite 260
Seattle, WA 98104

Feel free to email feedback as well: books@SasquatchBooks.com